Democracy and Economic Planning

ASPECTS OF POLITICAL ECONOMY
Series Editor: Geoffrey Harcourt

Published

A. Asimakopulos, *Investment, Employment and Income Distribution*
Pat Devine, *Democracy and Economic Planning*
Richard M. Goodwin and Lionello F. Punzo, *The Dynamics of a Capitalist Economy*
Marc Jarsulic, *Effective Demand and Income Distribution*
Peter Nolan, *The Political Economy of Collective Farms*
Bob Rowthorn and Naomi Wayne, *Northern Ireland*
Christopher Torr, *Equilibrium, Expectations and Information*
Warren Young, *Interpreting Mr Keynes*

Forthcoming

Grazia Ietto-Gillies, *Causes and Effects of International Production*
Ravi Kanbur, *Risk Taking, Income Distribution and Poverty*
Jose Salazar, *Pricing Policy and Economic Development*
Ian Steedman, *From Exploitation to Altruism*

Democracy and Economic Planning

*The Political Economy of a
Self-governing Society*

PAT DEVINE

Polity Press

First published 1988 by Polity Press
in association with Basil Blackwell

Editorial Office:
Polity Press, Dales Brewery, Gwydir Street,
Cambridge CB1 2LJ, UK

Basil Blackwell Ltd
108 Cowley Road, Oxford, OX4 1JF, UK

British Library Cataloguing in Publication Data
Devine, P.J.
  Democracy and economic planning: the
  political economy of a self-governing
  society.—(Aspects of political economy).
  1. Economic planning. Political aspects
  I. Title   II. Series
  338.9

  ISBN 0-7456-0515-X

Typeset in 10½ on 12 pt Times
by Opus, Oxford
Printed in Great Britain by T.J. Press, Padstow

Contents

Preface

After Karl Marx and Friedrich Engels, my greatest intellectual debts are to Rudolf Bahro, Wlodzimierz Brus, Maurice Dobb, Antonio Gramsci, David Purdy and Bill Warren.

I have received encouragement and support during this overlong project from many people but especially from Ian Gough, Phil Leeson, Elena Lieven, David Purdy, Roger Simon and Fred Steward.

My life formation and optimism of the will are due to my mother, Frieda Brewster, the international communist movement and the Marxist tradition; to Robin Jardine, Charlie Brewster and Ann Long; to Cath, John and Mike Devine; to the Eurocommunist and women's liberation movements of the 1970s; and to Elena Lieven.

I should like to thank Phil Leeson, Elena Lieven, David Purdy, Roger Simon and John Thompson for reading the entire first draft of this book and David Beetham, Sarah Benton, Dave Cook, Martin Currie, Ian Gough, Geoff Harcourt, Alan Hunt, Monty Johnstone, Norman Lee, Barbara MacLennan, Bob Rowthorn, John Salter and Fred Steward for reading part of the first draft.

I should also like to thank most members of the Department of Economics of the University of Manchester for making possible the two sabbaticals during which this book was conceived and written and the University as a whole for the intellectually and politically exciting sub-culture it has provided over the past twenty years. It has been a strength of our university system in this period that it has been able to accommodate people following unconventional trajectories, an era now sadly passing.

In addition to the above I have been helped in various ways by Jonathan Alexander, Marge Ben-Tovim, Gideon Ben-Tovim, Jude Bloomfield, Beatrix Campbell, Pete Coughlin, Pete Egerton, Diane Elson, Norman Geras, Judith Gray, Jose Green, Philip Hanson,

Martin Jacques, Trevor Marshall, Catherine Meredith, Dennis Ogden, Sheila Smith, Ian Steedman and David Wilkin.

Comments on the first draft of the book have suggested the need for two prefatory guidelines. First, although the concept of self-government is referred to throughout the book, it is not discussed in detail until chapter 6. Second, I use the term social division of labour to refer to the stratification of people into social classes or groups possessing differential social power and the term functional division of labour to refer to the performance of different tasks within a cooperative social activity.

Pat Devine
Manchester

PART I

Introduction

1

Introduction

1.1 Introduction

This is a book about transformation. It starts from two assumptions. The first is that neither the capitalist countries of the West nor the statist countries of the East[1] represent acceptable ways of organizing society. A third way is needed, and to create it involves the conscious transformation of existing societies. The second assumption is that people create themselves by acting on the circumstances in which they find themselves. Depending on the internal and external resources available to them, people transform to a greater or lesser extent both their circumstances and themselves.

The third way set out in this book is a model of democratic planning based on negotiated coordination. It is democratic, which distinguishes it from the command planning of the statist countries. It is planning, which distinguishes it from the instability and lack of conscious social purpose characteristic of capitalist countries. It is based on negotiated coordination, which distinguishes it from market socialism, the only reasonably worked-out alternative model of a third way that has so far been proposed.

In the most advanced modern capitalist countries political democracy has been won but not economic democracy. The political democracy so far achieved is of unparalleled historical importance but it is incomplete. It is primarily passive representative democracy in which most people elect others to act for them. The extent of active participation in self-government is very limited and in many countries the centralization of political power is increasing. Economic power remains highly concentrated and economic democracy, although now on the agenda, is still fragmentary and for the future.

Modern capitalism is not *laissez-faire* capitalism. The role of the state has increased inexorably during the twentieth century, notwithstanding the rediscovery of economic liberalism in the 1980s. Part of this process has involved attempts at economic planning, primarily during the two world wars but also in the period since the Second World War. However, planning has been limited, partial and largely unsuccessful. By the 1980s attempts at national economic planning had been effectively abandoned and macroeconomic management was in crisis. High levels of unemployment and inflation, persistent inequality, acute social divisions, environmental problems, the effects of unplanned technical change, international economic instability – all suggested a social system out of control.

The statist societies of the Soviet Union and Eastern Europe have centrally planned economies. Planning has enabled the mobilization of their human and material resources for the priority objectives of developing their backward economies and modernizing their societies. It has also enabled them to achieve full employment, low levels of inflation, and a more equal distribution of income than exists in capitalist countries at the same level of development. However, both political and economic power are highly centralized and neither political nor economic democracy exists in these societies.

As the level of economic and social development has increased, the statist societies have experienced endemic and periodically acute crisis. The absence of political democracy has resulted in a series of political crises, most dramatically in Poland in 1980. The combined absence of political and economic democracy, in a context of full employment and command planning, has resulted in lack of dynamism, economic inefficiency and labour indiscipline. Repeated attempts to deal with these systemic problems by introducing economic reform had come to very little by the mid-1980s, apart perhaps from in Hungary. The advent of Gorbachev in 1985 ushered in a new era in which for the first time in the Soviet Union the connection between economic performance and democracy has been officially recognized.

In both East and West overcentralization, bureaucracy and the exercise of arbitrary state or private power are now widely acknowledged to be major problems. The threat to personal freedom from the concentration of political and sometimes economic power in the state, the paternalism of nationalized industries and welfare state provision, the inefficiency of statist command planning, the power and lack of social accountability of large corporations, have between them led to a search for ways of decentralizing political power and economic decision-making.

Market socialism, in varying forms, has been increasingly advocated by reformers in the East and socialists in the West as the only way forward, the only viable third way. At a theoretical level the work of Lange (1938), Brus (1972) and Nove (1983) has been especially influential. At the level of historical experience the Yugoslav system of worker self-managed enterprises, whose activities are in principle coordinated by the market mechanism, is unique. There is also the Hungarian new economic mechanism, far less of a break with the command system than might appear and qualitatively different from the Yugoslav system.

The strongest argument for market socialism is that it is the only realistic, or feasible (Nove 1983), alternative to capitalism and, more particularly, to statist command planning. Its advocates accept that Yugoslavia has experienced the sort of economic instability and crisis more usually associated with the capitalist West and that Hungary's economic performance has not been noticeably better than that of other statist countries. However, the absence of political democracy means that neither country fully qualifies as an example of the sort of system recommended by market socialists. In any case, no one would expect market socialism, or indeed any system, to be perfect. The question is: is there a better alternative? Is there another third way?

This book is an attempt to show that there is, by developing a model of democratic planning based on negotiated coordination. In my view there are two fundamental problems with the model of market socialism which mean that it cannot constitute the economic part of a realistic vision of a self-governing society based on political and economic pluralism. The first is contingent. The case for planning is that it enables the conscious shaping of economic activity, in accordance with individually and collectively determined needs, and it overcomes the instability that is an endemic empirical characteristic of market-based economies. So far, neither historical experience nor the state of theory gives any reason to suppose that market-based economies can be managed or regulated effectively enough to achieve these objectives.

Second, the invisible hand, even if it could be steadied to avoid instability and guided to achieve broad social objectives, necessarily operates through an appeal to narrow individual or sectional self-interest and the coercion of market forces. It thus reinforces individualism and atomization and precludes conscious participation by people in the taking of key decisions that affect their lives. This, in turn, has far-reaching implications for motivation and the possibilities for linking the present and the future through transformatory activity and experience.

The fact that I reject market socialism as a model for the future does not mean that I necessarily regret the attempts currently being made to increase the role of the market in the Soviet Union, Eastern Europe and China. In my view, as argued in chapter 5, these are not socialist societies but rather societies with a non-capitalist social formation constituting an alternative to capitalism as a means for creating the material and cultural preconditions for socialism. It may be that a greater role for the market will be part of the process of undermining the monolithic political power of the state in these countries and moving towards political democracy, undoubtedly the central challenge facing them.

What is a matter for regret is the extent to which the doctrine of market socialism has achieved near hegemony among non-dogmatic, non-fundamentalist socialists in the West. The demise of capitalist planning and the breakdown of the post-war social democratic consensus on which it was based have not been replaced by a socialist trajectory. The crisis of the traditional socialist vision has enabled the new right's market-oriented project to gain the ascendancy. In my view, the increasing popularity of market socialism reflects the extent to which the ideology of the new right has succeeded in becoming dominant across the entire theoretical and political spectrum.

The rest of this introductory chapter assesses the Marxist socialist critique of capitalism and the crisis of credibility of the traditional model or vision of socialism. It then restates the case for socialism and planning in the light of historical experience and theoretical developments since the traditional model was developed.

Part II of the book looks in detail at the historical experience of planning, capitalist and statist, and examines the claim that market socialism enables effective planning to be combined with decentralized decision-making. Part III then sets out the objectives that I believe a desirable social system should seek to achieve. Part IV outlines the model of democratic planning based on negotiated coordination which, I argue, is a realistic third way whose logic works for the achievement of those objectives, unlike the logic of market socialism. Part IV is the core of the book. Part V then identifies trends present in today's capitalist and statist societies which might be developed as part of the process of transition to a democratically planned society.

1.2   The Marxist Socialist Critique of Capitalism

The traditional Marxist socialist critique of capitalism can be considered under three headings – exploitation, the anarchy of production and economic crisis, with the first two between them causing the third. The traditional case for socialism is that it abolishes exploitation and it replaces production for profit by production for use, that is, it replaces the anarchy of production for sale in the market by planned production for social need.

Under capitalism exploitation occurs as a result of the relationship between two classes: a minority class who between them own and control the means of production – capitalists; and a majority class who own no means of production – workers or wage labourers. Workers have no option but to work for one capitalist or another, on terms that produce a surplus in the form of unearned income, with the principal form of unearned income being profit. The market enters the picture in that workers' labour power, their ability to work, is bought and sold in the labour market and profit is only realized when what is produced is sold in the relevant product market. Thus, exploitation under capitalism results in profits and is mediated through markets.[2]

Marx used the term anarchy of production, Smith referred to the invisible hand. Both were talking about how society's productive resources come to be used in different branches of production and how changes in the pattern of resource use between different branches of production occur. Both were agreed that under capitalism this happens as a result of capitalists (also workers, landowners and moneylenders) responding to market forces. Capitalists take decisions about what, how and how much to produce with the intention of making as much profit as possible. Since each capitalist takes decisions independently of all other capitalists, and yet the outcome depends on the combined effect of all their decisions, the outcome of any individual decision cannot be known in advance.

If the result of all the independently-taken decisions is that too much or too little of any product is supplied, in relation to demand, the price at which the product can be sold, and therefore the profit realized, will be lower or higher than expected. Capital will move from low-profit branches of production to high-profit branches. Exit from and entry into branches of production will affect the balance between supply and demand in each branch and therefore the pattern of relative prices and profit rates. A new set of independent decisions will then be made, based on the new situation, with the outcome of each decision once again depending on the aggregate outcome of all decisions and therefore unknowable in advance.

In this way, resources are allocated and reallocated between different uses without any conscious overall decision or direction. The overall outcome is willed by no one. Independently taken individual decisions are coordinated but the coordination is unconscious, blind and invisible. Smith viewed the process as benign and so called it the invisible hand. Marx, while not denying the coordinating function of market forces, stressed the disruptive, wasteful, crisis-ridden character of the process and called it the anarchy of production.

Is there a connection under capitalism between exploitation and the anarchy of production? The standard Marxist argument is that the connection is provided by the institution of private property, by the private ownership of the means of production. Such private ownership is the basis for exploitation since it is the form through which the surplus produced is appropriated. It also necessitates the anarchy of production since the means of production are not owned collectively by the capitalist class but are divided into individual capitals, each privately owned by an individual capitalist with the exclusive right to determine its use. Private ownership of capitals and competition between them preclude any planned coordination before decisions are made and resources committed.

Marx's analysis of the law of motion of the capitalist mode of production is based on the coexistence of private property, private appropriation of the surplus and atomized decision-making. On the one hand, there is the need to maintain the conditions in which workers owning no means of production can be obliged to produce a surplus that is appropriated by capitalists owning the means of production and realized by them in the form of profit by being sold in the market. On the other hand, the increasingly social and interdependent character of production as a whole renders atomized decision-making increasingly disruptive and dysfunctional. It is the interaction of these two systemic features which gives rise to the economic crises and instability endemic to capitalism.

From this analysis has followed the traditional Marxist socialist, indeed general socialist, programme: the abolition of private ownership of the means of production and its replacement by social or common ownership. The emphasis has been on social ownership as a necessary condition for social control and the abolition of exploitation and the anarchy of production, that is, the replacement of production for profit for sale in the market by production for use in a planned economy. This programme, in varying forms, has been the bedrock of traditional socialist belief, rarely if ever challenged until recently. In the past decade or so, however, a crisis of credibility has arisen.

1.3   The Crisis of Credibility

The crisis of credibility of the traditional socialist programme has arisen as a result of over half a century's historical experience of what has been taken to be socialism in practice, and an even longer period of theoretical work. Three interrelated areas of reassessment can be identified: the relationships between legal ownership, actual control and exploitation; between planning and the market; and between individual freedom, planning and the market.

First, public, or state, ownership, whether in the public sector of capitalist economies or in the statist societies, has not in itself achieved what socialists have traditionally sought from common, or social, ownership. Nationalized industries and state-owned enterprises in the West have not behaved very differently overall from private sector enterprises, and they have been widely criticized for bureaucracy and inefficiency. The proper extent of direct state involvement in, and the criteria to be followed by, public sector enterprises remain unsettled and contested. Worker involvement in management has been token or non-existent, industrial conflict has not disappeared and the status of workers as wage labour is little if at all different from that of workers in the private sector.

It is equally true that workers in the statist countries, with the exception of Yugoslavia, play no part in management and are effectively wage labourers. Even in Yugoslavia unskilled workers play little part in the institutions of worker self-management and their actual status is hard to distinguish from that of wage labour, irrespective of the legal position. In the other statist countries the principle of one-person management has been rigorously operated and attempts to form workers' councils have been everywhere suppressed.[3] In this context, the issue of whether the control by the bureaucracy over the means of production carries with it some of the benefits traditionally associated with legal ownership has been the subject of continuing debate.

The traditional Marxist position on these issues is that everything depends on the character of the state. If, as in the West, it is a capitalist state, then state ownership is not social ownership. If it is a socialist state, as some socialists still argue is the case in what I have called the statist countries, then state ownership is the form taken by social ownership. There is no easy answer to this problem. The character of the state is certainly crucial. Yet this raises more questions than it answers. How democratic is the political system? How real is popular control over the decisions of state bodies? What sort of political and economic structure is necessary for self-government? This last question is really what this book is about.

What are the implications of this for the abolition of exploitation? The Marxist concept of exploitation is concerned with the extraction of a surplus product from the direct producers by an exploiting class. The traditional socialist programme assumes that with the abolition of private ownership exploitation is also abolished. Without at this stage considering the question of whether the controlling bureaucracy in the statist countries constitutes a new class, it is evident that workers in these countries have control neither of the production process nor of the use made of the social surplus, that is, the output not accruing to them directly in the form of household consumption.

Although not explicit in the classical Marxist analysis, it is surely implicit that the abolition of exploitation cannot mean just that the surplus product is no longer privately appropriated. It must also mean that the direct producers have some control over the production process and the use of the social surplus. For exploitation to be abolished in this sense requires some form of worker self-management and also democratic control over the state or the other institutions through which decisions over the use of productive capacity and the social surplus are made. In addition, there need to be processes or procedures that coordinate, or link together, the output decisions of production units and the demand for their output stemming from individually and collectively determined wants and needs.

This then connects with the second area, the relationship between planning and the market. Are the two antithetical, as in classical Marxism, or are they complementary, as argued by reformers in the East and market socialists in the West, with a regulated market mechanism constituting an essential instrument of planning? The traditional socialist programme envisaged the replacement of production for profit for sale in the market by planned production for use. This presupposes some way of determining what production is socially useful, some way for that information to be communicated to production units and reasonable confidence that they will respond to it.

For a small number of strategic objectives, given overriding priority, a centralized planning system in which the centre communicates its requirements directly to the production units has been shown to be effective, at least for a limited period, both in capitalist countries in wartime and in the Soviet Union. Increasingly, however, the authorities in the Soviet Union, Eastern Europe and China have been forced to recognize the need for reform. While this was initially couched primarily in terms of eradicating inefficiency and corruption, within a basically unchanged system, the balance has been shifting increasingly towards the need for systemic reform. The systemic problem has been identified as overcentralization, with the GDR pre–eminent in attempting administrative decentralization, and Hungary in pursuing market-based reform.

At the same time, theoretical work has increasingly tended to stress that resource allocation in a complex modern economy requires decentralized decision-making and that this can be coordinated only through the market mechanism. There are two interrelated strands to the argument. First, precisely because it does not involve a detailed blueprint being worked out in advance, it is claimed that only the market mechanism can convey sufficiently detailed information, in the form of market-determined prices, for individual production units to know what to do. Second, only through the market mechanism, it is said, can a system of incentives be operated such that individual production units respond to the information, or signals, available to them by producing what society individually and collectively wishes to use.

Profit, resulting from the relationship between the supply of and demand for a product, between the costs and revenues of production units, acts as a signal that more, less or the same quantity of a product is socially useful. At the same time, since the incomes of those working in the production units are related to profitability, there is an incentive for the production units to respond to the signal. Of course, most socialist advocates of the market mechanism, unlike the new right, are aware of the theoretical, not to mention empirical, shortcomings of the market: uncertainty, long gestation periods, indivisibilities, complementarities, externalities, monopoly power, inequality. They take it for granted that the market would need to be regulated.

In a regulated market socialist economy the market mechanism is used as a tool of planning. The pattern of prices and profit rates which makes up the economic environment to which production units respond is shaped by the use of economic regulators, by fiscal and monetary policy. The idea is that the market environment should reflect collectively determined as well as individual priorities plus any other information that would not otherwise be felt at the level of the individual production unit. It could be argued, therefore, that it would be better to refer to a regulated market mechanism (Brus 1972, ch. 5) rather than to market socialism, the most common current usage.

The issues raised in the discussion of plan and market are real and important. Any convincing model of planning must deal with them. Soviet and East European experience has almost universally been accepted as having demonstrated the need for movement in the direction of greater and more explicit decentralization. The reason why market socialism has increasingly come to dominate theoretical discussion of socialist planning is that the market has appeared to be the only means for achieving this. However, another reason for market socialism's attractive power has been the belief that it provides an alternative to the threat to individual freedom increasingly seen as inherent in highly centralized command planning and monolithic statist societies.

This, then, is the third area contributing to the crisis of credibility of the traditional socialist programme. Can a system of planning be devised that is not based on hierarchy and personal dependence? Is the market mechanism the only way in which the power of the state can be kept within bounds and individual freedom safeguarded? Few would argue that a market-based economic system is itself enough to guarantee individual freedom but, while it may not be sufficient, is it necessary?

If planning is identified with centralized command planning, in which the state issues directives which are passed down to and are binding on individual production units, then planning is necessarily hierarchical, based on relationships of superiority and subordination. If, in addition, all production units are state-owned and furthermore do not compete with one another, then individuals are dependent for work on the state and consumers and users of intermediate output are dependent on a single source of supply. In such a system, bureaucratic arbitrariness, on the one hand, and individual dependence on hierarchic superiors, on the other, are likely to be the norm.

At the economic level this type of planning displays systemic inefficiency, biased information flows, absence of adequate feedback mechanisms, low priority to consumer and user wants, private attempts to by-pass the formal system and official attempts to enforce it. Personal economic dependence carries with it a tendency towards risk avoidance and lack of innovation. It also undermines personal freedom, independence and self-reliance. If the society is politically monolithic, then the threat to freedom applies *a fortiori*.

A democratic political system is clearly a necessary condition for freedom. However, the argument that economic independence, in the sense of an absence of economic dependence on the state, is also a necessary foundation for political freedom has become increasingly convincing in the light of historical experience. Ironically for socialists, this argument can be thought of as implying a rehabilitation of the concept of property rights over the means of production. This would not in general be a rehabilitation of private property rights. Rather it would mean the creation of various forms of social ownership, such as workers' cooperatives or local community enterprises, with specified ownership rights, that is, rights of decision-making over the use to be made of the means of production involved.

Production units, no matter how owned, are necessarily involved in relationships with the suppliers of the inputs they use and the users or consumers of their output. Some means is therefore required for determining these relationships. Given the threat to freedom inherent in state determination through command planning, and the consequential need for socially-owned production units with rights that preclude arbitrary state interference or direction, the market mechanism, as a framework within which legally binding contracts are freely entered into, is seen by market socialists as indispensable. They see no other alternative to hierarchic command planning, no other way of coordinating decentralized decisions.

In my view, economic pluralism, in the sense of different types of social ownership and a multiplicity of decentralized, autonomous decision-making units, is essential in a free, self-governing society. However, there is a problem. Although individual private property might not exist, would not production units in such a system constitute *de facto* sectional private property, with decisions taken on the basis of sectional not social interest, whatever their *de jure* status as being socially owned? I shall argue that the logic of the market mechanism works precisely in that direction. By contrast, the logic of the model of negotiated coordination is for the tension between sectional and social interest to be made explicit when key decisions are being taken, with the possibility for at least partial reconciliation and also some transformation in the perceptions and level of social awareness of those involved.

1.4 The Case for Planning

At its most general the case for planning is that, through conscious social decisions and action, it enables more effective use of society's productive resources, in accordance with collectively and individually determined preferences, than would be possible without it. Planning provides a structure, a procedure, a form of social organization, that enables people to make most effective use of the possibilities open to them to achieve their objectives. It is a necessary condition for people individually and collectively to be able to control their lives, to exercise self-government. Thus, planning enables the maximization of positive freedom, by contrast with the wasteful and destructive automaticity of the unregulated market in which individuals and communities are buffeted by impersonal and coercive market forces beyond their control, or anyone else's.

It is a measure of the extent to which ideology dominates science in the discipline of economics that standard discussion of the case for collective action in relation to the economy starts from and remains within the paradigm of market failure. A perfectly competitive general equilibrium model is taken as the reference point and market failure is considered to exist when actual markets do not meet the conditions assumed by the model. Collective intervention is then assigned the task of correcting for the market failure. The model is based on methodological individualism, a doctrine in which social phenomena are explained solely in terms of the interactions of individuals acting to maximize their own narrow self-interest. There is no reason other than ideology to suppose that the conditions required for a competitive general equilibrium could ever be achieved, or that such a situation would be desirable even if it were possible.[4]

A competitive general equilibrium would be unlikely to be desirable, even if it were possible, for two reasons. First, the property of such an equilibrium that is supposed to recommend it is that it is Pareto-efficient. This means that resources are used in such a way that it is not possible to make one person better off without making another person worse off, a condition that is consistent with any degree of equality or inequality. Any Pareto-efficient equilibrium arrived at through a competitive economic system would have to incorporate significant inequality since such a system is motivated by the generation of inequality through rewarding success and penalizing failure. It would therefore be unlikely to be acceptable to many socialists.[5] Second, Pareto efficiency is defined in terms of people's existing preferences, assumed to be exogenous. However, preferences are in fact socially formed. All societies have structures, cultures and ideologies within which people grow up and live, and which shape their values and preferences. This is not a justification for paternalism, not an argument that the preferences of the state or planners should override people's existing preferences. It is, rather, an argument for democratically determined collective decisions and policies, based on existing preferences and values, to change the social determinants of preferences and so influence future preferences in socially desired ways.

Within standard economic theory market failure is recognized as a reason for collective action in cases when atomized self-seeking individual action cannot achieve the objectives of the individuals involved, namely, when prisoners' dilemma situations, externalities or public goods exist. In prisoners' dilemma situations, atomized decision-making prevents decision-makers from taking account of interdependencies that affect the outcome. The result is an outcome that none of the decision-makers would have chosen had they been able to get together to reach an agreed decision. It has been suggested that such situations make sense of Rousseau's notion of the general will, normally dismissed as a totalitarian concept by methodological individualists (Runciman and Sen 1965).

Prisoners' dilemma situations arise from the fact that in atomized decision-making people are by definition ignorant of the behaviour of others, yet to act effectively in their own narrow self-interest they need to know what the others are doing. In this they differ from situations in which externalities occur since externalities do not in principle arise from ignorance or uncertainty. Externalities exist because property rights are defined on too small a scale for the consequences of the use of property to be felt only by those who determine that use. They consist of costs or benefits that are not taken into account by narrowly self-interested decision-makers since some of the effects of using the property are borne by or benefit others. The extent and distribution of such external effects depend on the distribution of property rights. Externalities are the theoretical basis for the standard distinction between private and social costs and benefits.

Finally, there is the case for the collective provision of public goods. These are goods and services with two characteristics: first, everyone is affected by them, whether or not they are prepared to pay for them or want them, that is, no one can be excluded from their effects; and, second, their use by one person does not diminish their availability for use by others. The classic examples are law and order and defence. However, the concept of public goods can be extended to embrace collective provision contributing to the general fabric and ethos of a society, ranging from the prevailing level of education and standard of public health to a sense of solidarity and community.

The case for economic planning as a necessary condition for a self-governing society is more fundamental than that for collective action to deal with market failure. A democratically planned socialist economy has three essential advantages over an unplanned capitalist economy.[6] First, as already stated at the beginning of this section, the broad structure of resource utilization and the general direction of development of the economy can be planned in accordance with social priorities as determined through the democratic political process. At the national level, of course, only very broad priorities concerning economic development and social welfare can be decided, setting the framework for the more detailed decision-making by decentralized self-governing bodies that is characteristic of a self-governing society.

National decisions are likely to include: the rates of growth and investment, and therefore the overall balance between investment and consumption; the allocation of investment for the major expansion of key existing industries and the creation of new industries; the distribution of investment between regions; energy and transport policy; policy towards pollution control, environmental protection and resource conservation; the balance between individual household consumption and collective social provision; the distribution of personal income and a corresponding incomes policy; the coverage and character of social provision, including education and training, recreation, housing, health, social services and social security; science and research policy, in particular the sort of innovation to be encouraged; and the priority to be given to the promotion of more human social relations.

Of course, most of these issues are not left to the spontaneous workings of the invisible hand in modern capitalism. They are decided by the interaction of state policies, decisions of the large corporations and the struggles of the labour movement and other organized interest groups. Within this interaction, however, the private sector is favourably placed to dominate the outcome because of what Lindblom has called 'the privileged position of business' (Lindblom 1977, ch. 13). This privilege arises from the need for governments to create an environment that will induce the private sector to perform satisfactorily. It is supplemented by the economic power of business which gives it preferential access to the decision-making institutions and processes of the state.

If the private sector becomes too discontented with government policies there will be what may be called a capital strike or, in an international context, a flight of capital. For macroeconomic performance, the structure of resource allocation and the general direction of development of the economy to be determined democratically requires a fundamental redistribution of economic and political power. That is why socialists have historically sought the abolition of exploitation and private ownership and the abolition or democratization of the state. A redistribution of economic power is also a precondition for a more equal distribution of income, since investment would then no longer be motivated by the pursuit of unearned income accruing to private capital ownership.

The second argument for planning, indeed its principal technical advantage as a coordinating mechanism, arises from the fact that it enables the uncertainty associated with atomized decision-making to be overcome. Dobb, the most insistent and persuasive advocate of planning to date, has consistently stressed the significance for planning of the distinction between what he calls objective and subjective uncertainty. The former arises from our inability fully to know the future, the latter from the necessary lack of knowledge on the part of atomized decision-makers of their rivals' intended actions (Dobb 1955, p. 77; 1960, pp. 7–8; 1970b, p. 148). Koopmans refers to the same distinction as that between primary and secondary uncertainty (Koopmans 1957, pp. 162–3).

Primary uncertainty covers things like whether or not there will be a nuclear war, natural disasters, climatic changes, changes in social values and individuals' preferences, changes in technology, the discovery of new sources of energy or raw materials. Secondary uncertainty arises from 'lack of communication, that is from one decision-maker having no way of finding out the concurrent decisions and plans made by others' (Koopmans 1957, p. 163). It exists when enterprises make decisions independently of one another, the defining characteristic of an economy based on market forces.

Primary uncertainty is not system-specific in the sense that secondary uncertainty is. Of course, forecasts based on estimates or judgements of the likelihood of alternative primary outcomes can be made, as can contingency plans allowing for a flexible response depending on the outcome. Furthermore, collective social action can be taken to reduce the likelihood and/or consequences of undesired outcomes and increase the likelihood of desired outcomes. If the possibility of such collective action being taken depends to some extent on the characteristics of the society in question, then the degree of primary uncertainty is to that extent system specific. Indeed, an important aspect of the first advantage claimed for planning is precisely the possibility it affords for the conscious shaping of the general direction of development of the economy. However, while primary uncertainty may be less in some social systems than in others it will always be present. Secondary uncertainty, by contrast, is contingent on the existence of coordination through the market mechanism. It is unavoidable given such coordination but can be overcome by planning.

The consequences of secondary uncertainty for capitalism are severe, particularly in relation to investment. Investment decisions are made on the basis of expectations about future profitability. Future profitability depends in part on what other projects are being undertaken or planned simultaneously, since they will affect future supply and hence price and/or the degree of capacity utilization. However, in fragmented, atomistic, market-based decision-making, individual investment decisions are made on the basis of unavoidable ignorance of the actions of others. Hence, the expectations underlying them are in general unlikely to be realized.

Secondary uncertainty is one of the principal reasons for capitalism's macroeconomic instability. It is central to Keynes's analysis of capitalism and the macroeconomic demand management policies following from it. However, demand management is not based on the abolition of atomistic decision-making and the secondary uncertainty associated with it. Rather, it is a technocratic exercise seeking to compensate for the destabilizing consequences of such atomistic decision-making. Macroeconomic management is discussed in the next chapter. It represents an important recognition of the need for planning but it should not be mistaken for planning and it has been only partially successful in modifying capitalist instability.

In addition to their contribution to macroeconomic instability, atomized decision-making and secondary uncertainty are fundamental obstacles to rational decision-making about investment. Investment changes the distribution of productive capacity between different branches of production and, in the absence of constant returns to scale or when embodying technical change, may alter the relative production costs of different products. Investment decisions to be rational should be made on the basis of the future pattern of relative costs and prices not the existing pattern. Secondary uncertainty prevents atomized decision-makers from making as good estimates of the future as is possible in a planned economy. In a planned economy, major investments, those bringing about non-marginal changes, are planned together and coordinated in advance, thus substantially reducing if not abolishing secondary uncertainty.[7]

The third essential advantage of planning as an economic mechanism, then, is that it makes possible the coordination of interrelated decisions before they are implemented. It substitutes the conscious, planned coordination of decisions *ex ante* for the blind, anarchic coordination of the market mechanism *ex post*, operating through the changing reactions of atomistic decision-makers to continuously changing market prices. In a sense this is the essence of economic planning and constitutes the fundamental difference between a planned and an unplanned economy (Dobb 1955, p. 76; 1960, p. 5). It is this *ex ante* coordination that accounts for the superiority of estimates of the future in a planned economy. Those involved in carrying out particular investment projects know, rather than guess, hope or even expect, that projects being undertaken simultaneously are complementary to their own rather than in competition with them.

However, *ex ante* coordination is more generally advantageous for a wide range of decisions. The coordination in advance of investment not only enables rational decision-making, in the sense that decisions can be related to the future pattern of relative costs and prices, reflecting the desired future structure of production; it also economizes in the use of resources by reducing waste. Investment embodies resources in fixed capital equipment which cannot normally be dismantled and then reconstituted in a new form. Most capital equipment is fairly specific, with a limited range of uses to which it can be put. Thus, if more investment in a particular branch of production is undertaken than is needed, some of the productive capacity installed will be underused and the resources embodied in the fixed capital will be wasted.

In a capitalist economy, even if all the enterprises producing for a particular market agree on what total market demand is likely to be over the period relevant for current investment decisions, they are unlikely to agree on their individual shares of the market. Since they are competing against each other they will each be seeking to increase their share and they will make their investment decisions accordingly. Thus, total planned capacity will tend to exceed what all agree is needed to satisfy total expected demand. The result will be excess capacity, profits lower than expected, the scrapping of capacity and the waste of the resources embodied in it. If too much capacity is scrapped, which given the absence of coordination in advance is likely, shortage will occur creating anew the possibility of investment expected to be profitable.

A generalization of this process is what underlies the cyclical economic crises endemic to capitalism. In the upswing, when expectations are buoyant, enterprises invest in order to take advantage of the increasing demand. This occurs throughout the economy and for a time the growth of capacity in the different branches of production is mutually reinforcing, with respect both to the availability of necessary intermediate inputs and to the multiplied and accelerated generation of demand for their output. Eventually, however, wages rise, the accumulation of productive capacity outstrips the possibilities of selling its output profitably, expectations change and a cumulative downswing sets in. Boom gives way to slump, capital equipment is scrapped, workers are unemployed and resources are generally wasted. However, in the logic of capitalism economic crises have a function in that they eventually create the conditions for renewed profitable investment.

Waste in modern capitalist economies is not confined to periods of economic crisis. Most industries are not competitive in the sense used in standard analysis of perfect or monopolistic competition but are oligopolistic, that is, most productive capacity and output is controlled by a relatively small number of typically large enterprises. These enterprises are atomistic, however, in the sense in which I have been using the term, since ultimately they take decisions independently of one another. Their small number makes it possible, and their awareness of their interdependence makes it sometimes profitable, for them to get together to exchange information or to collude in restricting competition between them. Such contact or collusion constitutes a series of more or less temporary alliances in a war of all against all, normally at the expense of consumers and users, rather than a form of permanent cooperative coordination of decisions and actions in advance. Nevertheless, in a distorted way it is a recognition of the need for planning.

Oligopolistic rivalry gives rise to characteristic forms of waste arising from the forms of non-price competition typically associated with it. The common feature of non-price competition is the attempt by each enterprise to differentiate its products from those of its rivals and thus insulate the markets for them from rivals' incursions. The principal forms of product differentiating activity are sales promotion, most visibly but not necessarily most importantly advertising, and minor innovation, such as a new shape, colour or package. While some of this may be socially useful, in that it provides information or variety, much of it involves the proliferation of essentially identical products, the duplication of mutually cancelling sales promotion and product development activity, and the systematic promotion of misinformation and appeal to irrationality.[8]

Lastly, the coordination of decisions in advance that planning enables is of immeasurable importance for regions, local communities, individual workplaces and the people who live and work in them. Decisions about the distribution of economic activity, about where it is located, where it expands and contracts, have a major effect on people's lives. If participatory democracy and self-government are to be real people must have the opportunity to be involved in taking these decisions – and that requires planning.

In an unregulated market-based economy, the geographical distribution of economic activity is determined by the aggregate outcome of the uncoordinated decisions of individual enterprises, each motivated by the expectation of profitable investment. In theory, capital moves from regions where profitability expectations are lower to those where they are higher. This evens out the balance between the demand for and supply of productive resources in each region and therefore equalizes regional profit rates, in the same way that capital mobility between industries is supposed to equalize industry profit rates. In fact, the regional problem, in the form of persistent inequalities in employment opportunities, unemployment and income levels, is acute in virtually all capitalist countries, as it is in Yugoslavia, the only statist country that is market-based.

The essential reason for the persistence of the regional problem is that the market mechanism rewards success as calculated on the basis of existing and expected future patterns of relative profitability. Analysis of this process has led to the generalization of an argument first applied to individual industries, the so-called infant industry argument. The argument is that while a new industry in a particular country is being established it must be protected from the more competitive exports of the same industry already established in other countries, or it will never get off the ground. This argument has been extended to the case of newly developing countries facing competition from already established modern economies, with the development of the Japanese economy behind a highly effective protective wall being perhaps the best known example. More recently, the argument has been extended further to the situation of developed economies that have begun to decline relatively.

Thus, discussing deindustrialization in the United Kingdom, Singh (1977) has distinguished between successful, internationally competitive economies enjoying the dynamic of a virtuous circle and unsuccessful, uncompetitive economies, like that of the UK, locked into a vicious circle of cumulative relative decline. Uncompetitive economies, whatever the initial causes, experience balance of payments problems which enforce a slower rate of growth and therefore a lower rate of investment. Since most new technology is embodied in capital equipment, low investment results in increasing technical backwardness, the initial lack of competitiveness is reinforced and the vicious circle is given a further twist. The process works in reverse for initially competitive economies.

Geographical inequality is due to an uneven rate of economic development or decline within a country or between countries. In all cases, free trade, the logic of market forces, favours the more competitive enterprises, regions or countries at the expense of the less competitive. To break the logic of a system that combines cumulative relative prosperity for some with cumulative relative decline for others requires, at least, determined collective action and, at best, the planned implementation of an interrelated set of mutually reinforcing measures, coordinated in advance.

Regional or national development or decline is made up of changes for better or worse at the level of individual local communities and places of work. The anarchy of production, even when called the invisible hand, closes workplaces, undermines communities and destroys valued cultures and ways of life. In doing so it causes misery and despair and also the bitterness and anger which have motivated struggle against closure and unemployment through the ages. It also creates new jobs, skills, workplaces, communities and opportunities. Change is not always bad, nor of course good, and there will always be changes that are judged to be desirable. The point is that market forces act blindly and those affected are not involved in taking the decisions that affect them. The only way in which they can have any influence in a market-based economy is if they are able to apply political or industrial pressure, if they are able to bargain or negotiate.

This outline of the case for planning has ended where it began. Planning is necessary if people are to be able to shape their own lives, if they are to exercise self-government. Most major and many minor decisions have consequences for others. Interdependence is the defining feature of social existence, not in the sense of atoms bouncing off one another, but in the sense that our relationships with others shape both us and them. If we are to act rationally, in the fullest possible awareness of all the factors relevant to our actions, we must place our interdependence with others at the centre of our considerations. In the economic sphere this means that major decisions that affect one another should be coordinated in advance by those affected by them. Conscious, planned, *ex ante* coordination needs to replace the unconscious, blind, *ex post* coordination of the unregulated market mechanism.

1.5   Models of Planning

At the start of this chapter, I stated that this book is based on two
assumptions: first, that neither capitalism nor statism is the way
forward and a third way is needed; and, second, that people create
themselves and have the capacity for self-transformation. To these I
now add a third assumption: that planning is necessary for self-
determination and self-government. The rest of the book is about the
form of planning.

Although capitalist countries do not have planned economies there
are elements of planning to be found in them from which we can learn.
These elements, discussed in the next chapter, are concerned primarily
with ways of modifying the operation of market forces and the
consequences of uncoordinated decision-making. Economic planning,
however, is normally associated with the statist countries. The rapid
rate of economic development in the Soviet Union during the 1930s is
evidence of the formidable ability of its centralized command planning
system to mobilize and concentrate resources. The experience of the
Soviet Union and Eastern Europe until recently in maintaining full
employment and avoiding inflation suggests the different order of
control over an economy made possible by planning. Much can be
learned from the experience of statist planning, which is discussed in
chapter 3. Yet the absence of democracy, the human cost involved and
the mounting problems now evident suggest that the lessons are as
much negative as positive.

What is needed is a form of democratic planning combining centrally
taken decisions where necessary with decentralized decision-making
wherever possible. Market socialism, discussed in chapter 4, is widely
held to be the only way in which this can be achieved. Regulated
market socialism, its advocates claim, would dispense with capitalist
social relations and thus enable market forces to be harnessed to
planning. I believe, on the contrary, that the argument developed in
the previous section establishes a strong *prima facie* case against the
possibility of using the market mechanism as an instrument of planning.

It is important to be precise here since the term market is used in
very different ways and the crucial distinction between market
exchange and market forces is often obscured. Holesovsky defines the
institution of the market as 'stabilized patterns of buying or selling' and
argues that 'being a sale–purchase transaction is the essence of market
exchange' (Holesovsky 1977, pp. 25, 69). Here, the market is being
defined in terms of exchange, with no reference to decisions about
production. This is the sense in which market exchange in prisoner-of-
war camps has been discussed, with the set of tradeable goods being

what the prisoners received from home in parcels. Cigarettes emerged as money, people exchanged things that they valued less for things that they valued more and everyone ended up better off (Radford 1945).

A formally identical situation, although slightly more complicated, is a model in which the starting point for exchange is a set of intermediate goods, that is, of capital equipment and material inputs, that already exists. These intermediate goods have alternative uses and their ownership is distributed among the participants in the economy on an arbitrary basis. Since available intermediate goods and labour services are given, the different alternative structures of output that can be produced are determined. Analysis then consists in demonstrating that exchange motivated by self-interest results in the particular structure and distribution of output that is Pareto-efficient. This structure and distribution, of course, reflect the initial distribution of ownership of intermediate goods and labour services. However, the crucial point for the present argument is that the underlying structure of resource allocation, the initial set of intermediate goods, is taken as given and not discussed. There is production in the economy but only from existing capacity. There is no investment to change capacity, to change the set of capital equipment and material inputs, no fundamental redeployment of resources. In this crucial sense, market forces do not operate in this model, there is no change in the underlying structure of resource allocation.

I wish to distinguish between market exchange, on the one hand, and market forces, or the invisible hand, or the anarchy of production, on the other. By these latter terms I mean a process whereby change occurs in the pattern of investment, in the structure of productive capacity, in the relative size of different industries, in the geographical distribution of economic activity, in the size and even the existence of individual production units, as a result of atomized decisions, independently taken, motivated solely by the individual decision-makers' perceptions of their individual self-interest, not consciously coordinated by them in advance. It is to this process that I am referring when I argue against the use of market forces or the market mechanism as an instrument of economic planning.[9]

No contemporary model of planning, whether statist, regulated market socialist or the model of negotiated coordination developed in Part IV, incorporates the direction of labour or the rationing or free distribution of all consumer goods. The continued existence of labour markets, in which people agree to participate in production in exchange for income, and of consumer markets, in which consumer goods and services are bought and sold, is not at issue. At issue between statist and regulated market socialist models is whether all decisions affecting the activities of production units are taken centrally and communicated

vertically downwards as instructions or whether some decisions are
arrived at by horizontal interaction. At issue between regulated market
socialist models and the model of negotiated coordination is whether
horizontal interaction must necessarily involve market forces, the
market mechanism.

Nove thinks it must: 'it is clear that someone (some institution) has to
tell the producers about what the users require. If that "someone" is
not the impersonal market mechanism it can only be a hierarchical
superior. There are horizontal links (market), there are vertical links
(hierarchy). What other dimension is there?' (Nove 1983, p. 226).

I think Nove is mistaken. Of course, if horizontal links are defined as
market links involving the market mechanism there can be no
argument. However, what is the essence of the point Nove is making?
Is it that horizontal links involve exchange between producers and
users or that horizontal links involve producers in taking decisions
without reference to any higher level body or to other producers in the
same line of production? Is he referring only to decisions involving the
use to be made of existing capacity, that is, current production, or
would he also include decisions about investment and the expansion of
existing capacity, about contraction and closure? Nove's outline of his
model of feasible socialism (Nove 1983, Part 5) is vague on these
questions. Yet they are crucial and the answers to them, in my view,
determine whether or not a model is based on the use of market forces.
They determine whether major interdependent decisions would be
made in isolation, with the advantages of planning being lost, or would
be planned together and coordinated in advance.

At the moment, in all economies, most transactions between
enterprises are based on an established pattern of horizontal relationships which are only reassessed when they cease to satisfy the
requirements of those involved.[10] These relationships are between
producers and users and in market economies constitute what I have
called above market exchange. Change in the established pattern
resulting from reassessment typically involves negotiation. The model
of negotiated coordination is a qualitative development of this existing
reality. In it, such horizontal relationships and reassessments continue
to be the basis of transactions concerned with current production, that
is, most transactions. However, the crucial difference by comparison
with market economies is that negotiation is extended to embrace
relationships between enterprises in the same branch of production
when changes in capacity are at issue. Thus, while market exchange
exists market forces do not.

This crucial difference enables decisions about changes in the size of
production units and branches of production, about investment or
contraction, to be coordinated in advance. It enables decentralization

of routine, day-to-day decisions to be combined with coordinated decision-making when significant interdependence is present. Thus, when decisions potentially affecting the future of individual workplaces and communities are being taken, those potentially affected can participate consciously in taking them. In this way, negotiated coordination, unlike command planning instruction and market force coercion, creates the possibility for people consciously to transform their perceptions, values and motivation by confronting their own interests with those of others and seeking a resolution. As is elaborated in Part IV, the process of negotiated coordination can be generalized to incorporate all interests affected by major decisions and to cover all major decisions affecting people's lives. The interests participating in negotiation can be constituted narrowly or broadly, involving more or less (de)centralization, according to the issue.[11]

It will, I hope, be clear that the model of negotiated coordination is not based on the assumption of perfect knowledge or optimality. In relation to neoclassical theory's 'myopic concentration on problems of marginal adjustment', Dobb has referred to the 'Perfectibility Fallacy' (Dobb 1970b, p. 121). In Ellman's view, the waste and inefficiency of statist planning arise because it is based on the false assumption of 'a perfect knowledge, deterministic world, in which unique perfect plans can be drawn up for the present and the future' (Ellman 1979, p. 73). More generally, Lindblom has distinguished between two models, with different assumptions about the nature of social reality: Model 1, based on the possibility of perfectibility and the scientific discovery of correct solutions in the interests of all – the paternalist model; and Model 2, based on the permanence of fallibility and on preference-guided choice through a process of social interaction – the pluralist model (Lindblom 1977, ch. 19).

The process of negotiated coordination in my model has similarities with the 'social processes or interactions that substitute for conclusive analysis' in Lindblom's Model 1 (Lindblom 1977, p. 253). However, in the economic sphere, although not unaware of the problems associated with private property and atomized decision-making, Lindblom espouses the market mechanism as the way of organizing preference-guided, pluralist social interaction. He sometimes also gives the impression of underestimating the role that knowledge and reason can and should play in the process of self-determining, self-governing democratic decision-making. My model of negotiated coordination is not based on perfectibility, whether of knowledge or solutions, but it is based on a belief in reason and in the possibility of transformation and progress.

PART II

Historical Experience

2

Capitalist Planning

2.1 Wartime Planning

The British economy during the Second World War was planned to an extent greater than ever before or since and greater than the economy of any other capitalist democracy has been to date. The British war economy was administratively planned which meant '*not* that there was rationing and price control of consumer demand, but that a major part of the economic decision process at "intermediate stages" took place not through influencing prices and incomes – planning through the price mechanism – but by administrative decision, allocation, direction and specific decision what to produce and where' (Devons 1970, pp. 103–4). However, this did not mean that there was a detailed blueprint covering the economy as a whole. Instead, there was a set of interlocking sectoral plans which were rendered more or less consistent a complex process of iteration and negotiation.

The overriding objective was to mobilize the entire economy for the war effort. This was done in real not financial terms with all major allocations determined directly in physical units and financial flows subsequently shaped to parallel them. As the official war history put it when summing up, 'The reckonings of national achievement to which people had accustomed themselves had been in physical terms. Finance had lost its traditional significance as a criterion and a method of control' (Hancock and Gowing 1949, p. 553). Direct allocation in real terms was necessary because the speed with which resources had to be redeployed and the need to achieve redeployment with reasonable equality of sacrifice, in order to maintain the national consensus, precluded the use of market forces.

The absence of any need for a comprehensive, economy wide blueprint is an important lesson of British wartime planning. Cairncross refers to 'The lesson that planning was essentially a technique of grappling with uncertainty, and that it rested on readiness to replan' (Cairncross 1970, p. 18). Robinson, discussing the overall allocation of resources, argues, 'The main purpose of economic planning, in war as in peace, is to foresee difficulties sufficiently in advance for it to be possible to diminish their impact and, if practicable, to avert them entirely' (Robinson 1951, p. 56). Indeed, in the absence of change, planning would not have been necessary. Reflecting on his experience in the Ministry of Aircraft Production, Devons writes, 'One of the main features of the task of co-ordination was that it was easiest when least needed, i.e. when conditions were fairly stable, and most difficult when it was most necessary, i.e. when conditions were changing rapidly' (Devons 1951, p. 114). The speed of response to changing circumstances was a major advantage of the wartime planning system: 'the power to make rapid changes in the disposition of the nation's resources was the greatest war-winning weopon of all' (Robinson 1951, p. 36; see also Devons 1970, p. 108).

Decisions covering the economy as a whole were made only in relation to the allocation of resources between 'broad classes of uses – military, home, export' and did not require detailed knowledge within each use (Chester 1951, p. 12). By the end of 1941 effective full employment had been achieved, employment in less essential civil industries was reaching an irreducible minimum and the question of having to make choices within the war zone of the economy itself had increasingly to be faced (Robinson 1951, p. 43). The allocation of 'manpower' was the key to the overall allocation of resources: 'It was, in fact, the only method the War Cabinet ever possessed of determining the balance of the whole war economy by a central and direct allocation of physical resources among the various sectors . . . every economic enterprise needed manpower, and to control its distribution from the centre signified direct central planning of the whole economy' (Hancock and Gowing 1949, p. 452).

Manpower planning operated through a series of manpower surveys, starting in 1941, and manpower budgets based on them. The surveys estimated both total labour availability, after expected wastage, new entry and any change in the participation rate, and also the possibilities for transfer out of less essential industries. The budgets set those estimates against forecasts of manpower requirements from the armed services, munitions industries and essential civil production. The inevitable excess demand for labour was then resolved in broad terms at the top level, frequently involving fundamental policy changes. Once the broad allocation had been decided, the government departments involved revised their production targets within each broad heading and contracts and labour allowances were then agreed with firms.

The implementation of changes in the use of labour, in accordance with the final budget that emerged from this process, was the responsibility of the network of labour exchanges. In addition to military conscription, a system of industrial conscription operated. Workers in certain categories could be compulsorily transferred to other jobs. In specified industries they could not leave or be sacked without official agreement. All new employment in certain industries had to be obtained through the employment exchanges. There was, in effect, formal direction of labour, although available labour was normally steered, rather than directed, to the most urgent use for which it was suitable, in a system of 'manpower allocation, supported but not distorted by preferences' (Robinson 1951, p. 51).

The system operated reasonably well. It depended very heavily on consent and goodwill. Firms had to cooperate in not requesting more manpower than their contracts warranted, despite the fact that the penalty for failing to meet production targets was normally greater than that for exceeding labour entitlement. Ministry of Labour staff in the employment exchanges required constantly changing, up-to-date information about the relative importance of the work being undertaken by the firms they dealt with, which had to come from the different national supply departments through their local representatives. Regions with complementary labour surpluses and deficits had to cooperate with each other, although in general it proved more effective to take work to the workers than to seek large scale movement of labour between regions. There were, of course, biases in the information supplied to the decision makers, stemming from people's perceptions of their own self-interest, but the system was difficult to police and could not have worked as effectively as it did had not most people been committed to the war effort and cooperated honestly with the authorities.[1]

The change to a war economy had dramatic effects on the suppliers of 'manpower' and the households in which they lived. The bitter irony that the achievement of full employment under capitalism seemed dependent on mobilization for war was not lost on people, although the consequences of that realization were postponed until the war was over and the whole of Europe moved to the left, in what was seen by many at the time as a socialist direction. In the meantime the war had to be waged, working-class cooperation was essential and the conditions for that cooperation had to be created.

A shortage of skilled workers meant that dilution was required. This involved the crash-training of unskilled workers to do skilled jobs and their acceptance by skilled workers and the relevant trade unions, despite their not having served an apprenticeship and the potential threat they posed to hard-won conditions of work. More generally, the changes necessary in hours of work and work practice required the cooperation of workers and the organized labour movement at all levels. Bevin, the leader of the largest unskilled workers' union, was Minister of Labour, a member of the five-strong War Cabinet and effectively in charge of the home front. In some factories Joint Production Committees were formed, consisting of representatives of workers and management, to find ways of increasing production. Collective bargaining was not abolished but was used with moderation, although strikes did occasionally occur.

With the economy mobilized to the full for war the standard of living fell, on average. The extent to which it could be reduced depended on what was necessary to maintain people's ability to work and on public opinion. It was rapidly realized that a condition for working-class cooperation was a sense of equality of sacrifice. An extensive system of price control and rationing was operated, with specified standards and a utility scheme for clothing and furniture. Although the average standard of living fell, what was available was more evenly distributed and overall people were healthier than ever before, in part contributed to also by greater attention to welfare at work. While prices were controlled wages were not and, although collective bargaining was used with restraint, money incomes crept up. Inflationary pressure was contained by taxation, compulsory saving, price control and rationing.

The war economy was planned on the basis of conscious direct allocation, even though production was undertaken by firms that remained predominantly privately owned and motivated by profit. This gave rise to a tension between the residual need for profit-based incentives to achieve production targets and, if the national consensus was to be maintained, the need to prevent profiteering in conditions of excess demand. Equality of sacrifice was also threatened by the, in the circumstances inevitable, 'black' marketeering. Even so, the social contract held and present privations were expected to lead eventually to a new era, the welfare state: 'There existed . . . an implied contract between Government and people' (Hancock and Gowing 1949, p. 541).[2]

Although manpower became the scarcest resource and the basis of the most general level of overall planned allocation, material inputs and transport and, associated with these, imports were also scarce and for particular purposes might constitute the binding constraint. Robinson sums the situation up as follows:

> any attempt to work out an overriding allocation in terms of manpower as the scarcest of all resources or of money as a general common measure of all resources was foredoomed to failure. It was necessary to work simultaneously in terms of all the scarce resources, to give each its paramountcy in the field in which it particularly applied, and to see that, so far as human intelligence was capable of providing, the decisions made

under one head were reasonably consistent with the decisions made under other heads (Robinson 1951, p. 57)

The method used to do this was that of budgeting, similar to the manpower budgeting outlined above and, in a different context, to the material balances used in Soviet central planning. There was no overall plan integrating the budgets for each separate material input. Instead there was a process of continuous interaction, negotiation and revision of allocations. In many ways it was a process of negotiated coordination between the officials responsible for controlling the allocation of materials, on the basis of their budgets and their collectively constructed view of the most urgent needs. Specific allocations were not made on the basis of technical coefficients or any formula, but on the best judgement of those involved, taking into account all the information available to them.[3]

What conclusions can be drawn from wartime planning in capitalist Britain? It was immensely effective in the short run in deploying the nation's resources for the war effort. The task was to make the best use of available resources, domestic and imported, to achieve the overriding objective of surviving and winning the war. However, the disaggregation of this one national objective into detailed guidance on what production best contributed to its achievement at each stage of the war was not easy and the procedure for doing so was complex and constantly subject to revision. Furthermore, the task was seen as essentially short-term so the problem of long-run investment did not arise. In 1941 the length of the war was not foreseen, while in 1944 the manpower allocations were based on the maximum possible military effort and the assumption of victory that year (Hancock and Gowing 1949, p. 451).

Two important lessons emerge. No detailed overall blueprint was required for planning. It proved possible for current production and investment with limited gestation periods to be coordinated in advance through a complex process of negotiation. The changes in the pattern of output that needed coordinating were determined by the judgement of an interrelated set of government officials, responsible for interpreting how the changing requirements of national strategy could best be met. These changes were implemented by the same officials, through an iterative negotiation between those responsible for different branches of production, leading eventually to contracts between government bodies and individual firms. Within the portion of resources allocated for civil consumption, changes in the pattern of output were determined 'through consumer surveys and by watching statistics of stocks and sales. Production was then organized to meet demand' (Hancock and Gowing 1949, p. 494).

The system worked primarily through consent and the commitment of people to making it work. The social contract on which it rested represented an uneasy compromise. Production had to be profitable enough for the private sector to cooperate but not so profitable as to offend people's sense of equality of sacrifice. Workers could be involved in discussing ways of increasing output in Joint Production Committees but not to the extent of undermining the prerogatives of management. Fundamental changes in the pattern of ownership and, assumed to go with it, control had to wait for the end of the war. As the official history put it, 'Requisitioning of the mines might well have made not only production control but also financial control much easier. But the politics of coalition . . . ruled it out' (Hancock and Gowing 1949, p. 510). Yet the system did work.

The conclusion to be drawn from the experience of wartime planning is that, in the exceptional conditions prevailing, with a single overriding objective, the two conditions necessary for coherent planning were both fulfilled: adequate information and adequate motivation. The two are of course connected. Furthermore, they were fulfilled without recourse to market forces and could not have been fulfilled had market forces been operative.

The information needed for the negotiated coordination of current production was generated because of the commitment and motivation of the people involved. The information about production possibilities and input requirements on the basis of which decisions were made was supplied by firms. It was distorted to some extent by biases reflecting residual narrow self-interest but by and large it was adequate. Firms were effectively instructed from above what to produce and did not decide this on the basis of horizontal negotiation with one another. Decisions were made through horizontal negotiation between what amounted to industry-wide coordinating bodies, informed by a view of the national interest. Financial flows were shaped to provide adequate profit and wage incentives at firm level but did not determine production decisions. Markets existed but in any significant sense market forces did not. There was planned production for need, as it was defined by the nation at war.

2.2   Macroeconomic Management

The fact that neoclassical economics dominated the discipline from 1870 until Keynes and has recently made a comeback with monetarism and the new classical school, despite its doctrine that unemployment is all due to market imperfections and state interference, is another measure of the power of ideology. Keynes sought to save capitalism from itself and from its supporters by providing a theoretical basis for state intervention to achieve and maintain full employment, within an otherwise essentially unchanged capitalist economy. He argued that, in a context of atomized decision-making, the split between decisions about saving and investment, made possible by the use of money to postpone expenditure as a hedge against uncertainty, created not only fluctuations in the rate of investment but also a tendency for such fluctuations to be around an equilibrium level lower than that required for full employment.

It followed that the state should intervene to compensate for the instability of investment and to boost the underlying level of expenditure to the full employment level. It should do this directly by itself undertaking expenditure in excess of its revenue, preferably on socially useful projects, but if necessary on paying the unemployed to dig holes and then fill them up again. It should also intervene indirectly by seeking to influence private sector expenditure through taxation, transfers and monetary policy. In these ways, the state should act to maintain the total level of effective demand, or expenditure, in the economy at a level just sufficient to buy the full employment volume of output valued at existing prices. A lower level of expenditure would mean unemployment, a higher level would result in inflation and balance of payments problems.

In Britain the implicit wartime contract discussed in the previous section and the theoretical and policy impact of Keynes reinforced one another. Together they resulted in a broad consensus that it was the responsibility of the government to ensure full employment, defined as three per cent unemployed (Beveridge 1944, pp. 126–8), and that it was possible for government action to achieve this. The change in perception marked by the near-universal rejection of the previous fatalistic view that unemployment was due to objective economic laws, and the government could do nothing about it, was a major historic advance. It placed on the agenda the possibility of conscious collective social action to control the economy, instead of having passively to accept the outcome thrown up by uncontrollable market forces.

However, although macroeconomic demand management may have been stabilizing in the short run [4], it was potentially subversive of capitalism in the longer term. If social control is acceptable at the macro-level, why not also at the micro-level? Furthermore, if macroeconomic management proves unable to maintain an acceptable macroeconomic performance, if it perhaps even contributes to the accumulation of economic and political forces that prevent it from doing so, what then?

In fact, the decline in the intellectual status, though not the technocratic elaboration, of macroeconomics in the 1970s and 1980s, as macroeconomic instability and crisis reasserted themselves in the capitalist world, has been accompanied by two opposing responses. The ideologically dominant response has been a recrudescence of neoclassical doctrine in new forms – rejecting state intervention in the form of macroeconomic demand management and emphasizing monetary control, the conditions of supply and the primacy of market forces. The alternative response has been to seek ways other than, or in addition to, macroeconomic management to exercise social control over the economy.

There are three interrelated reasons why the promise of macroeconomic management has not been fulfilled, all stemming from the fact that it seeks to compensate for the social irrationality of atomistic decision-making based on private ownership and the pursuit of narrow self-interest, rather than to replace it. First, in class and interest group divided societies, with narrow self-interest as the motivating force of behaviour, competition between groups possessing roughly equal power produces stalemate and paralysis.[5] Full employment in a capitalist society is dysfunctional for the economic system. It strengthens the position of workers in the labour market and the production process and obstructs the creative role of economic crisis in recreating the conditions for profitable production. The result is inflation and relative stagnation (Devine 1974; Rowthorn 1980; Bleaney 1985).

There is thus an element of plausibility in the new neoclassical attack on Keynesianism and on the role of the state in capitalist society more generally. Its critique is in part directed at the real inefficiencies and irrationalities associated with the intervention of a paternalistic state into ever more areas of economic and social life. However, the new doctrine depends theoretically on the assumption of atomistic decision-making on the basis of adaptive or rational expectations and flexible market clearing prices (see Tobin 1980, Ch. II).[6] People are assumed to behave as if they were in a neoclassical world where changes in monetary magnitudes have no long-run effect on the real economy and all unemployment is voluntary. The new theorists have unlearned the profound insight of Keynes, and Marx before him, that the existence of money affects the real economy by enabling people in the aggregate to postpone expenditure. At the theoretical level they have not refuted Keynes's fundamental argument, they have ignored it (Bleaney 1985, p. 199). In modern capitalist economies, when unemployment exists, an expansion of monetary demand is likely to remain central to any policy aimed at reaching full employment.

However, whether demand expansion by itself is sufficient to maintain full employment, or in some circumstances even to achieve it, is another matter. In the long run the social relations of production cannot be ignored. Keynes did ignore them and, although aware of the problem of inflationary pressure in a fully employed economy, did not consider or was not interested in the long-term compatibility of full employment and capitalism. An early response to the problem of inflationary pressure stemming from full employment was the proliferation of various forms of incomes policy. An incomes policy would, of course, be an essential part of a democratically planned economy. However, incomes policies in the post-war capitalist world have been used primarily as a means of incorporating and neutralizing the increased power of workers in the labour market due to full employment. Their failure has contributed to the abandonment of full employment as an objective and its replacement by the restoration, through mass unemployment, of discipline in the labour market and the labour process as the central objective.[7]

The second reason why macroeconomic management is necessarily limited in its effectiveness is that it fails to engage with the process of production. Microeconomic decisions concerning what is produced, how it is produced and for whom are essentially left to market forces to determine. Since the Second World War, production has increasingly been organized on an international scale and competition between the major capitalist countries has intensified as the task of post-war recovery was completed, protected ex-imperial markets were opened up and liberalization of international trade and payments occurred. Most capitalist countries sooner or later adopted policies at the micro-level directed towards increasing international competitiveness throughout the economy and towards particular firms or industries considered to be of special national interest.[8] These policies are discussed in sections 2.3 and 2.4.

The final reason why macroeconomic management in capitalist economies is likely to prove of limited value is its view of people. Applied macroeconomics shares with applied microeconomics the failing of treating people instrumentally. On the basis of analyses of the way in which people have behaved in the past and the assumption that they will continue to behave in the same way in the future, both seek to make quantitative predictions about what will happen in response to certain policy changes. They fall into the category of scientism, rather than science, by abstracting from the reality that people are conscious subjects who learn and modify their behaviour by reflecting on their experience. This may also turn out to be a problem for advocates of regulated market socialism, since the regulation envisaged is essentially the application of the policy instruments used in macro- and micro-intervention.

There is an important distinction to be drawn here. The fact that people's behaviour in a less than certain world depends in part on their expectations about the future has long been recognized. Expectations, formed by animal spirits, were central to Keynes's analysis. Adaptive and rational expectations are central to monetarist and new classical doctrine respectively. Keynes was concerned to emphasize that the future is, to a significant extent, inherently unknowable and that this contributes to instability and the need for state intervention. The monetarist and new classical doctrines, by contrast, are concerned to establish a case against state intervention, on the grounds that it will modify expectations in a way that renders the intervention ineffectual in the long or the short run. In the case of monetarism's adaptive expectations it is ineffectual in the long run, because people learn from experience; in the case of the new classicals' rational expectations it is ineffectual in the short run as well, because the consequences of intervention are anticipated and discounted.

However, recognition of the importance of expectations and how they are formed must be distinguished from understanding of the way in which people behave given the situation as they perceive it, including of course their expectations. At a formal level people's behaviour can be said to be determined by their objectives, yet to say only that is empty of content. People's behaviour is influenced by their perception of their narrow self-interest but also by their more general view of the world, by their values. If, as in wartime Britain, people share a general commitment, they will tend to cooperate with policies and seek to observe and make work the regulations and policy instruments applied by the government. They will be motivated by their interpretation of what is in the public interest and by what is fair, rather than only by their narrow self-interest.

If, on the other hand, people find themselves in a situation of inequality, generated by competition and what is perceived as an unfair distribution of wealth and power, with the pursuit of narrow self-interest as the sole or dominant value, behaviour will be different. Instead of co-operating with and seeking to make work the macro- and micro-policies of the government, people will tend to seek ways round them, to frustrate them, to turn them to their own advantage. This is what underlies the unending contest between those responsible for implementing economic policy and those affected by it, with tax avoidance and evasion as the most obvious examples. The technocratic approach of seeking to run the economy by remote control, through manipulating people's narrow self-interest, cannot escape from the paradox that it will be in people's narrow self-interest to find ways round that control. The point is not that people's expectations are influenced by government policy, although of course they are, but that narrowly self-interested people will actively use their human creativity to frustrate government policy.

I am not suggesting that macroeonomic policy under capitalism can have or has had no influence on the course of events. In the two decades after the Second World War Keynesian theory and demand management played a progressive role, asserting the possibility of conscious social control over the economy and to some extent exercising it. However, this role has now been undermined by the interaction of the underlying *modus operandi* of the capitalist system and the considerations discussed in the last paragraph. The pressures of intensifying international economic instability, distributional conflict and inflation have led to the use of macroeconomic policy to recreate mass unemployment, in order to allow impersonal market forces to contain the socioeconomic conflict that demand management policies both helped to create and were themselves unable to contain. The attempt at partial social control of capitalism proved unstable. Demand management had been set an impossible task.

Attempts at macroeconomic management in capitalist economies do not qualify as planning in the sense used in this book. However, macroeconomic planning is normally taken for granted as an integral part of models of planned market socialist economies. Yet the way in which macroeconomic planning would work in a regulated market socialist economy has never been clearly set out. The usual assumption is that macro-regulation would be through the instruments of macroeconomic management developed in capitalist economies, even though they have been unable to maintain full employment and macroeconomic balance in those economies. It could reasonably be argued that the task would be easier if major investment were coordinated and implemented centrally. It might also be the case that people would be more prepared to accept government policies and cooperate with them, rather than seek to frustrate them, if they had been involved in deciding the overall priorities to which those policies were giving effect.

However, I remain unconvinced by this line of argument. If people are told to pursue their narrow self-interest within a set of constraints shaped by the government, even a democratically controlled government, and are rewarded or penalized according to their success in competing against one another, will they not try to break out of the constraints or even try to influence in their favour the way in which the constraints are shaped in the first place? Is it reasonable to assume that people can be encouraged to pursue their narrow self- or sectional interest within the regulated economic sphere and yet not do the same in the sphere of social and political decision-making and behaviour? The model of democratic planning through negotiated coordination developed in Part IV of this book is based in part on the assumption that it is not. It tries instead to incorporate a transformatory dynamic in the direction of people's creativity and energy working with the grain of collectively determined social objectives rather than against it.

2.3   Indicative Planning

The only comprehensive economy-wide planning to have been undertaken in the advanced capitalist countries since the Second World War has been indicative planning. Formal planning has been most prominent in France, present but largely irrelevant in Japan and, in the first half of the 1960s, fleetingly on the agenda in Britain. There has, however, been fairly widespread partial planning – of incomes in Holland and Sweden, of education and training in West Germany, of particular sectors of the economy in all countries.

The theoretical rationale for indicative planning is that, by improving the information available to decision-makers, it alters expectations and thereby behaviour. The idea is that the government and the key sectors and enterprises in the economy should get together to discuss their plans for the future. By exchanging information about what they have in mind they make it possible for each of them to modify their intentions in the light of what the others are proposing to do. The process is then repeated until eventually a consensus emerges over target growth rates for the economy as a whole and for individual industries. In principle, all the separate plans of the independent decision-makers are then consistent with one another and between them add up to the agreed overall outcome, in terms of which they each individually make sense. Indicative planning is intended to remove or reduce the secondary uncertainty that arises from atomized decision-making. It is an iterative process designed to achieve *ex ante* coordination in the hope that this will improve both the quality and quantity of investment (Meade 1970; Cave and Hare 1981, ch. 7)

If indicative planning is to work, it must affect expectations and thereby modify behaviour. Expectations may be affected in two ways. First, the planning exercise itself may create conviction that the growth rate of the economy as a whole will be higher than previously expected, which is likely to increase the expected rate of growth of demand for the output of individual industries. Second, discussion between firms active in the same industry may influence the expectations of each firm about its likely share of total industry demand, and therefore its investment plans. However, although expectations may be modified there is no guarantee that behaviour will change accordingly.

The problem with pure indicative planning is the absence of policy instruments able to ensure that overall and individual industry target growth rates and firm shares are met. Everything depends on each individual decision-maker really holding expectations that will only be realized if the plan is fulfilled, and voluntarily acting on them. However, what if there is doubt about whether the overall and industry growth targets will actually be reached, or about whether firms will accept their target shares of industry demand, as there must be in an economy made up of fully independent enterprises? The rational thing for a narrowly self-interested decision maker to do then may well be to wait and see. Yet if enough enterprises behave in this way they will ensure that the targets are not reached, the plan is not fulfilled.[9]

The process and problems of indicative planning can be illustrated from the British and French experience. In Britain, the 1945–51 Labour governments presided over the dismantling of the machinery of planning that had proved so effective during the war (Dow 1964, ch. II). Planning had come to be associated with austerity and controls. It was also incompatible with the arm's length tradition, stemming from the classical economists' doctrine of *laissez-faire*, which became dominant during the period when the British economy was the workshop of the world and British capitalism benefited from free trade. By contrast, the French etatist tradition, reflecting a history of highly centralized economic development, led easily into the first post-war plan for recovery and a continuing series of plans thereafter, albeit of a changing character (Shonfield 1965, chs V, VII).

By the end of the 1950s concern over the increasing lack of international competitiveness and the relative decline of the British economy, together with awareness of the French experience, had produced a new near-consensus on the need for planning. In 1960 the Federation of British Industries proposed a five-year indicative plan. In 1962 the Conservative government set up the National Economic Development Council (NEDC), which was followed in 1963 by a series of Economic Development Committees (EDCs), each responsible for a key sector of industry. Between 1962 and 1964 the NEDC, in discussion with seventeen key industries, explored the implications for different sectors of the economy of a growth rate for the economy as a whole of four per cent. In 1964 the newly elected Labour government transferred responsibility for planning from the NEDC to a newly created (and short-lived) Department of Economic Affairs which a year later published the National Plan (Department of Economic Affairs 1965).

The National Plan was based on the assumption of an overall growth in GNP of 25 per cent in the six years 1964–70, or 3.8 per cent a year. Discussions were held with individual industries, through the EDCs where they existed or in other ways, in order to discover what a growth rate of 3.8 per cent for the economy as a whole implied for the growth of demand for each industry, how this compared with existing plans for expanding capacity, and what inputs would be needed if the industry were to increase its capacity at the rate implied by the overall rate of growth. At the same time, the government was estimating what would be required for macroeconomic balance, given its expenditure plans, projections for consumption, the investment rate thrown up by the industry discussions, and projections for exports and imports.

The results of the discussions were then examined and where inconsistencies were discovered further discussions were held, in order to convince individual industries that it was in their interests to revise their estimates in the light of the more extensive information available from the overall picture. Although the process was rushed, the eventual plan was reasonably consistent internally, apart from two major unresolved problems. First, the plan envisaged a growing shortage of labour but proposed no measures for dealing with it. Second, the rate of growth of exports required by the plan was 5.25 per cent, compared with the then prevailing rate of 4 per cent, and again there was no indication of how the necessary increase might be achieved. This was especially serious since it was the increasingly acute problems of international competitiveness that had given rise to the planning attempt in the first place.

In the event, the National Plan lasted under a year. In the summer of 1966 the most serious sterling crisis since the war developed. The government refused to contemplate devaluation and instead imposed a package of severely deflationary measures. There was now no prospect of the overall growth rate of 3.8 per cent being achieved and shortly afterwards the National Plan was formally abandoned.

Although short-lived, the British attempt at indicative planning is instructive. There were no policy instruments harnessed to the implementation of the targets set out in the National Plan, neither sticks nor carrots. As soon as the demands of short-term exchange rate policy asserted themselves the illusory nature of indicative planning was revealed and the plan was forgotten. Furthermore, the plan embodied no collectively determined strategic view of a desired direction of development for the economy as a whole, or for particular industries or sectors, apart from a faster rate of growth. In all these respects, British capitalism's brief encounter with indicative planning contrasted with French experience, where at least the early plans gave expression to national strategic priorities and were to some extent backed up by industrial policy.[10]

The first post-war French plan, the Monnet Plan 1947–53, covered only the six industries considered most vital for recovery: coal, electricity, cement, steel, agricultural machinery and transport. It was expressed in physical terms and government financing was concentrated on these six priority industries. The plans during the 1950s and 1960s covered the whole economy, moved away from physical quantities, became steadily more technically sophisticated, and were decreasingly effective. From the 1970s onwards, with a brief interlude under the socialist government in the early 1980s, planning rapidly ceased to be a major focus of discussion. Plans became less quantitative, were no longer concerned with inter-sectoral coherence and ended up as little more than general expressions of government intentions with respect to the public sector and macroeconomic policy.

At the height of its influence, during the 1950s, French planning took the form above all of 'concertation', a process in which sectoral or issue-based commissions discussed the projections of the national Planning Commission drawn up on the assumption of existing trends and policies. The commissions in principle consisted of representatives of all who would be involved in carrying out, or would be affected by, a particular part of the plan, together with planning officials and experts. Their purpose was to engage those with local knowledge of and responsibility for a particular area in the task of resolving inconsistencies, agreeing targets and, in the course of doing so, developing a commitment to the plan. There were several rounds of concertation during which the results of previous discussion in the commissions were brought together by the national Commission, any remaining inconsistencies were identified, and the commissions were then asked to have another look. Thus, the objective of concertation was coherence and consensus.

The trade unions, particularly the most important grouping, the communist-led CGT, largely refused to participate in concertation, arguing that it amounted to incorporation. Despite this, it is possible that the combination of discussion in the concertation process and government commitment to the plan, in particular to the pursuit of macroeconomic policies consistent with it, may have contributed to a belief in and an atmosphere conducive to economic growth, and so may have influenced behaviour. However, expressing the general consensus, Brown concludes that in fact the early plans 'were successful precisely because industrial policy was used alongside them and referred to them as a framework within which decisions about which sections of the economy should be supported should be taken. The force of industrial policy gave force to the plans – it provided the instruments which made possible the achievement of plan objectives' (Brown 1980, p. 72).[11]

Although the French experience is generally considered to have been the most successful example of indicative planning, the reason why French indicative planning appeared to be successful is that it was closely linked to an effective industrial policy. In Japan, by contrast, an even more effective industrial policy proceeded without reference to the simultaneously undertaken formal planning exercise, which therefore appeared irrelevant. In both cases, what mattered was the industrial policy, not the indicative planning (Brown 1980). Indicative planning and industrial policy may be connected but they need not be. Indicative planning is unlikely to work on its own but can provide a framework to guide industrial policy. Effective industrial policy needs to be guided by criteria, which may derive from indicative planning but have more usually been provided in some other way.

Capitalist planning of the economy as a whole in peacetime has been limited to attempts at indicative planning and has been ineffective. No one would claim that capitalist economies have been planned economies. There have, however, been more serious attempts at sectoral or partial planning, undertaken as part of industrial policy. These attempts reflect the inescapable reality that the uncertainty and lack of consciously coordinated action associated with unregulated market forces give rise to an unacceptable economic (and social) performance. They are discussed in the next section.

Watson has identified two distinct modes of planning in capitalist economies, technocratic and corporatist, which coexist in differing proportions according to circumstances. Technocratic planning is concerned with the technical problems of achieving consistency, in the sense of attempting to ensure an adequate balance between supplies and demands in a set of interlocking industries and markets. Corporatist planning, by contrast, is concerned with the political problem of achieving consensus between potentially conflicting social classes or interest groups. With the important exception of incomes policies, attempts at capitalist planning have been primarily technocratic (Watson 1977, pp. 42–3).

Technocratic partial planning has by definition no overall technical planning function, but it does have an overall ideological function. It accustoms people to think of economic problems and their solutions as technical in nature, rather than as social or political issues, and thereby performs the ideological function of legitimizing the status quo. Technocratic planning is also profoundly undemocratic in that it encourages people to leave decisions to the experts and discourages participation. In the long term, of course, this may be its undoing since if people have not been involved in taking decisions, and do not understand or accept the reasons for them, they are unlikely to cooperate fully in their implementation.

The one area in which the technocratic mode has not been dominant is that of incomes policy. In bodies concerned with sectoral planning any trade union presence has typically been token and largely unconnected with its supposed constituency. However, if incomes policies are to have any chance of long-run success the cooperation of the trade unions and their members is indispensable. Trade union centres have typically been involved in agreeing guidelines and have sometimes even been involved in implementing the policy. The experience has been one of the state seeking to incorporate the unions into the process of managing a fundamentally unchanged capitalist economy. However, explicit or implicit negotiation over the agreement that has underpinned most incomes policies has at times provided the means for genuine discussion of social priorities. Corporatist planning may contain within it the possibility of transformation into genuinely democratic planning.

2.4 Industrial Policy

Pure indicative planning, in order to achieve an outcome different from what would have occurred in its absence, relies entirely on changing the expectations of decision-makers at the level of the firm. Industrial policy, by contrast, seeks to induce decision-makers to behave as they would not otherwise have done by providing incentives, or imposing restrictions, directed at specific sectors, industries or firms. Indicative planning, by improving information, seeks to change perceptions about what course of action is most conducive to narrow self-interest. Industrial policy, by altering the real pattern of rewards and penalties accruing from different courses of action, seeks to change directly the most profitable course of action. The one is a 'virtuous confidence trick' (Brittan 1969, p. 280), the other a combination of bribery and threat.

Historically, industrial policy emerged whenever the development of capitalism within a country required state assistance, that is, wherever an inadequate infrastructure, an inappropriate financial system, or foreign competition, rendered the consequence of reliance on market forces either stagnation or external domination. However, the standard theoretical justification for industrial policy is market failure due to uncertainty, with a perfect market solution as the benchmark for comparison (Morris and Stout 1985, p. 856). In situations in which socially desirable investment is inhibited by uncertainty, the state is assigned the task of ensuring that finance is available on sufficiently favourable terms to bring the private profit making interest of firms into line with the social interest.

The principal instrument of industrial policy has been the provision, directly or indirectly, of long-term capital. The extent to which the state has been involved directly in this, or has played a supporting or facilitating role, has depended on the nature of the financial system. Zysman has classified the financial systems of capitalist countries into three basic types: capital market, in which financial institutions channel capital to industrial companies on a competitive short-run basis, with no long-term commitment, as in Britain and the United States; negotiated credit, in which financial institutions are closely linked to industrial companies on a long-term basis and guide investment, as in West Germany; and credit based, in which the state has a central role in allocating credit and shaping the pattern of investment, as in France and Japan (Zysman 1983, pp. 16–18).

It is the central role of the state in France and Japan, fulfilled in very different ways, that underlies the success of industrial policy in these two countries. However, it is important to note that West Germany, where the state has had a less prominent role, has been one of the two most successful capitalist countries in the post-war period, with a much stronger economic performance than France. This has been contributed to by the strength of its industrial banking structure, which dates back to the mid-nineteenth century, when *laissez-faire* was rejected in favour of a national strategy for economic development based on a partnership between finance and industry. The state, even so, has played a more important role in Germany than is often realized, particularly since 1945 (Shonfield 1965, ch. XII; Dyson 1986).

The crucial conclusion to be drawn from the experience of post-war capitalism is that the more successful economies have been those in which economic development has not been left to be determined by market forces. In the end, as Cox has argued, what has mattered has been the extent to which a country has arrived at a national consensus over the long-term financing of industry (Cox 1986, p. 57). This has been more important than the particular relationship between the financial system and the state through which that financing has been achieved. West Germany and Japan have both had such a consensus, made possible in part by the incorporated position of and lack of political challenge from their labour movements. France has had a partial consensus, between the state and industry, but challenged by the trade unions. Italy has had an uneasy and economically irrational consensus, due to a corrupt state and a strong political challenge from the left. Of the major capitalist countries, that leaves Britain and the United States, where reliance on unguided market forces has been greatest and economic performance worst.

The successful long-term financing of industry necessarily involves selectivity. Neither the state nor privately-owned financial institutions can provide long-term support for all companies or all sectors. Resources are limited. The use of both public and private funds has sooner or later to be accounted for. Furthermore, a long-term commitment involves not only taking a view on long-term developments that are, potentially, socially desirable or privately profitable, but also acting to ensure that as far as possible the potentiality is realized. This may mean both committing resources on a large enough scale to be effective and coordinating major investments within and between sectors. Advocates of reliance on market forces criticize the policy of picking winners on the grounds that it implies that the state knows better than the market. However, what is at issue is not passive crystal ball gazing but the identification of desirable directions of development that are realizable if appropriate action is taken, and then the taking of that action.

This raises the question of the criteria that have been used to guide industrial policy. Three categories found in all capitalist countries to a greater or lesser extent can be distinguished. First, there have been policies towards specific industries judged to be in need of restructuring. These have covered both declining capital-intensive industries, whose slow rate of adjustment results in financial losses and social and regional problems, and industries whose structure was considered too fragmented for international competitiveness. Second, financial assistance has been provided to individual firms where it was judged to be in the national interest to rescue them from bankruptcy, or to enable them to undertake investment or research and development too large or too uncertain for private capital to finance. Third, there have been incentives for particular categories of investment, almost universally in agriculture, most recently in new technology, that governments have wished to encourage.

These categories are all of an *ad hoc* nature, concerned with peripheral although not unimportant matters, and can just about be analysed within the framework of market failure. However, to be effective in shaping the overall direction of development of an economy, industrial policy must be informed or guided by a view of the future structure of the economy it is desired to achieve. One way of putting this might be to say that investment should be guided not by present comparative costs or relative prices but by those expected to prevail when the investment comes to fruition. However, this is too limited. Private sector decision-makers make investment decisions on this basis already. The case for an effective general industrial policy, as opposed to *ad hoc* intervention, must be more than the need to base investment decisions on expectations about future relative prices.

The weak case is that the government has an overall view, and therefore better information, on the basis of which to form its expectations. However, this is merely to say that the government is better at predicting the future than private sector decision-makers or analysts. This may or may not be so, but it is not really the point. The strong case for a general, as opposed to *ad hoc*, industrial policy is the argument that, if individual acts of intervention are related to a coherent strategy, and are therefore coordinated and reinforce each other, the future structure of the economy and the future pattern of comparative costs will be different in desired ways from what they would otherwise have been.

In France, coherence was lent to industrial policy by the priorities set out in the early plans and the plans were broadly successful because they were supported by effective policy instruments. State ownership in France was much more extensive than in any other major capitalist country, largely due to the post-war expropriation of wartime collabora- tors, with complete ownership of public utilities, ownership of major firms in most industries, a dominant presence in the financial sector, and widespread minority shareholdings. The public sector accounted for a high proportion of investment and was a major purchaser from the private sector. Furthermore, the state was indirectly the major source of finance for private sector investment, with about 80 per cent of private sector borrowing during the 1950s at low interest either from or guaranteed by the state. During the early plans the economic power that went with this state presence was used to a significant extent to shape investment in accordance with national priorities (Brown 1980).

During the 1960s, however, the character of planning changed and industrial policy became less interventionist and coherent. For a time during the 1960s the negotiation of planning contracts was envisaged, as a means of obtaining agreement over investment and pricing policy in exchange for a package of incentives, but this never really got off the ground. In the early 1980s, under the socialist government, there was a temporary revival of interest in planning and state intervention. However, the French economy was by then much more integrated into the international economy and therefore vulnerable to international competitive and monetary pressures. In the context of the international recession, the entire economic strategy of the socialist government was swept away by the pressures generated by its reflationary policy. A relatively weak economy, although not as weak as the British economy, had been brought into line by the coercion of market forces.

The dazzling post-war success of the Japanese economy has been widely attributed to its industrial policy. This was unique, in that it combined very clear objectives, not determined by current market conditions, with very close collaboration between state and industry in the realization of those objectives. The principal instrument of industrial policy was the Ministry of International Trade and Industry (MITI), with a structure not unlike that of the British National Economic Devel- opment Office which serviced the NEDC. It consisted of sectoral bureaux, which drew up targets and were responsible for implementing the policies directed towards achieving them. However, while the British arrangements were tripartite, involving the state and both sides of industry, MITI was based on bipartite consultation between government and private enterprise management.

Although Japan has had a system of formal planning, the operative strategy underlying its industrial policy has been developed and implemented by MITI. The civil servant who had been in charge during the 1950s summed up the strategy at that time as follows:

> [MITI] decided to establish in Japan industries which require intensive employment of capital and technology, industries that in consideration of comparative costs of production should be the most inappropriate for Japan, industries such as steel, oil-refining, petro-chemicals, aircraft, industrial machinery of all sorts, and electronics, including electronic computers. From a short-run, static viewpoint, encouragement of such industries would seem to conflict with economic rationalism. But from a long-range viewpoint, these are precisely the industries where income elasticity of demand is high, technological progress is rapid, and labour productivity rises fast. (Quoted in Brown 1980, p. 61)

Three principal means of implementing the strategy can be identified. First, the structural changes desired were promoted, in the 1950s and 1960s, by an extensive system of protection, as emphasized by Boltho:

> The importance of this protective network cannot be underestimated. Control of raw material imports gave MITI the power to cajole firms to move in desired directions. Control of technology imports allowed MITI to select the industries and processes it wanted to see develop. Control of manufactured imports, combined with selective exemption from import duties for foreign machinery and indirect tax systems geared to favour domestic purchases of certain products, meant that MITI could create hot-house conditions for the expansion of pre-determined sectors. Finally, control of inward investment, preserved the Japanese nature of these sectors by sheltering the under-capitalised Japanese firm from the danger of foreign take-over bids. (Boltho 1985, p. 190)

The second way in which MITI's strategy was implemented was through the financing of investment. Unlike in France, there has not been a large public sector, nor has a high proportion of private sector investment been state financed or channelled through state-owned financial institutions. However, Japanese industry has operated on the basis of a high gearing ratio, with some 80 per cent of capital borrowed. Borrowing has been primarily from the banks, which have been heavily supervised by the Ministry of Finance and the Bank of Japan, working closely with MITI. As a result, MITI's priority sectors and firms have been favoured, a tendency reinforced by the fact that the state-funded Japan Development Bank, although financing only one or two per cent of fixed investment, effectively guarantees lending to priority sectors which is therefore virtually risk-free.

Finally, there is the network of consultative bodies and informal contacts through which the broad consensus that underlies the system of administrative guidance is continuously renegotiated. Japan is of course not unique in having a system of informal contact and administrative guidance. However, the distinctive feature of the Japanese system seems to be the extensive interchange of personnel between the civil service and industry. Civil servants tend to retire in their late forties or early fifties and then frequently take up leading positions in the companies they used to supervise. Thus, the informal contacts are typically between erstwhile leading civil servants, now leading industrialists, and the new leading civil servants who were previously their juniors.

Japanese industrial policy has depended above all on the broad bipartite consensus established between the state and business. Resources have been channelled to priority sectors but this has been primarily through persuasion and facilitation not compulsion. In the two decades after 1945 priority sectors were selected and developed behind a protective wall. The structure of individual sectors was carefully controlled by MITI, with the number of firms only allowed to increase as the domestic and later the export market expanded. Thus, competition, as a spur to efficiency and innovation, was promoted but market forces were not allowed to determine the structure of priority sectors. During the 1970s and 1980s the formal system of protection began to be dismantled as a result of international political pressure. However, by then Japanese industry had established itself at the frontier of international achievement. Administrative guidance has continued, with the challenge now no longer to select priority sectors with a view to catching up but to identify the crucial sectors for the future.[12]

It is important not to be starry-eyed about the Japanese experience. Its enormous economic achievement was achieved at enormous personal, social and environmental cost. The socio-political balance of forces was very different from that in most European capitalist countries, reflected in the exclusion of independent workers' organizations from the process of consensus formation. Nevertheless, the conclusion that I draw from the Japanese experience of industrial policy is that the development of criteria and methods of implementation not primarily derived from or relying on market forces is essential if a country wishes to shape its own future and not be dominated by forces beyond its control.

This conclusion is reinforced by the negative example of British experience. During the 1960s and 1970s the attempt was made to use industrial policy to reverse the long-term relative decline of the British economy. There were two cycles, separated by a brief period of half-hearted disengagement at the beginning of the 1970s. The first cycle consisted of the indicative planning exercise discussed in the previous section and the work of the Industrial Reorganization

Corporation, a body established to promote industrial restructuring through merger. The second cycle was primarily an exercise in channelling public money into the private sector on the private sector's terms, under the provisions of the 1972 and 1975 Industry Acts. There were also leisurely and largely inconsequential discussions intended to develop strategies for individual industries. Neither cycle made any noticeable impact on the deep-seated problems of the British economy and they were followed, in the 1980s, by a prolonged period of determined disengagement (Devine et al. 1985, chs 9, 12).

At one level this failure was due to the absence of appropriate criteria and methods of implementation, in particular to a refusal to take a view on a desirable long-term structure for British industry and a reluctance to override private sector decisions (Young with Lowe 1974, pp. 87, 208). Policy was piecemeal. It sought to supplement rather than supplant market forces and consequently remained 'limited to a peripheral role of tidying up at the edges of the economy, rather than providing any central thrust to alter and improve industry's performance and that of the economy as a whole' (Mottershead 1978, p. 483).

At another level, the reason for the failure must be sought in the historically evolved relationships characterizing the political economy of British capitalism: the traditional arm's length relationship between the state and the private sector; the relationship between finance and industry; and the balance of class forces which, for a time, produced a situation of stalemate and paralysis. The social consensus that underlay the creation of the welfare state reflected a socio-political balance within which state intervention in the economy, apart from peripheral tinkering, was confined to the infrastructure and the macro-level. To go beyond that, given the balance of class forces, would have threatened to undermine the post-war settlement and the basis of the prevailing capitalist hegemony.

2.5 Conclusion

What overall conclusions relevant to the development of a model of democratic planning can be drawn from the discussion in this chapter of the different ways in which planning can be said to have been attempted in capitalist countries? In so far as there have been conscious attempts to take a view on the desired future structure of the economy and serious attempts to bring that structure about they have taken the form of industrial policy. Wartime planning, while very effective, was essentially short-term. Macroeconomic management has necessarily been concerned with short-term exigencies and has become decreasingly effective, while indicative planning has been more or less wholly ineffective. Neither can count as serious planning.

I think there are three important lessons to be learned. The first is that effective planning requires clearly specified criteria related to the objectives society has set itself. This does not mean a detailed blueprint nor does it imply perfect knowledge about the present or the future. However, it does require a view about the desired shape and direction of economic change and development. It requires a strategy related to society's objectives. Of course, both the objectives and the strategy have to be realistic, in the sense that it must be possible to move towards the objectives through a strategy that is both consistent with them and capable of being implemented. The inevitability of imperfect knowledge means that deterministic models of planning, with analytic general equilibrium solutions whose properties can be formally compared, are irrelevant. The only realistic model of planning is one in which decisions taken in the light of continuously changing circumstances are neverthel-ess informed by a strategy related to longer-term social objectives.

Japanese experience is the positive example of this, British experience the negative example, and French experience somewhere in between. The Japanese objective was to build a modern industrial economy able at least to hold its own in international competition with the most advanced capitalist economies. This objective dictated the strategy developed by MITI in the 1950s, which was then pursued flexibly, taking into account changing market, technological and socio-political conditions. An alternative national objective for a country might, in principle, be to isolate itself from the rest of the world and pursue objectives related solely to its internal situation, although for socio-political reasons this is unlikely to be a viable long run possibility, to say nothing of its desirability. In practice, as the experience of the British government in the mid-1960s and the French socialist government in the early 1980s shows, the international context inevitably imposes constraints on national objectives and strategies which cannot be ignored. A self-governing planned society ultimately requires a self-governing planned world.

The second lesson I draw from the analysis of this chapter is that in the most successful capitalist countries, even in those apparently most private enterprise and market-oriented, the long-run development of the economy is not left primarily to the determination of market forces. Some degree of *ex ante* coordination is attempted, both within and between industries and sectors. In Japan, there are the sectoral bureaux within MITI and the administrative guidance based on the consensus emerging from the system of informal negotiation. In West Germany, the system of industrial banking has enabled some coordination to be undertaken without the direct involvement of the state. In France, there have been the sectoral commissions and the administrative guidance based on the network of informal contacts. Even in Britain the necessity for such coordination has found expression, in the Economic Development Committees and the subsequent Sector Working Parties, although to very little effect.

What has distinguished relatively effective from ineffective industrial policies has been the extent to which a country has evolved ways of implementing its broad strategy in a more or less coordinated way at the level of individual sectors and ultimately firms. In Japan, it is unlikely that companies would undertake major developments without first discussing them through the informal consultation process and taking account of the ensuing administrative guidance. Of course, even in Japan agreement is not easily reached. MITI's guidance has sometimes reflected the need to accommodate the competing claims of rival companies and companies have sometimes gone their own way. Nevertheless, the system has broadly speaking worked because of the ability to reach a consensus at least about the broad structural framework within which corporate rivalry is then fought out.

This is a crucial point whose significance appears to be widely unrecognized by advocates of market-based reform in Eastern Europe and market socialists more generally. In Hungary, for example, parametric regulation is the objective, although not so far the practice. What this means is the setting of a framework of taxes, subsidies and other regulations which in principle applies without differentiation to all enterprises, at least to all within the same category. This is recommended precisely in order to avoid negotiation between enterprises and state officials designed to take account of the individual circumstances of enterprises, on the grounds that such negotiation amounts to special pleading and encourages dependence rather than self-reliance. While this argument may have some substance in the context of statist command economies, care is needed. In all modern economies interdependence is such that negotiation does, must and should occur. The real issue is not how to abolish it but between whom and on what basis the negotiation should take place.

This brings me to the importance of consensus, the third lesson to be learned from the experience of attempts at capitalist planning. The success of Japanese industrial policy stemmed from the ability of the relevant decision-makers to reach broad agreement. The relevant decision-makers are those with the power to further or frustrate a course of action. In Japan, this meant state and private sector management but not the unions, because of their lack of power and their ideological incorporation. Hence the bipartite character of Japanese negotiation. In Britain, the defensive strength of the unions gave them the power to frustrate decisions (Kilpatrick and Lawson

1980) so they had to be included. Hence the tripartite character of British negotiation, at least until the exclusion of the unions in the 1980s.

In the end, to be effective planning must be based on consensus and must ultimately be democratic. All groups with an interest in the outcome of a decision need to be involved. Furthermore, those who represent interested groups in the process of negotiation need to be chosen in such a way that they really do represent their constituents. Without genuine participation in the decision-making process people cannot be expected to, and in the long run do not, cooperate in the carrying out of decisions. Of course, the determination of who has a legitimate interest in any particular category of decision, the distribution of power between the groups involved in negotiating over decisions, the information available to people, the objectives and values of those participating – all remain to be considered. What I think is clear, however, is that the alternatives to democratic planning based on negotiated coordination are coercion by market forces, or administrative coercion by the state, or in practice a combination of the two.

3

Central Planning

3.1   Administrative Command Planning

The planning system in the statist countries of Eastern Europe in the 1980s still closely resembled that developed in the Soviet Union in the 1930s and exported to the other countries after the Second World War. Yugoslavia, which broke politically with the Soviet Union in 1948, and Hungary, which adopted a partially market-based economic mechanism in 1968, are the exceptions and are considered in the next chapter. For the rest, although there are many differences between their planning systems and there have been many changes since the end of the 1950s, they exhibit sufficient similarity and continuity for them to be regarded as variants of a centrally planned and administered command system with clearly defined characteristics.

In this system, production is organized and coordinated within an administrative hierarchy, with decisions being made at the centre and passed down through intermediate levels of the hierarchy to the production units (enterprises). Transfers of goods and services between enterprises are determined vertically, by superior levels in the hierarchy, not horizontally, through direct contact and agreement between the enterprises themselves. Each enterprise receives from above instructions detailing the total quantity of output it is to produce and the enterprises or other destinations to which that output is to go. It also has allocated to it from above the quantities of the different inputs it is allowed to use to produce its output: quantities of material inputs, with the supplying enterprises specified; permitted expenditure on wages which, given centrally set wage rates, determines the possible range of quantity/quality combinations of labour; and new investment.

These instructions, or targets, are arrived at in the course of the plan being drawn up. Operational annual plans are related to medium-term, typically five-year, plans which are in turn loosely related to longer-term plans. The political leaders decide on broad objectives and priorities for the period of the plan and pass them to the planning authorities. The planning authorities draw up a provisional plan, expressed in terms of output targets, designed to achieve those objectives and priorities to the greatest extent possible, given their knowledge of the economy's productive capacity. These targets are then passed down through the hierarchy to the individual enterprises. The enterprises then estimate the inputs they would need to fulfil the output targets they have been set and pass that information back up through the hierarchy to the planning authorities.

The principal method used by the planning authorities in drawing up the plan is that of material balances. A material balance is a statement of the estimated potential availability of a good or service set against its estimated use. Availability is made up of output, imports and stocks. Use consists of use as intermediate input in production and use for consumption, export or stockbuilding. When the planning authorities receive from the enterprises their estimates of the inputs they would need to fulfil their provisional output targets, it is in general unlikely that total estimated use and total estimated availability for each separate good and service will balance. Since the norm has been to set ambitious growth targets estimated use has typically exceeded estimated availability. The planning authorities then have the task of modifying targets in order to achieve consistency between estimated use and estimated availability.

They may adjust targets for exports and imports, they may reduce targets for lower priority output and reallocate inputs to higher priority output, and they may ask enterprises to produce more output with no more inputs, or the same output with fewer inputs. In principle, the revised targets should then be passed down the hierarchy and the whole exercise repeated since the new set of output targets will in general involve a new set of input requirements. In practice, however, there is normally not time for successive iterations to take account of these secondary effects. The output targets and input allocations on which the revised, approximately consistent, material balances are based become the definitive plan and are passed down through the hierarchy to become binding instructions to the enterprises.

The centre itself is only able to administer the material balances for the more important material inputs and consumer goods and services, with the rest being administered at intermediate levels within the hierarchy. The centre is also responsible for ensuring external and macroeconomic balance. It controls foreign trade, sets wage rates and capital charges and also determines prices, apart from those in the markets for collective farm and private produce. Output targets and input allocations, although during the 1930s set in physical units, have increasingly been expressed in value terms. The more developed and complex an economy becomes, the more aggregated information has to become as it passes up the administrative hierarchy. For the same reason, targets and allocations determined by the centre are necessarily highly aggregated and have to be disaggregated at each lower level in the hierarchy before they become instructions to individual enterprises.

As well as output targets, enterprises are also set financial targets, as part of a financial plan for the economy as a whole which parallels the physical plan based on the material balances. Transfers of goods and services between enterprises are valued using prices set by the centre (or intermediate levels in the hierarchy) and are paralleled by transfers between money balances held for enterprises by their branch of the state bank. Enterprises keep cost and revenue accounts and are given financial targets, particularly for expenditure on wages and cost reduction. They have to pay a capital charge on capital employed and a turnover tax. They also obtain short-term credit from the bank if it is needed to finance production of targeted output.

It is important to realize that, in relation to transfers of goods and services between enterprises, money is in principle passive. Such transfers are determined vertically from above, through the administrative hierarchy. Financial flows are shaped to parallel the predetermined physical flows set out in the enterprises' plans, and the requirement that enterprises transfer money balances between them to 'pay' for physical transfers enables the state bank to monitor plan implementation. However, while money is passive in relation to transfers between enterprises, it is active in the labour market and the market for consumer goods and services. Workers are not directed to jobs and the pattern of relative wage rates is consciously adjusted to influence job choice in accordance with the requirements of the plan. Similarly, most consumer goods and services are neither free nor rationed, so the pattern of relative consumer prices influences consumer choice.

The basic structure of administrative command planning determines the shape of its incentive system. Income consists of wages or salaries plus bonuses of various sorts. Wages and salaries are based on centrally determined rates that vary according to skill, geographical location and industry priority. Within an enterprise they are sometimes related to individual or group contributions to output. Bonuses are related to an enterprise's performance, assessed against its planned targets, and accrue partly to individuals and partly to the enterprise as a whole for collective use. The primary performance indicator has been the extent to which output targets are met. Given the material balance method of coordinating the output of the different enterprises it could hardly be otherwise since, in general, one enterprise's output is another's input and failure to fulfil targets has ripple effects throughout the economy.

The importance attached to planned output fulfilment is reflected in the fact that, typically, no bonus is received if the output target is not achieved, by however small an amount, whereas if the enterprise fulfils its planned output a large bonus is received and overfulfilment attracts only a small additional bonus. In addition to the primary target of output quantity, typically measured by value of sales, each enterprise's plan normally contains other targets, designed to motivate the enterprise to behave more finely in accordance with the centre's wishes. Although these have varied between countries and at different times they have usually included targets for output composition, input use (including the wage fund), investment, innovation, payments to and from the state budget and, since the 1960s, profitability. While in principle all targets have been binding, in practice, as a result of the material balance system, total output has been the most important.

So far, the official, formal, but also very real, structure of centralized command planning has been considered. There are, however, two further characteristics that are integral to the way in which the system works. Both involve bargaining and negotiation. The formal account of the construction of the plan suggests a straightforward flow of provisional targets down the administrative hierarchy, with an equally straightforward flow of information about input requirements up the hierarchy, leading to adjustments in order to achieve consistency. In fact, at each stage in the process there is 'plan bargaining', that is, negotiation over output targets and input allocations. This vertical bargaining is between hierarchical superiors and inferiors, of course, but, since in the end a more or less workable outcome has to be achieved, the bargaining is none the less real. In general, targets cannot just be imposed on enterprises without the agreement of their directors.

The significance of this is emphasized by Augustinovics:

> It turns out that plan coordination is much more than the technical procedure of iteratively approximating consistency: it is the ground where views and values, interests and priorities are confronted and gradually synchronized. The result of traditional coordination is more than a technically feasible variant: it also implies a more or less general agreement on what should be done, that makes the particular variant feasible in the social and political sense. (Augustinovics 1975, p. 147)

Of course, given the absence of political and economic democracy in the statist countries under discussion, the agreement reached is between different sections of the ruling bureaucracy and reflects their interests and priorities. It does not consciously reflect the interests of society – the diverse interests of people as citizens, members of communities, consumers and workers.

Nevertheless, although very imperfectly for reasons discussed in the next section, the system has at some level worked. That it has depends crucially also on the second, horizontal, form of bargaining and negotiation that is integral to it. Although output targets with destinations and input allocations with sources are specified in general terms in each enterprise's plan, the details have to be worked out between the enterprises concerned. The results of this bargaining and negotiation over precise quantities, qualities and delivery dates are then incorporated in a contract. In addition to this legal horizontal bargaining between enterprises, there is also unofficial bargaining, resulting in unplanned transactions between enterprises, of dubious legality but in general officially tolerated. Enterprises employ people (known variously as expediters, fixers or pushers) to seek out and acquire vital inputs that cannot be obtained from their designated suppliers but are available elsewhere in the economy. Finally, there is the secondary economy consisting of corrupt transactions between enterprises, 'black' markets and private transactions.[1]

The administrative command planning system, based on vertical flows of information and instructions, lubricated by vertical and horizontal bargaining and negotiation within the ruling bureaucracy, is generally accepted as having impressive achievements to its credit. Historically it made possible in three decades, interrupted by the unprecedented destruction wrought by the Nazi invasion, the transformation of the Soviet Union from a backward society with an underdeveloped economy into one of the world's two superpowers. It has been the vehicle for rapid economic growth and regional development, maintained full employment and low rates of inflation, and been associated with some increase in standards of living and cultural development. It has also coexisted with appalling repression and violation of individual freedom and been the vehicle for arbitrary decision-making, inefficiency and waste, endemic shortage and lack of consumer satisfaction.

Since the late 1950s the statist countries have experienced mounting economic problems, recognition of which has led to a series of attempts at economic reform, considered in the next section. The extent to which the failings of the administrative command planning system are due to the absence of political and economic democracy, and whether or not the system is actually compatible with democracy, are then discussed in the rest of the chapter.

3.2   Economic Reform

Just as capitalist countries have inherent economic characteristics and
problems associated with the nature of the capitalist economic system,
so too statist societies have their own inherent characteristics and
problems associated with their administrative command planning
system. These were already evident by the 1950s and have resulted in
successive movements for economic reform. The first wave was in the
late 1950s and early 1960s, followed by renewed attempts at intervals of
roughly a decade. The reasons for this pattern, which inevitably involve
the interaction of economics and politics, are discussed in the next
section. However, in order to draw some conclusions from the
experience of command central planning of relevance to the possibilities for democratic planning, the nature of the problems that have
emerged and the remedies proposed for them are first considered.

The manifestations of the underlying systemic problems are evident
enough: falling rates of economic growth; continuing difficulties in
agriculture; poor innovative performance; rising capital–output ratios
and evidence of unemployed fixed capital; low labour discipline and
morale; low quality output; generalized inefficiency; and low levels of
consumer satisfaction. Simultaneously, in the social and political
spheres, social problems associated with alienation, cynicism about
public life, and a preoccupation with privatized consumerism, are
widely observed.[2] The extent of these problems has varied from
country to country, and between different periods, as has the
willingness of the political leadership to recognize them. However, the
increasingly frank statements by Gorbachev and others in 1987,
insisting on the need to face reality and referring to a pre-crisis
situation, perhaps marked a turning-point.

What, then, are the systemic problems inherent in the centralized
administrative command model of planning? They can be discussed
under two interrelated headings – information and motivation. A
modern economy consists of individuals or groups, organized in
production units, whose activities are coordinated so that as far as
possible between them they produce the goods and services that people
individually and collectively want, in the proportions in which they
want them. The productive capacity of the economy sets a limit on how
much can be produced, and the distribution of power, mainly but not
only economic power, determines what is produced and how it is
distributed. For production to be socially valuable, as defined by the
society in question, it has to be informed by two types of information:
first, the detailed local information that is known only to the person or
small group of people on the spot; second, information about how each

local act of production fits into the activities required from the economy as a whole.

Hayek has argued that, in central planning, local knowledge has to be supplied by producers to the planners, who then consciously decide how local activity should be fitted into the picture as a whole and inform the producers what to do; whereas, in the market mechanism, producers decide what to do with their local knowledge themselves, on the basis of market signals in the form of relative prices, and this, without anyone having to think about how, results in local activity fitting into the overall situation (Hayek 1945). The problems with the market mechanism, in particular the fact that it cannot in practice provide adequate information for rational decisions about investment, have already been discussed. Nevertheless, the question of information is absolutely crucial for any model of planning. Indeed, Ellman has argued that the fundamental systemic problem of the administrative command economies is that their planning system attempts to mimic a planning model based on the assumption of perfect knowledge, thus ignoring the inescapable realities of 'partial ignorance, inadequate techniques for data processing and complexity' (Ellman 1979, p. 79).

The complexity of a modern economy means that it is not possible for the centre to gather in all the local information in the whole economy, construct a model on the basis of it that is an exact replica of the real economy, work out a planned set of interlocking transfers that is consistent and optimal, and instruct each production unit what to do in order to fit in with it.[3] Nor, of course, is that what the planning authorities in the statist countries try to do. As information passes up the administrative hierarchy it becomes increasingly aggregated, with more and more detailed information being lost. The centre takes decisions in a highly aggregative form and even then only in relation to what it regards as the more important sectors and outputs. The detail and the gaps are filled in at successively lower levels of the hierarchy and much remains for the enterprises themselves to settle. In addition, as outlined in the last section, the formal vertical planning process is lubricated by informal vertical and horizontal interactions.

The fact that the centre cannot plan everything, that even its necessarily limited plan depends on vertical negotiation and plan bargaining, and that overall plan targets are typically not achieved, has led some people to question whether the administrative command economies can really be regarded as planned economies at all. However, their direction of development, certainly that of the Soviet economy, has broadly corresponded with the intentions of the planners and, as Nove has argued, the fact that plans are not fulfilled does not mean that what actually happens is not the result of the planning process (Nove 1983, p. 80). Since uncertainty can never be completely eliminated, plans are unlikely ever to be fully achieved.

Nevertheless, the extent and persistence of the shortcomings that have been encountered do suggest that there is something fundamentally wrong with the system in the centrally planned statist countries. In relation to both information and motivation, the problems have been identified as stemming from overcentralization.[4] Authority always remains with the superior level in the hierarchy which can and does frequently intervene at lower levels, ultimately in the form of changed instructions to the enterprises. This is inevitable since the superior levels have to react to unforeseen, changing circumstances and so seek to modify the overall plan, or the part of it for which they are responsible, in the light of the new situation. However, such changes appear arbitrary to the enterprises concerned and are frequently disruptive of planned production at the enterprise level. Furthermore, the need for enterprises to obtain hierarchic approval before they can adjust their output targets in response to changing local circumstances inhibits the effective use of local knowledge.

The centre suffers from information overload and the enterprises from lack of sufficient autonomy. The conclusion to be drawn is that an effective planning system, in order to be able to deal with imperfect knowledge and the need for flexibility and continuous revision, has to incorporate an appropriate balance between centralization and decentralization. The centre can only carry out effectively its role of taking the decisions that affect the economy as a whole, thereby setting the framework within which local decisions are made, if it is not overwhelmed by responsibilities it cannot fulfil and swamped by information it cannot use. Enterprises can only make proper use of local knowledge if they are able to act reasonably rapidly in response to changes in their circumstances, which means that they must be relatively autonomous. The command planning system incorporates the wrong balance between centralization and decentralization and needs to be decentralized.

The case for decentralization is equally strong in relation to the problem of motivation. The discussion of the problems arising from imperfect knowledge has so far implicitly assumed that people wish to behave in accordance with the overall social good and that the problem is how they become aware of what that means in detail for what they should do. However, once it is recognized that although people may be interested in the social good they are also interested in their own narrow sectional or self-interest, the problem of motivation and incentives arises.

In the command planning system, the output and input use targets for each enterprise are not merely to inform those running and working in the enterprise what they should do to fit in with what other enterprises are doing, so that between them they produce a planned pattern of overall output. The targets are also used as the basis for rewarding or penalizing enterprises, their managers and their workers. They are the data on which the incentive system is based. The assumption is that without a system of rewards and penalties people will act to further their own narrow self-interest, even if they know that the general social interest requires them to do something different. Thus, an incentive system has to be devised and operated in order to shape narrowly self-interested behaviour so that it corresponds with what is in the social interest, defined as the fulfilment of plan targets.

The market mechanism is said to be incentive compatible since the local knowledge of producers is used by them to further their narrow self-interest within the constraints set by market prices that are assumed to reflect relative scarcity and consumer preferences. The fact that this is only so in a competitive general equilibrium and requires such restrictive assumptions as to be irrelevant for the evaluation of any actual or potential economy has already been discussed. Nevertheless, as with information, the question of motivation is central for any model of planning. A model based on an unrealistic view of people, a misleading assumption about human motivation, is as likely to give rise to a dysfunctional system of planning as is one based on an assumption of perfect knowledge.

Although the administrative command planning system has made use of moral incentives, such as public recognition and social esteem, it has relied primarily on material incentives at the level of the individual, the group or the enterprise as a whole. The problem of devising an effective incentive system for command planning is analogous to that of shaping a regulated market mechanism. In both cases, the challenge is to create an environment within which people pursue their narrow self-interest and in doing so contribute to the general interest. In the command planning system and, as is argued in the next chapter, in a regulated market mechanism, the problems of motivation and information are in practice inseparable.

In the command system, the administratively set targets are based on local information supplied by the enterprises. The information supplied by self-interested enterprise directors and senior management to the next level in the hierarchy is inevitably shaped by their perceptions of their self-interest. Typically, they understate productive potential and overstate input requirements so that their output targets are more easily achieved, they avoid any penalties associated with non-fulfilment, and they reap the rewards associated with fulfilment. Since the performance of each successive level in the hierarchy is evaluated in terms of its success in achieving the output target at the level of aggregation for which it is responsible, the same process is repeated at each stage in the flow of information up the hierarchy from enterprise to centre.

Thus, the problem of adequate information arises not only from the necessary loss of local knowledge as aggregation proceeds. It is also inseparably associated with the bias imparted to the information flow arising from the self-interest of those supplying the information. Of course, each level of the hierarchy is aware of what is happening and seeks to take account of it. Higher levels mark down lower levels' estimates of input requirements and mark up lower levels' estimates of productive potential. The centre imposes taut plans not only because of its desire for ambitious growth rates but also to compensate for the concealed slack it assumes to be present. Plan bargaining and negotiation are not just to achieve consistency but, perhaps primarily, also constitute a game of bluff and counter-bluff.

Since the incentive system has been geared to the achievement above all of output targets, enterprise behaviour has been shaped to that end. In the conditions of endemic shortage that have generally prevailed in the administrative command economies, it has not been possible to rely on input suppliers to deliver on time, or even at all. The consequence has been that enterprises have tended to build up excessive reserves and to instal their own capacity to make essential spare parts and other key manufactured inputs. They have also at various times, depending on the precise form of the incentive system operating, produced heavy products when quantity has been measured by weight, identical standard products when it has been measured by number, products using expensive materials when it has been measured by gross value, and so on. The incentive system has not rewarded quality or attention to user or consumer requirements.

In addition to the inefficiencies in relation to the use of existing productive capacity arising from an incentive system based on quantitative output targets, a deep-seated problem over innovation has also been experienced. Administrative command planning was initially, in the period of extensive growth, considered to perform well dynamically but poorly in terms of static allocative efficiency. More recently, this evaluation has been reversed and the system has increasingly been seen as incompatible with dynamic innovative performance. In part, this is because the premium placed on planned output fulfilment understandably inhibits innovation, with its unavoidable short-term disruption for what is inevitably an uncertain long-term outcome.

However, it has also been argued that innovation depends on the creative use of local knowledge and that this will only occur if those who possess that knowledge are given the incentive of being able to benefit personally from its successful use. On this view, dynamic innovative performance is inseparable from a degree of inequality incompatible with the values so far associated with the actually existing socialism officially proclaimed to exist in the statist countries (Gomulka 1986, ch. 3). The corollary, with implications for advocates of regulated market socialism that are not always recognized, is that the effective use of local knowledge in general, and a dynamic innovative performance in particular, require private property rights.[5] These implications are considered in the next chapter.

An alternative explanation for the poor innovative performance of the administrative command economies, one which I find more convincing, is that the absence of political and economic democracy promotes alienation and privatized self-seeking behaviour which, in the case of enterprise management, takes the form of conservatism, risk-avoidance and creative conformity. The implications of the creation of all-round democracy and a self-governing society for motivation and innovation are considered later in this book. At the moment, the conclusion I draw from the analysis of the problem of motivation under command planning is that, for effective use of local knowledge, as much decentralization as possible is needed, so that the interests of the system as a whole engage with people's immediate individual interests as far as possible at the levels over which they have most direct control.

As has already been argued, it is inherent in administrative command planning, not accidental, that the fulfilment of enterprise output targets is the central performance indicator on which the incentive system is based. The success of the plan as a whole depends on the achievement of its interlocking parts. Not surprisingly, therefore, quantitative output targets have remained central in virtually all the attempts that have been made to change (reform) the system. For the same reason, although attempts have been made to decentralize decision-making within the administrative hierarchy, with more decisions being devolved to lower levels, an apparently inexorable tendency towards recentralization has been evident.

In the Soviet Union, starting with the Kosygin reforms in 1965, there have been a series of attempts to change the incentive system. These have included: the replacement of gross value of output by value of sales or value added as the target variable, in order to encourage quality; the inclusion of synthetic indicators, such as productivity and profitability, which relate inputs or costs to output or revenue; the specification of some targets for a five-year rather than one-year period, in order to overcome the disincentive of the ratchet effect, whereby overfulfilment of one year's target results in a higher target the next year; the creation of separate funds (typically for managerial bonuses, decentralized investment and collective social provision for enterprise workers), with payment into each depending on the fulfilment of different targets, in order to generalize the incentive and discourage concentration on any one performance indicator; and the option of receiving a higher than normal rate of bonus with respect to targets offered by the enterprise in excess of those proposed by the planning authorities, in order to encourage full use of hitherto undisclosed productive potential. However, 'little systemic innovation has been preserved from the 1965 reform. A shift back to more centralization, to the application of more administrative methods, has occurred' (Adam 1980, p. 362).

The attempts at economic reform in the Soviet Union had come to very little by the mid-1980s and it remains to be seen whether the Gorbachev reforms, discussed in section 3.5, will result in more far-reaching changes. Reflecting on the experience of economic reform in Eastern Europe up to the mid-1970s, Bornstein distinguished between the comprehensive, major reform designs of Czechoslovakia and Hungary and the partial, minor reforms of the Soviet Union and the other countries (Bornstein 1979, p. 290). The former were market-based and the Hungarian experience is considered in the next chapter, on market socialism.[6] The latter were based on administrative decentralization to associations and on modifications to the incentive system. These minor reforms are generally evaluated as having failed, in the sense that the economic system in the countries concerned remains essentially that of administrative command planning, the systemic problems have not been overcome and their manifestations have not disappeared.

In one case, that of the German Democratic Republic, it could be argued that the attempt at administrative decentralization was comprehensive and major, rather than partial and minor as Bornstein suggests. In the early 1960s, a far-reaching administrative reorganization resulted in the creation of powerful associations, or supra-enterprises, working on a profit-maximizing basis, but nevertheless expected to fulfil centrally determined output targets. Associations were obliged to contract to sell all their targeted output to other associations, with severe financial penalties for failure to meet the quantities, qualities and delivery dates specified. The modified system in the GDR could only operate effectively in the absence of taut planning and has proved vulnerable to pressures for rapid growth rates. It remains an administrative command system, but one in which economic decision making has perhaps shifted away from the political section of the ruling bureaucracy and towards the technocratic section to a greater extent than in the other statist countries.[7]

The attempts so far to reform the administrative command system have fallen within three broad areas – incentives, decentralization and prices. Changes to the incentive system and limited decentralization of the administrative structure have been concerned to address the systemic problems that have been identified with respect to information and motivation. There have also been changes to the price system intended to bring the pattern of relative prices more into line with the structure of comparative costs, including the closer alignment of domestic and international prices. The first two areas have been discussed in this section. The importance of a rational price structure and the problems associated with achieving it are considered in the next chapter.

Before looking at the reasons for the relative lack of success of attempts to reform administrative command planning, what conclusions can be drawn from the discussion so far? In my view, it is important to distinguish between the systemic problems of information and motivation. Both require decentralization, but for different reasons. Information is needed at the local level but also at the level of the system as a whole. It is to enable local decisions to be taken consciously in the light of their consequences for the system as a whole that planning is necessary. The balance between centralization and decentralization, or, to put it another way, the size of the system within which local decisions have significant effects, must depend on the nature of the activity in question. Different types of activity have to be organized at different levels. Decentralization is required because at the moment there is overcentralization, with decisions taken by the centre, at least in principle, which need not be and are not most effectively taken there. The result is that the centre is overloaded and cannot take even the decisions that need to be taken by it effectively, while enterprises are prevented from making effective use of local information by the hierarchic straitjacket within which they operate.

There is a sense in which the problem of information is a technical one. The technical problem of deciding on the level at which different types of decision are most effectively taken, on the appropriate balance of centralization and decentralization, would remain even if there were no problem of motivation. The problem of motivation, however, is inseparable from a view of human beings and their potentialities. It is inherently human not technical, although this distinction is normally obscured in the standard literature on planning and economic reform. This occurs because in the literature human beings are normally viewed instrumentally and the problem of motivation is in fact cast as a technical one of devising an incentive system that will manipulate people to behave as the planners would like them to. Of course, to categorise the problem of information as technical is not intended to minimise its importance. On the contrary, the problem of arriving in each area of social activity at the balance between centralization and decentralization that enables the most effective use of information by self-activating people to achieve their individual and collective objectives seems to me the real challenge. The point is that it can only be properly addressed on the basis of a view of human beings, about which there is room for discussion and disagreement.

What, then, is the relationship between decentralization and motivation? In the standard analysis decentralization is necessary so that responsibility for the use of local knowledge rests clearly with the narrowly self-interested people who possess it. They are then rewarded or penalized according to the use they make of it. If the incentive system is properly designed it will shape the narrowly self-interested use of local knowledge in conformity with the wishes of the planners. An alternative view of the relationship between decentralization and motivation, which I hold, is that fully developed participatory democracy and the non-narrowly self-interested motivation associated with it, require as much decentralization as is consistent with the involvement in decision-making at each level of all those affected by the decisions taken at that level. This is because, although there will always be decisions in which people can be only indirectly involved, through the process of representative democracy, self-activation is most readily developed through direct involvement in decision-making. This approach is discussed in Part III.

3.3   The Political Economy of Reform

As Nuti has observed, most Western literature on the 'socialist' economies has been concerned with 'capitalism without capitalists' (Nuti 1979, p. 228), rather than with analysis of the mode of production of the statist socio-economic system and its laws of motion. This is what underlies comparison of models of planning involving different forms of (de)centralization with the idealized Pareto-efficient allocation of resources in a competitive general equilibrium. In so far as any attempt is made in this literature to explain why economic reform came onto the agenda, it is in terms of transition from the phase of extensive to that of intensive economic growth and development. Extensive economic growth is achieved by transferring labour from lower to higher productivity sectors, intensive growth by increasing labour productivity in all sectors through education and technical and organizational innovation.

Within the Marxist tradition, recognition of systemic problems in the administrative command planning system, the emergence of a cyclical pattern of attempts at economic reform, the appearance of investment cycles (Nuti 1978, p. 199; Ellman 1979, pp. 143–7), and a succession of political crises – all point to the need for an analysis of the socio-economic dynamic of the system. This was recognized by Dobb (1970a, ch. 5), but not really developed by him. Such analysis must ultimately be based on a view of the type of social formation existing in the statist countries, a matter touched on at the start of this book and discussed further in chapter 5. In this section, however, I consider the work of Nuti, Gomulka and Brus analysing the political economy of what they refer to as socialist societies. Between them they identify crucial questions for any model of democratic planning.

Nuti's model is based on 'the interaction between capital accumulation, economic decentralization and political liberalization' (Nuti 1979, p. 235). He argues that a combination of self-interested motivation, akin to the growth preference of capitalist managers, and residual ideological influence results in the ruling bureaucracy undertaking a higher rate of investment than the majority of people would have chosen for themselves. This gives rise to the familiar pattern of ambitious growth rates and output targets, concentration on investment in the capital goods sector at the expense of consumer goods, and generally taut planning. Thus, there is

a fundamental difference between economic systems. Capitalism has a tendency to chronic under-investment . . . frustrating democratic institutions because private ownership and free enterprise take capital accumulation away from parliamentary and government control. Socialism creates the preconditions for a public control over accumulation, given public ownership and macro-economic planning, but economic and political centralization equally take accumulation away from public control; thereby generating chronic over-investment even . . . in conditions of full employment. (Nuti 1979, p. 249)

Overaccumulation accentuates the systemic drawbacks of administrative command planning. The mounting economic problems, exacerbated by rising consumer aspirations, have resulted in various attempts to improve central planning, such as the use of mathematical methods and the creation of large corporations (associations). They have also led to massive imports of foreign technology and pressing international indebtedness. These developments have coexisted with cycles of largely unsuccessful attempts at economic reform, intended to decentralize more decision-making to the level of the enterprise. Nuti certainly does not regard the emergence of acute economic problems as being in itself sufficient to give rise to successful economic decentralization. In fact, he points out, it has generally been the case that economic crisis and acute shortage have resulted in a tightening not an easing of central control.

Nuti envisages two alternative trajectories for the laws of motion of centralized socialism, a virtuous circle of harmonious development and the vicious circle that has so far prevailed. The virtuous circle starts with an autonomous initiative of political democratization that establishes genuine social control over accumulation and therefore results in a lower rate of investment and growth. This in turn, by ending taut planning and chronic excess demand, creates the conditions necessary for successful economic decentralization, which then leads on to further democratization. In the vicious circle, by contrast, economic problems lead to inadequate economic decentralization in conditions of continued overaccumulation. The reform is a failure, economic performance deteriorates, recentralization takes place and economic problems continue, leading, after an interval, to the next unsuccessful attempt at decentralization (Nuti 1979, pp. 258–60).

What is unclear in Nuti's model is where the impetus for the initial political democratization in the virtuous circle comes from, although he cites the Twentieth Congress of the CPSU in 1956 and the Prague Spring in 1968 as examples and would presumably include the Gorbachev initiatives in 1987. Nuti is anxious that political democratization should not be confused with 'bourgeois liberalism' and that the danger of excessive decentralization should be recognized. Restoration of private ownership or the evolution of syndicalism would carry with it the re-emergence of the problems of capitalist economies: 'chronic underinvestment, inflation, personal and regional inequalities, unemployment' (Nuti 1979, pp. 259–60). As well as pivoting his virtuous trajectory on the need to establish democratic control over the rate of investment at the national level, Nuti also identifies the other dimension of economic democracy, when he points to the complete absence in the centrally planned economies of any real participation by workers in enterprise decision-making.

Nuti's political economy builds on that of Brus, to be considered shortly. However, a different view of the relationship between democracy and economic progress underlies Gomulka's more pessimistic appraisal of the prospects for the centralized socialist countries. Gomulka argues that the rate of growth of the most technically advanced countries is limited by the growth of the technological frontier, that is, the rate at which new technological possibilities can be created. The rate at which technically less advanced countries grow depends on how far they are behind the leaders, that is, on the size of their technological gap, and on the non-economic factors that determine the rate at which they are able to close the gap. In his view, the statist socialist countries, incorporating neither political nor economic democracy, are a social formation dedicated to catching up with the most advanced country in the world, the United States.[8]

From this springs Gomulka's pessimism about the prospects for democratization and evolution towards 'true' socialism in these countries. He argues that the revolutionary group, in its role as a manager of the pursuit of the technological frontier, begins immediately after the revolution . . to turn from a revolutionary into a 'leading' group. Organising a less or more drastic form of state-run economy, the group takes over the role of capitalist not only in the area of decision-making, but also as an agent of the 'culture of growth', propagating its values. Indeed, in the USSR and Eastern Europe strong material incentives dominate; relatively large income differentials are maintained, ideals of competition, promotion, success, power and economic efficiency are cultivated. (Gomulka 1986, p. 17)

According to Gomulka, the Soviet Union's rate of innovation is now roughly equal to that of the world's technological leader, the United States, but with a gap in technological level that is no longer closing, due to systemic socio-political characteristics that preclude market competition, financial discipline, and the degree of inequality inherent in them. If this gap in level persists in the long run, then Gomulka would expect pressure to develop for major economic reform conducive to innovation, irrespective of the inequalities that might be involved (Gomulka 1986, ch. 3). What he does not expect is democratization: 'At present, catching up with the United States in each field of importance, especially perhaps in the military field and in material standard of living, appears to be the dominant goal of the Soviet nation, not just of its "leading group". As long as this continues to be the case, the prospects for democratisation in Eastern Europe must in my view remain poor' (Gomulka 1986, p. 19).

Brus, who has provided the most sustained and, in my view, most profound analysis of the political economy of the statist countries (Brus 1973; 1975; 1980; 1985), takes the opposite view to that of Gomulka, arguing that democratization is likely to be a necessary condition for a qualitative improvement in economic efficiency. Brus operates within a Marxist historical materialist theoretical framework, in which at the most abstract level the dynamic giving rise to societal change is contradiction between the social forces and social relations of production. His analysis leads to the conclusion that the resolution of that contradiction, as it exists in the statist countries, requires democratization (Brus 1975, p. 209).

The forces of production have historically been defined as the means of production, that is, capital equipment and material inputs, together with the workers, including their skills, who work with the means of production in the labour process. The relations of production have been interpreted primarily as the relationship between the owners of the means of production, or their agents, and the workers, although relations between workers themselves within the labour process have sometimes also been included. Brus's argument is that modern methods of production, both the complexity of the processes involved and the extent of interdependence and associated need for coordination, mean that information and motivation have become, in a qualitatively new way, crucial inputs into the productive process. Since unbiased information and the necessary level or quality of motivation require democracy, democracy itself is now one of the forces or factors of production.

In the statist, administrative command planning, mode of production there is no class owning the means of production. They are publicly owned by the state. Primary relations of production are, therefore, the relationship between people (society) and the state, with respect to decisions at the level of the economy as a whole, and between workers and the agents of the state (director and top management), at the level of the enterprise. These primary relations of production in the statist countries are an obstacle to the fullest potential development of the forces of production, in particular to the generation of unbiased information and committed self-activating motivation, since that requires political and economic democracy. Hence, the resolution of the current contradiction between the forces and relations of production involves changing the relations of production by democratization (Brus 1975, ch. 4).

Political and economic democracy, involving pluralism and the participation of workers in decision-making at the level of the enterprise, are necessary for what Brus means by the socialization of the means of production, to be discussed in detail in chapter 5. He stresses particularly the importance of political democracy at the national level:

> Lack of political pluralism seems to be the major cause of blockage of information flows in Eastern Europe, and hence the major cause of misallocation of resources on a long-term macro scale. Here, and not so much in the absence of the market which . . . cannot nowadays be relied upon to make long-run allocative decisions, I see the main source of *arbitrariness* of economic decisions – shown in the disregard of constraints and the neglect of alternative courses of action . . . the autocratic syndrome goes a long way toward explaining not only the imprecisions but also the lack of elementary coordination in the construction and implementation of the plans. The ensuing 'planned chaos', and particularly the investment cycles peculiar to this form of socialism, seem to be firmly rooted in the political system. (Brus 1980 in Gomulka 1986, pp. 28–9)

Brus advocates use of the regulated market as an instrument of planning, although he has not gone beyond a sketchy outline of how it might work (Brus 1972, ch. 5; 1973, ch. 1). Unlike many advocates of (regulated) market socialism, he is very conscious of the limitations of the market mechanism. His principal concern is to insist on the centrality of democracy and that is the conclusion I take from this discussion of the political economy of reform. My project is to develop a model of democratic planning based not on market forces but on negotiated coordination. Given political and economic democracy, I believe the problems of information and motivation can be resolved.

Let Brus set out the objective: 'democratization of the centre, mutual integration of the "system" as a whole with the "sub-systems", through participation of the latter in general decisions . . . this is the only direction which offers a proper solution, since it permits rational proportions of centralization and decentralization to be maintained, and favours the coordination of group interests (and through them individual interests) with general social interests, the definition and implementation of which is the task of the community' (Brus 1975, p. 204).

3.4 Alienation and Democracy

The absence of political and economic democracy in the statist countries of Eastern Europe takes the form of totalitarianism or universal generalized paternalism. In every aspect of their lives people are more or less dependent, typically more, on the bureaucratic apparatus – the enterprise, the state and ultimately the party. Not surprisingly, the most convincing accounts of the system come from those who have experienced it. Bahro's characterization of actually existing socialism is striking: 'It regularly and inevitably reproduces precisely those barriers that block the way to the free development of self-conscious subjectivity and individual autonomy. It precisely embodies all the structural conditions of individual subalternity . . . the mentality and behaviour of dependent "little people" alienated from the overall totality' (Bahro 1977, p. 10).

All sections of society are affected, 'the indolence of the bureaucrat corresponds to the lack of interest of the worker and the dissatisfaction of the specialist' (Bahro 1978, p. 235). The political leadership, what Bahro calls the politbureaucracy, commands; lower levels in the bureaucracy passively receive commands from superiors and actively issue them to subordinates; workers and citizens are commanded. The problem of motivation is normally discussed at the level of the bureaucracy, particularly of enterprise management. Risk-avoidance, resistance to innovation, transmission of biased information, accumulation of hidden reserves, conformism towards superiors, arbitrariness towards subordinates, indolence, inefficiency, corruption – all are widely accepted, since Gorbachev not least in the Soviet Union itself, as deep-seated characteristics of bureaucratic behaviour in the statist countries.

However, the consequences of generalized dependence for workers and citizens are at least as profound, probably more so. All organized activity needs an adminstrative structure. The problem is to ensure that such structures are controlled by and accountable to society, rather than society being controlled by and accountable to the administrative bureaucracy. This problem is discussed in detail in chapter 7, but it is self-evident that dependent, passive, psychologically subaltern workers and citizens lack both the capacity and the desire to participate in economic decision-making, at the enterprise level as much as at the national macro-level. This is the most intractable problem inherent in 'revolution from above'.

Far from incorporating a process of self-transformation through active participation in enterprise decision-making, the administrative command planning system was from the beginning based as a matter of principle on one-'man' management. In the economic sphere this is the most important way in which the system, for all its rhetoric about the 'new man', reproduces dependence and subalternity and actively prevents the development of autonomy and self-government. The status of workers in the statist countries is little different from that of wage labour under capitalism and the evidence suggests that workers 'continue to regard themselves as wage workers rather than as co-owners of the means of production' (Ellman 1979, p. 172).

There are, however, differences between the position of workers in the statist and in the advanced capitalist countries. On the one hand, 'the position of workers in state socialism with respect to opportunities for improving qualifications, work intensity, social security, hours of work, security of employment and availability of employment, compares favourably with that in comparable capitalist countries' (Ellman 1979, p. 176). The legitimacy of the system rests on its claim to represent the interests of workers, who are accorded a privileged position in its ideology. Full employment has so far been necessary to maintain that legitimacy and workers have come to regard it as inviolable, although the logic of some of the more far-reaching reform proposals, occasionally made explicit, is such that the situation may change.

On the other hand, workers in the statist countries lack independent trade unions and the experience of Solidarity in Poland suggests that the system may be incapable of accommodating them. Workers' enjoyment of the benefits listed by Ellman depends on acquiescence in the benevolent paternalism of the state and ultimately the party. Feher, Heller and Markus give a chilling account of the economic situation of workers in the command economy. The right to employment is accompanied by a legal obligation to undertake administratively recognized work, an obligation that is enforced by administrative measures as well as by the absence of unemployment benefit. For people with limited job opportunities, whether due to specialization (especially white-collar or professional), place of residence (especially small town or rural), or domestic circumstances (especially women), this can lead to 'degrading and humiliating forms of personal dependence' (Feher, Heller and Markus 1983, pp. 73–4).

The relative security enjoyed by workers is the opposite side of the coin to the prohibition of independent organization and the consequential atomization and dependence on paternalistic benevolence. Benevolence can always be withdrawn:

> If conflict with the management of a particular enterprise regularly involves demotion or loss of job, conflict with the apparatus as such, that is, 'political misbehaviour', generally results in a stigmatization of the person concerned for the whole of his or her professional career. In the context of a generally prevailing job security this attaches such a high risk to any such act (even leaving other possible consequences aside) as to make it appear irrational. In this way state paternalism in both its aspects constitutes an important element in the legitimation, and therefore in the reproduction, of the social system. (Feher, Heller and Markus 1983, p. 76)

The situation is one of alienated labour, with workers approaching their jobs instrumentally, interested in obtaining maximum income with minimum effort. Although in this respect no different from the situation of alienated labour under capitalism the context is different. The absence of independent organization means that organized industrial disputes and industrial action are virtually non-existent, although spontaneous strikes do occur. However, the privileged position accorded to workers in official ideology and the associated job security mean that the discipline provided by unemployment under capitalism is absent. It is this which largely accounts for the work intensity of alienated labour in the statist command economies being so much lower than that in developed capitalist economies. Workers engage in passive resistance, regulating work intensity through a variety of informal practices familiar in the West, and there is not much management can do about it, within the constraints of the existing system. Of course, given managerial indolence, managers may not wish to do anything about it. The resultant mutual complicity in inefficient cosy paternalism, at the expense of society as a whole, presents a formidable obstacle to economic reform.

What are the options for the way forward? Much of the discussion around economic reform is concerned with increasing efficiency by rewarding effort and the more effective use of local knowledge. From where the administrative command economies are now it is difficult to see how this can be achieved without increasing differentials within enterprises and inequality between them. This is already being justified by the argument that socialism should reward people according to the work they do. However, there is likely to be opposition from those who will lose out or who are ideologically committed to equality. A particular problem is that those who gain are likely to be professionals and the more entrepreneurial managers rather than the skilled manual workers who have traditionally constituted the ideologically privileged proletariat.

A second option, so far rarely mentioned openly in discussion of economic reform, is acceptance of unemployment as a discipline. If forced labour is ruled out, what is to be done about inefficient, lazy or incompetent workers who do not respond to the carrot of higher material rewards or promotion to more responsible and fulfilling work? If dismissal, with little prospect of alternative employment, is not a possibility, how is passive resistance by alienated labour to be overcome? Similarly, with respect to enterprises. If they do not face the real possibility of bankruptcy and closure, if they are not faced with a hard as opposed to soft budget constraint (Kornai 1980b), how are inefficient enterprises to become efficient? One of the so far unacknowledged reasons for the at first sight surprising trend in the statist countries to establish embryonic stock exchanges is presumably the hope of creating a means of bringing pressure to bear on enterprise management.

These two options, the carrot of greater inequality and the stick of unemployment, both persist in treating people instrumentally, as objects to be manipulated, and therefore reinforce and reproduce the alienation of labour. Neither begins to confront the challenge of how to initiate a realistic process of transformation, starting from recognition of the existing situation in which workers are alienated – an 'us and them' situation prevails – but setting in motion a prolonged period of transition in which people's lived experience enables them to become autonomous and self-activating. The fatal weakness of classical Marxism was to assume that this would happen overnight, once the revolution occurred. Its enduring strength was to believe that it was possible.

The third option, the only worthwhile option in the long run, is democratization. Alienation can only be overcome, non-coercive human social relations can only be achieved, when people are autonomous, self-activating and self-governing. In the economic sphere, this requires political democracy, enabling people individually and collectively to be involved, on the basis of adequate knowledge and understanding, in deciding at the national level the strategic issues and priorities that set the broad outlines of the plan. It also involves industrial democracy, with workers participating in decision-making at the level of the enterprise. Both are necessary for economic democracy. The challenge of participating in decision-making, at both levels, is that it is potentially transformatory. However, for the potential to be realized participation must be real not formal or token. Only as people learn how to exercise responsibility can they bring bureaucracy under control and move towards self-government.

3.5 Conclusion

It is only through the consistent development of the democratic forms inherent in socialism, through a broadening of self-management, that our advancement in production, science and technology, literature, culture and the arts, in all areas of social life, is possible. It is only this way that ensures conscientious discipline. Restructuring itself is possible only through democracy and due to democracy. It is only this way that it is possible to give scope to socialism's most powerful creative force – free labour and free thought in a free country. (Gorbachev 1987, p. 24)

Gorbachev's speech to the January 1987 meeting of the Central Committee of the Soviet Communist Party represented a qualitative change in discussion of economic reform in the statist countries. In general terms the above quotation is a vindication of Brus's argument, discussed in section 3.3, that democratization is necessary to resolve the contradiction between the forces and the relations of production that exists in statist societies. Gorbachev's open advocacy of democracy was a landmark in his campaign for glasnost (openness) and perestroika (literally reconstruction; used to mean a new way). It was apparently triggered by the need to overcome opposition to the process of moving towards a new attempt at economic reform, made urgent by growing awareness of the deep-seated problems of the Soviet economy and their social consequences. The prospects for real democratization in practice, crucial for the fate of the economic reform, are considered in chapter 11. Here the reform proposals as they had emerged by the end of 1987 are briefly outlined.

During 1986 and 1987 there was much discussion about the need for economic change and the form it might take. Gradually, the outline of a reform package intended to be operational by the beginning of the 1990s began to emerge, although much remained unclear. The elements of this package were as follows. First, worker participation at the level of the enterprise was to be encouraged by provision for the election of workforce councils and of directors and top management.

Second, enterprises were to be grouped into associations which would be self-financing and were to be allowed some scope for obtaining their inputs and disposing of their output through horizontal negotiation with one another, with increased scope for negotiating prices. Enterprise association plans were to be fixed for five years, as were payments to the state and allocations to the different enterprise funds. The intention was to provide an incentive to increase efficiency and reduce costs by guaranteeing that success in one year would not lead to the ratchet effect of increased targets, payments and allocations the following year. Third, there were to be policy changes, in particular reduced subsidies, increased differentials and rigorous quality control – all designed to increase incentives by relating income more closely to results. Fourth, small scale cooperatives and self-employed private enterprise were to be encouraged.[9]

The package of reforms as it stood at the end of 1987 consisted primarily of elements that had either been tried before or were already in operation in other statist countries. Hanson has suggested that the proposals are closer to the GDR model, discussed in section 3.2, than to the Hungarian model, discussed in the next chapter (Hanson 1986, p. 322). The possibilities for worker participation, although real, are limited by the provisions for hierarchic approval of those elected to manage the enterprise and by the leading role legally assigned to the party organization in the enterprise. The scope for enterprise association autonomy is restricted by the continuing role and responsibilities assigned to the overseeing ministries. The intention to pursue a policy of acceleration, of ambitious growth targets, with the associated taut planning and tendency towards excess demand, suggests that the economic environment will not be conducive to decentralization.

In Hanson's view,

> The reorganization scheme that has emerged so far is close to the 'moderate' or 'rationalizing' brand of Soviet reform instead of the more radical market reform that some Soviet economists have espoused. Rather than make a complete break with the hierarchical system, as the Hungarians tried to do in 1968, the rationalizers aim at a blend of market relations with central administration while keeping the authorities' control over enterprises limited to broad, aggregated totals, within which enterprises make their own plans and pursue their own (workers' and managers') financial advantage in a stable framework . . . In keeping with the half-way house character of the scheme, many prices would still be centrally set, and supply and use of a number of 'most important' products would still be centrally planned. A recent short summary of this scheme, by two members of the Gosplan research staff, envisages 250–300 product groups being centrally planned and 'most' prices continuing to be centrally set. (Hanson 1987, p. 7)

It is too soon to be able to form a judgement about the possibilities of success for this latest attempt at economic reform of the command planning system. On the basis of past experience the prospects cannot be good, since the present reform package in itself is limited, has effectively been tried before and is inevitably meeting opposition. On the other hand, there are two new elements in the situation. First, the state of the economy is such that there now appears to be very widespread agreement inside the Soviet Union, almost a consensus, that something has to be done about it, even if there remains major disagreement about what. Second, Gorbachev's insistence on placing the issue of economic reform firmly in the context of the need to democratize Soviet society as a whole is quite unprecedented. The fate and future course of the reform are bound up with the extent to which the process of democratization is real, gathers momentum and begins to transform social relations and the consciousness of the Soviet people.

There are important lessons, positive and negative, to be learned from the experience of administrative command planning and the attempts to reform it. The system has proved to be an effective vehicle for concentrating a country's economic resources on the strategic priority of achieving rapid development in a backward country. In this ability to mobilize national resources for a clearly specified overriding objective it has similarities with the system of planning developed in wartime Britain. However, although the planning system in both cases was a necessary socio-technical mechanism it depended for its success in both cases on the existence of socio-political control, albeit resting on very different combinations of coercion and consent.

Administrative command planning has so far also achieved a degree of macroeconomic control over the economy that is not present in capitalist countries, nor in market socialist Yugoslavia. Full employment and an absence of serious inflation are impressive achievements, as is the avoidance of balance of payments and exchange rate crises. Here too, however, a distinction must be drawn, this time between an enabling socio-technical mechanism and the consequences of its use in a particular socio-political context. The corollary of the macroeconomic control achieved in the statist countries has been inefficiency, shortage, reliance on foreign technology and international indebtedness.

The reasons for this have been identified as the systemic problems of information and motivation. However, the system of administrative command planning has existed in a context of totalitarianism or universal paternalism, in the absence of political and economic democracy. Are the systemic problems in fact problems of the planning system or of the socio-political system, or can the two not be separated?

Presumably, any system of planning would involve consideration of the implications for the future structure of the economy of strategic, non-marginal decisions about the future direction of development of the society. Unless non-marginal sectoral changes are coordinated in advance too much of some categories of output will be produced and too little of others. The system of material balances, or something like it, operated at a sensible level of aggregation, may turn out to be of enduring value for this purpose. Similarly, in any system of planning there must be some way of coordinating in advance major investment decisions within a particular industry or sector. Some sort of association of enterprises will presumably be needed.

Could the systemic problems of information and motivation be overcome if a system of administrative command planning existed in a context of political and economic democracy? At the national level it would mean that genuine social control existed with respect to strategic macroeconomic priorities and people could therefore be expected to be committed to the microeconomic implications for their individual enterprises entailed by the plan. At the level of the enterprise it would mean that workers, experts and managers could all be expected to use their abilities and local knowledge to fulfil the targets laid down by the plan. The problem of motivation would have been solved by the existence of political and economic democracy. The problem of information would be purely technical, to be solved by a combination of computerized data processing and devolved decision-making.

There are three reasons for discounting this approach as a possible model for democratic planning. First, it amounts effectively to a resurrection of the possibility of planning on the assumption of perfect knowledge. Second, it assumes that the overall social interest can be decided at the national level, albeit democratically, in sufficient detail to be conveyed to individual enterprises in the form of instructions on what they have to do in order to fit into the overall picture. The result of these two assumptions is Lindblom's Model 1 planning, a technical procedure operated by experts for arriving at optimal solutions in everyone's individual interest once society's objectives have been decided through the democratic political process (Lindblom 1977, ch. 19).

Such an unproblematic view of the relationship between overall social interest, group interest and individual interest is untenable. There is an analogy here with the distinction between knowledge about the system as a whole and local knowledge. Even when people agree with the social priorities decided at the national level, or agree to go along with them because they have taken part in the decision-making process, they still have their own local interests about which no overall plan can have anything to say. The harmonization of these local interests with other people's local interests, in a way that takes account of overall social interests and priorities, can only take place through a process of negotiation. Harmonization is unlikely ever to be complete but a process of negotiation enables people to become aware of other people's interests and, in a situation of equality, obliges them to take account of the interests of all who are affected by the decision.

The third reason why administrative command planning is unsustainable, even in a democratic political and economic context, follows from this. If such a system could ever work properly there would be nothing to do at the enterprise level except carry out detailed plan directives received from above. There would effectively be nothing to decide. However democratic the process through which the plan was arrived at, it could not involve people directly in taking decisions about and assuming responsibility for their local activities. They would have to take on trust that what they were directed to do was in the general interest. They would not be involved in a process of negotiation through which the general interest was constructed in detail from below rather than being passed down from above.

Such a situation would contain no transformatory dynamic. Participation in the detailed construction of the social interest, taking account of the interests of all involved, is a central part of the process through which people cease to be objects, to be manipulated by administrative command or economic incentives, and become self-activating subjects who do what they do because they think it is right. The argument is not that people become unworldly altruists with a quixotic disregard for their own interests. Rather, it is that narrow self-interest gives way to a broader self-interest, in which people's own interests are redefined to include the interests of others. This is not such a novel view, although in the company of economists one might be forgiven for thinking it was. The reason why an increasing number of relatively privileged people favour equality is not for the sake of others but for the sake of themselves.

I am not suggesting that a model of planning for now could be based on the assumption that people in general have completed such a process of transformation. What I would like to insist on, however, is that any model of democratic planning worth the name should have a dynamic that promotes self-transformation and movement towards self-determination and self-government, rather than one that reinforces narrowly self-interested motivation and reproduces people as alienated objects to be manipulated.

4

Market Socialism

4.1 Introduction

Market socialism is a term it would probably be best to avoid. It has been misleadingly used to describe the family of decentralized planning models which seek to arrive at a Pareto-efficient competitive general equilibrium through an iterative process – what Bliss has called 'the Economics of Fairyland' (Bliss 1972, p. 100).[1] It has been used, somewhat misleadingly, to describe the Hungarian economy under the New Economic Mechanism introduced in 1968 and, perhaps less misleadingly, the Yugoslav worker self-managed system introduced in 1950. Finally, it has been used, again sometimes misleadingly, to describe models for further economic reform in the East (Kornai 1986b, section VII) and evolution towards democratic socialism in the West, in which the market is used as an instrument of planning.

Nevertheless, despite its varied usage, indeed possibly because of it, the term market socialism does focus on something very real in most current attempts to work out a third way somewhere between managed capitalism and statist command planning. The conjunction of socialism and market is significant. Socialism is intended to contrast with capitalism and incorporates a rejection of the exploitation, inequality and injustice associated with capitalism. Market is intended to contrast with comprehensive central planning and reflects recognition of the need for decentralization and the dangers of statist authoritarianism. There is, however, a very real sense in which the attractive power of market socialism is primarily negative. It is advocated above all on the grounds of realism, because there is no alternative, but no one is really enthusiastic about it.

It could be that this lack of enthusiasm is due to residual fundamentalism. It may be part of the more general difficulty the

socialist left has had in coming to terms with late twentieth century
reality and an indication of how far the process of renewal still has to
go.[2] This would be consistent with the fact that, while at a general level
market socialism has become almost a new orthodoxy on the
non-dogmatic left, discussion of how it might work in detail, how the
problems that would arise might be dealt with, remains sketchy and
tentative. In an essay on the future of British socialism published in
1984, Lukes is still posing the question, 'exactly *when* should market
forces operate and how should they be constrained and guided?'; and
he continues, 'our social analysis must . . . begin to distinguish between
capitalism and the market principle, and between different types of
markets' (Lukes 1984, pp. 275, 280). However, I believe that a lack of
enthusiasm for market socialism is well founded and reflects a justified
unease about the extent to which the effective operation of market
forces is compatible with equality and self-government. I share with
Nove the view that fundamentalism is a substitute for thought, though
not, I hope, the vituperative tone of his polemic (Nove 1983, passim). I
also share with Kornai the view that there are unsolvable dilemmas
requiring pragmatic compromises (Kornai 1986a, p. ix). Nevertheless,
recognition of the need for realism, of the inevitability and desirability
of significant decentralization, of the fact that there are no unproblematic optimal solutions, of the dangers of statism – none of this in itself
establishes either the possibility or the desirability of using market
forces as an instrument of planning.

In my view, the current vogue for market socialism on the
non-dogmatic left in the West reflects the ideological hegemony of the
new right, the fact that the left has not gone beyond a legitimate
rejection of statism and, in the absence of any alternative, has fallen for
the market. Similarly, most democratic reformers in or from the East
have seen the market as the only alternative to state domination and
personal dependence. They have drawn the wrong conclusion from the
fact that, historically, direct interpersonal relationships, between
people as state functionaries and people as workers or citizens, have
involved personal dominance and domination. The reaction has been
to seek to depersonalize interdependence through recourse to the
impersonal market mechanism. The alternative I advocate is to
democratize interdependence, through a process of negotiated coordination between equals, the subject matter of Parts III and IV of this
book.

The rest of this chapter examines the experience of Hungary and
Yugoslavia, whose economic systems are usually thought of as being
the closest yet to market socialism in practice, and then considers
theoretical models of democratic market socialism, so far unrealized in
practice. It is important to keep in mind that what is under discussion is

the use of the market mechanism as an instrument of planning. Brus
has distinguished between three categories of decision: basic strategic
and macro-level decisions, concerned with major investment, income
distribution and macro-stability; decisions concerning job choice and
personal, not collectively provided, consumption; and current economic decisions, concerned with the size and structure of enterprise and
industry outputs and inputs, the destination of outputs and the source
of inputs, and minor investment.

He argues that the first category of decision must be taken centrally
in any economy that can be called planned and that, except in times of
national emergency, the second category will remain decentralized for
the foreseeable future, through labour and consumer goods markets, as
they are at the moment in both capitalist and statist economies. Only
the third category is at issue in discussion of economic reform, or
market socialism: *'models of the functioning of a socialist economy, if
they are truly to correspond to the foundations of the system, can only
differ from each other by the centralization or decentralization of the
decisions in this third group'* (Brus 1972, p. 63). I agree with Brus that
planning necessarily involves some centralization of decision-making
and also with his view that current economic decisions should be
decentralized. The question is how that balance between appropriate
centralization and decentralization can best be achieved.

4.2   The Hungarian New Economic Mechanism

In the mid-1980s, Hungary was the one centrally planned country in
Eastern Europe whose economic system was significantly different
from that existing before the reforms of two decades earlier. In only
two countries, Czechoslovakia and Hungary, was the momentum for
change that developed in the mid-1960s primarily towards market-
based reform. In Czechoslovakia, the momentum for economic reform
came together with pressure for political reform in the Prague Spring of
1968, forever associated with Alexander Dubček. The Soviet invasion
in August 1968 cut off any sort of reform for a generation in a tragic
closure of the most exciting opening towards democratic socialism that
the world had then seen. Hungary's economic reform had developed
without any hint of associated political reform and so was allowed to
continue.

The post-war statist regime in Hungary was imposed by the Red
Army in 1945 after the defeat of fascism. The Hungarian uprising in
1956, which followed the acknowledgement of Stalinism and its
consequences at the Twentieth Congress of the CPSU earlier that year,
was suppressed by Soviet troops and Kadar emerged as the new leader.

Kadar succeeded in consolidating the situation and creating a stable political and economic environment. Nevertheless, economic problems developed, as in the other administrative command economies, and in 1965 it was decided to draw up plans for a comprehensive economic reform, known as the New Economic Mechanism (NEM). A radical economic programme was possible because the prospect of major political change could not arise. The question of basic political system had already been settled in Hungary, unlike in Czechoslovakia in 1968.

The fundamental content of the NEM introduced at the beginning of 1968 was the abolition of central determination of output targets and central allocation of intermediate inputs. Instead, enterprises were to negotiate contracts with one another in pursuit of profitability, which was to be the primary criterion of success and the basis for enterprise reward. It was recognized that the preconditions for an effective reform were, first, a rational price structure related to real costs and, second, an incentive system that would motivate enterprises to produce efficiently. Given these preconditions, profitability calculated in terms of rational prices would reflect the relationship between the social value of resources used (costs) and the social value of output produced (revenues). The state would collect a capital charge, related to the value of assets employed, and a payroll tax in order to finance central expenditure. Residual profits would then be divided between enterprise self-financed minor investment, collective social provision for employees, and the personal income of managers and workers.

The role of the centre in the NEM can be considered under three headings: institutional structure; plan formulation; and plan implementation, or regulation. First, the centre was responsible for the foundation, division, integration and liquidation of enterprises and for defining their field of activity. It was also responsible for the appointment or dismissal of enterprise management and for the supervision of their activities through annual auditing and evaluation. Second, the centre was to draw up five-year and annual plans, expressed in terms of quantitative output targets, which the relevant ministries were then responsible for achieving. The centre, through the ministries, was also responsible for major new investment.

However, although ministries were to be set output targets, enterprises were not, nor were they to be allocated inputs. The plan was to be implemented not directly, through central administrative instruction, but indirectly, through regulating the environment within which enterprises pursued profitability, that is, by manipulating the framework within which they made their profit-motivated decisions about what to produce and where to obtain inputs. Thus, the centre's third role in the NEM was to implement the plan by operating the system of remote control, the regulators. The principal regulators or policy instruments available to it were fiscal and monetary policy, prices and incomes policy, and foreign trade and exchange rate policy. It also controlled major investment, financed by taxation of enterprise profits.

A fundamental principle underlying the NEM was that as rapidly as possible regulators should become parametric, that is, should apply on a non-discriminatory basis to all enterprises in the same category. With parametric regulation it would be legitimate to distinguish between different categories of enterprise in order to take account of longer-term planning objectives, or on social grounds. Thus, the target rate of return (capital charge) could differ between essential and non-essential industries, as defined by the plan, and their products could be further subsidized or taxed to encourage or discourage production. The same principle would also apply between regions if the plan gave priority to some at the expense of others. However, it would not be legitimate to discriminate between enterprises in the same category, in the same industry and/or region. That would be non-parametric regulation.[3]

How has the NEM worked in practice? Three periods can be distinguished: the introductory period around the turn of the decade, during which economic performance improved; the 1970s, during which growth continued at a high rate, despite the turmoil in the international capitalist economy, but economic problems began to accumulate and a recentralizing process became evident; and the period from the end of the 1970s, during which successive attempts were made to renew the impetus of the reform in the face of relative stagnation, severe balance of payments problems and pressure on living standards (Galasi and Sziraczki 1985). An evaluation of the effect of the NEM on Hungary's economic performance would have to take account of the interaction between the international economic context, relevant structural characteristics of the Hungarian economy, such as its heavy dependence on international trade and its high level of industrial concentration, and the NEM itself. I shall concentrate on the way in which the NEM has worked from the standpoint of the implications for a model of democratic planning.

The problem confronting those responsible for the NEM has been how to combine overall central control with enterprise autonomy, that is, with a situation in which enterprises take their own decisions and bear the consequences of them. For enterprises to bear the conse-quences of their own decisions they have to be confronted by hard rather than soft budget constraints. Essentially, this means that enterprises must not be able to influence the external determinants of their profitability, the basis on which their performance is assessed. They must not be able to influence prices, taxes or subsidies, or the terms on which credit is available. Faced with such hard budget constraints the behaviour of profit-motivated enterprises really would be determined by an exogenous environment. If the centre were then able to shape that environment it would be shaping enterprise behaviour.[4]

In fact, under the NEM enterprises have not been fully autonomous and have not faced a hard budget constraint. During the 1970s a trend towards recentralization set in. The original intention was for inputs to be bought from other enterprises without reference to the centre. However, in practice the centre continued to influence input allocation to a large extent, initially through informal pressure, later through a system of advisory committees. There appear to have been three reasons for this. First, until the end of the 1970s a high rate of investment continued, if anything higher than in the earlier period. Excess demand and shortages persisted, with the consequence that some system of rationing was necessary. In the absence of any significant decentralization of price formation, rationing by price did not occur. Instead, central guidance replaced formal central allocation. Although output targets were not formally set, output was in fact largely determined by centrally guided input allocation.

Second, ministries were formally assigned quantitative output targets even though enterprises were not. Ministries were responsible for evaluating enterprise performance, in particular managerial performance, and were able to award additional bonuses to managers on top of any that they received out of enterprise profits. Ministries had reserve powers that enabled them to issue administrative instructions. Not surprisingly, enterprise managers had an interest in keeping their overseeing ministry happy by cooperating with its informal guidance. Third, informal guidance from the centre was a practical possibility because of the high level of concentration in Hungarian industry. In 1970 there were roughly 800 enterprises and in 1979 roughly 700, with about half of these organized into associations or trusts. Furthermore, most products were produced by only one or two enterprises.

Enterprises under the NEM, then, have been less autonomous than had been intended. They have also faced soft rather than hard budget constraints. Although profitability is formally the principal performance indicator, and the basis for the incentive system, the link between profitability and reward has been much weaker than intended. The central plan has included targets for wage differentials and money wage increases consistent with avoiding inflation. Wage increases, along with collective social expenditure financed by the enterprise and minor investment, are a claim on profits net of central charges, taxes and subsidies. There has been no limit on the wage increase an enterprise could pay but increases in excess of the centrally determined targets have been subject to very steeply progressive taxation. In effect, there has been a tax-based incomes policy.

In addition to wage increases, which have been permanent, one-off bonuses have been possible, also paid out of net profits. Initially, maximum bonus rates were set at 80 per cent of salary for managers, 50 per cent for leading workers and 15 per cent for other workers. The increase in income differentials that this produced led to worker unrest and a modification of the bonus system. In 1972 the maximum was reduced to 30 per cent for managers and 10 per cent for workers, although managers could still receive additional bonuses directly from their supervising ministry. The dependence of the regime on workers' acquiescence has also meant that, in general, unprofitable enterprises have not been allowed to disappear, nor even to contract significantly. They have also been expected to pay the target wage increase. Thus, profitable enterprises have been highly taxed and unprofitable enterprises have received subsidies.[5]

Associated with the absence of full enterprise autonomy and hard budget constraints has been a tendency for the economic regulators to become less not more parametric. There are two reasons for this. First, the centre has wanted to influence the behaviour of individual enterprises and has therefore shaped the regulators applied to them in the light of their particular circumstances. Second, enterprises have sometimes wanted their particular circumstances to be taken into account and so have sought, and often obtained, special treatment.

The first reason for the tendency towards non-parametric regulation has generally been regretted in the literature, not least inside Hungary itself. Yet why is it necessarily a bad thing? Is this not just what would have to happen if the market mechanism is to be regulated as an instrument of planning? One of the lessons from the operation of industrial policy in capitalist economies is precisely that non-discriminatory policies are relatively ineffective and that effective policy must engage at the level of the individual firm. If this does not happen through direct interpersonal contact, whether official or informal, then it must happen through the use of enterprise specific regulators. At a formal level, it does not in principle matter which method is used. The centre requires the same information on the basis of which it makes the same decision. The only difference is in the way in which the decision is conveyed to the enterprise, by direction or by non-parametric regulation.

However, in reality there is a crucial difference. In the case of interpersonal contact the technical problem of information can be overcome, although not necessarily the problem of information bias. There is no need to make the impossible assumption of perfect knowledge. The centre does not need all the local knowledge available to the enterprise and the enterprise does not need to supply it. The local information relevant for a given decision will emerge from the discussion. Of course, the same process could occur as a basis for the centre to arrive at a set of enterprise specific regulators, which it then imposes on the enterprise, but what would be the point? Why introduce a redundant stage? The only point of a system of enterprise specific regulators, as opposed to direct instructions, would be if it had different information requirements and resulted in different behaviour.

If the centre is prepared to confine itself to macro-management, major investment, and concern with broad industrial and regional structure, leaving the fate or fortune of individual enterprises to the outcome of regulated market forces, then parametric regulation might conceivably work, although that has yet to be established. If, as is likely, the centre wishes to have an influence on what happens to individual enterprises, then either direct interpersonally-based decisions or non-parametrically regulated decisions are unavoidable. In this context, the centre stands for any authority or interest outside the enterprise: it may be the capitalist state claiming to represent the national interest; or the higher levels of the statist administrative bureaucracy; or, in the future, representatives of the self-governing communities affected by the enterprise's decisions and performance.

If the first reason why parametric regulation has not developed in Hungary is that the centre has wished to influence the behaviour of individual enterprises, the second is that enterprises have not wished to be bound by such inflexible regulation and have sought to circumvent it. They have done this either by using local knowledge not available to the centre or by persuading the centre that their specific circumstances merited special treatment. Such persuasion has typically occurred either through the top management of large enterprises becoming integrated into the central planning and management structure or through a continuation in the new circumstances of the old plan bargaining. In these ways, relatively unprofitable enterprises have sought special subsidies and reduced levels of capital charge and taxes, and to a large extent have obtained them.

Unlike the first reason for non-parametric regulation, the centre's wishes, this second reason for enterprise specific regulation is in general likely to be undesirable. Enterprises that are inefficient in resource utilization, or are failing to produce what customers want, will tend to spend their time in lobbying for favourable treatment rather than in doing something about the reasons for their poor performance. However, although the attempt by enterprises to obtain special treatment is likely to be undesirable, it may not always be so. It will sometimes be the case that the reasons for an enterprise's relatively low profitability are beyond its control. In such situations, it might sometimes be thought socially desirable for enterprises to receive special subsidies to enable them to pay socially agreed minimum wages or to maintain employment in particular communities.

The problem is how to distinguish between conceptually distinct situations that, at the level of regulation, have the same outcome in the form of enterprise specific packages of regulators. Is an enterprise facing regulators tailor-made for its circumstances because the centre wishes to influence its specific behaviour? If so, the enterprise faces a hard budget constraint even though regulation is non-parametric. Is an enterprise receiving special treatment because it has sought it? If so, while regulation is again non-parametric, the enterprise faces a soft budget constraint and the favourable treatment may or may not be socially desirable. It will be desirable if the centre has been legitimately convinced that the enterprise merits special treatment but not if the centre has been conned.

The problem can be illustrated from the experience of the attempt to impart a new impetus to the Hungarian reform at the end of the 1970s. Among the new measures was a revised set of regulations for price formation. When the NEM was introduced three categories of price were established: centrally set prices; prices set by enterprises within centrally determined limits; and prices set by enterprises without limits. The intention was to increase the third category as quickly as possible. However, largely because of the problem of monopoly power arising from the highly concentrated structure of Hungarian industry, most prices continued to be determined by the centre, either directly, or indirectly through detailed rules. From the beginning of 1980 the rules for price formation were changed in an attempt to move from an internal cost-plus basis to a situation in which prices corresponded more to world market prices in convertible currency (Kornai 1986a, p. 82).

Kornai cites a study by the Ministry of Finance which examined the effect of this price revision on profitability. The initial impact was to increase the profitability of enterprises whose prices had been relatively low, compared to world prices, and to decrease it where they had been relatively high. What happened then was a marked tendency for the relative profitability of enterprises to revert rapidly to the pre-revision situation. In particular, where profitability calculated in terms of the new prices initially fell, it soon rose again (Kornai 1986a, pp. 83–4). As Kornai points out, this could have been because inefficient enterprises successfully adapted to the new situation and increased their efficiency, as defined by the new set of input and output prices. However, it could also have been because they found ways round the new situation, which he thinks more likely.

In the context of the Hungarian economy, Kornai has discussed the related phenomena of the 'regulator game' and 'regulation illusion'.

The regulator game consists of a continuous interaction between the centre, seeking to constrain enterprise behaviour by manipulating the regulators, and the enterprises, which use their local knowledge to get round the regulators. As Kornai puts it: 'One of the teams – the ensemble of the central organs – devises new tactics, new clever combinations, how to "get" the adversary. But the other team – the ensemble of enterprises – immediately works out countertactics and tries to get around the adversary' (Kornai 1986a, p. 89).

Will the game ever end? Between 1968 and 1978 in Hungary 'over one hundred orders and legal rules were issued to regulate the profit and profit-sharing of the firm' (Kornai 1980a, p. 156). However, the centre can never win, because it does not have the local knowledge available to the enterprise and can never get access to it in an adversarial situation. The result is regulation illusion, the mistaken view that effective regulation is possible. Discussing the price reform of 1980, Kornai argues, 'We have to put up with the fact that *it is the relatively smaller part of production where the method of price calculations can be prescribed in an administrative manner. With the greater part of production this is sheer illusion, only pseudo-administrative prices come about*' (Kornai 1986a, p. 89).

The regulator game and regulation illusion are widely observed in the state enterprise sector of the Hungarian economy. Enterprises seek to avoid hard budget constraints either by bending the rules for price formation or by bargaining with the centre. Kornai has compared the profits of state enterprises in 1978–80 before and after tax and subsidy and has also examined the relationship between original profitability and profit-linked income. He concludes:

> Subsidy is still of a compensating or levelling nature; this is indicated by the fairly strong negative correlation between pure profitability and subsidies. Profits distributed to employees (as profit sharing) are almost *independent of the 'true', 'original' profitability of the enterprises*. We may add further that *the bonus of the manager of the enterprise also does not depend on the 'original' profitability, but on the actual profitability after receipt of the subsidies*. The manager is thus forced not only by the interest of the enterprise, but by his own immediate financial interest, to acquire as much subsidy as possible. (Kornai 1986a, p. 91)

Subsidies may or may not be justified in terms of a country's values and objectives. Kornai on the whole seems to think that in Hungary they mainly represent featherbedding. Bending the rules can rarely be justified on social grounds. Yet if managers are encouraged to pursue their narrow self-interest within a regulated environment they must be expected to seek subsidies, justified or not, and bend the rules if they can. Hungary, of course, is not unique in this. The regulator game between the authorities and those whom they instruct and/or seek to regulate is played everywhere.

Thus, there are two reasons why parametric regulation is generally considered to be desirable – it precludes special pleading and it makes it easier to avoid the regulator game. The argument is that it gets as close as seems possible to confronting enterprises with hard budget constraints. It is acknowledged, of course, that there would be costs in parametric regulation. Less successful enterprises and those who work in them, even if the reasons for their lack of success were beyond their control, would have to accept the consequences and inequality would be bound to increase. However, that would be the price that would have to be paid for efficiency. Whether this approach could actually be adopted in the existing Hungarian situation is another matter. Kornai doubts it, because of 'the *artificial nature* of the system of rules and regulations. Real market competition is not devised by anybody: living organizations compete with each other for the buyer, ultimately for profit, for survival, and for growth. In our country, however, the intention is to simulate live competition with extremely complicated legal rules devised on a desk – with little success' (Kornai 1986a, p. 86). In other words, at the moment market forces do not really operate.

This analysis is consistent with the direction of the new round of reforms initiated in Hungary in the late 1970s. The price reform trying to link domestic prices to world market prices has already been discussed. In an attempt to break the informal vertical links between the centre and enterprises the three existing industry ministries were merged and much responsibility for regulation was transferred to the prices office. Many trusts were broken up and new state enterprises were created in order to increase competition. New forms of joint, cooperative and small private enterprise were permitted, partially at least in recognition of the second economy that had developed during the previous decade (Marer 1985).

However, although the direction of change has been towards a greater role for real as opposed to simulated competition there is a long way to go. The industrial sector is still dominated by large state enterprises facing relatively soft budget constraints. The logic of this line of argument is that budget constraints will only be hard, enterprises will only be forced to be efficient, when losses lead to liquidation or to takeover by more profitable enterprises.[6] What starts as an attempt to operate a regulated market mechanism, using the market as an instrument of planning, turns out to have a logic leading to primary reliance on market forces, with 'planning' confined to macroeconomic management and possibly a shadowy industrial policy.

I think there are three possible conclusions that might be drawn from this analysis of the unique and rich Hungarian experience. The first is

Kornai's, the second what I take to be Brus's, and the third is my own. Kornai has concluded that efficiency and socialist values are bound to be incompatible in some situations. His argument is that, given '*the true behavioural characteristics of people, communities and social groups*' (Kornai 1980a, p. 157), it is not possible to combine all the best features from different economic systems and avoid all the worst. The choice is between different packages, which represent different compromises between different desirable objectives. The best that can be done is to discover what the bedrock trade-offs are, so that people can chose the package, the social system, they prefer.

Brus accepts that the Hungarian experience has 'exposed the difficulties of combining central planning with a regulated market mechanism' and that because of the incentive problem there is a 'need to re-think and re-interpret the ownership issue, in the context of a wider use of the market mechanism' (Brus 1985, pp. 61, 62). However, his general analysis continues to give central importance to the question of democratization. Hungary remains a statist society, enjoying neither political nor economic democracy. Worker participation in enterprise management has not been part of the NEM. Managerial indolence, worker alienation and privatized behaviour appear to be as prevalent in Hungary as in the other statist countries. Although the Hungarian economy until the mid-1980s performed relatively well with respect to personal consumption, this was not due primarily to the NEM but to the fact that since 1956, for political reasons, government policy gave priority to living standards and the non-state sphere grew significantly (Kornai 1986a, pp. 109–10).

It seems likely that Brus is more optimistic than Kornai over the prospects for regulated market socialism, without too many cruel dilemmas, in that he believes democratization would greatly widen the options. Noting the fact that debates on the reform within Hungary never discuss that possibility, he writes: 'It may well be, however, that the political framework is simply treated as a given in the debates, so that remedies have to be sought elsewhere. If this is so, we would be faced with quite a paradox: marketization of a socialist economy as a substitute for pluralization of its polity' (Brus 1985, p. 61). This is precisely what I think has been happening. Whereas Brus thinks that democratization would make the prospects for regulated market socialism with a human face more likely, I think it would make it unnecessary, even supposing it were possible.

Real democracy, self-government, would, in my view, change those behavioural characteristics which Kornai takes as given. As people cease to be manipulated objects and become self-activating subjects the incentive problem is likely to be increasingly resolved and the information problem can then be dealt with through cooperative as opposed to adversarial negotiation.

4.3　Yugoslavia's Worker Self-managed Economy

Unlike Hungary, Yugoslavia was liberated from fascism by its own communist-led Partisans, with some help from the Allies and the Red Army. In 1948, after three years as part of the Soviet bloc, Tito's refusal to accept Soviet domination resulted in Yugoslavia's expulsion from the Cominform. Faced with a relatively underdeveloped economy and extensive war damage, forced into economic links with the capitalist West by a Soviet-led economic blockade, committed to socialist ideals and enjoying massive popular support, the Yugoslav communists embarked on a unique historical experiment – the attempt to create a self-governing society. The economic institution on which this was based was the worker-managed enterprise; the political institutions were the local commune, the regions, the republics and the federation.

Yugoslavia is a one-party statist country but since the early 1950s it has not had an administrative command planned economy, indeed since 1965 it has not had a planned economy in any real sense at all. However, although it has not enjoyed democratic political pluralism, self-government has not been an entirely empty concept. Given a need to maintain popular support and federal unity, in face of the early Soviet threat, Yugoslavia's national and ethnic diversity has resulted in a degree of autonomy on the part of its constituent republics and regions far greater than that in any of the other statist societies. In fact, since the death of Tito in 1980 there appears to have been increasing difficulty in holding the country together. The worker-managed enterprises have also enjoyed more autonomy than enterprises in the administrative command economies. Thus, there has been a significant measure of geographic and economic pluralism, although not democratic political pluralism, and this may account for the relatively unoppressive character of the society.

The worker-managed enterprise is what has made the Yugoslav system unique. The basic institutional arrangements are by now well established. Enterprises are created by social bodies: the federal, national or regional governments, or the commune (local government). They are then handed over to their workers to be held on trust as social property.[7] Workers elect a Workers' Council which in turn elects a Management Board and appoints a Director from a list of candidates approved by the commune. The Council is responsible for general policy decisions, the Board and the Director for day to day operational decisions. The Yugoslav experience of seeking to achieve worker participation in management is more extensive than any other. How has it worked?

Up to 1965 the evidence suggests: '(1) widespread worker desire to influence enterprise decision-making, (2) a growing expectation to participate in decision-making concerning production as well as personnel, income and welfare issues, and (3) high attendance at worker assemblies and meetings of other participatory bodies' (Zimbalist and Sherman 1984, p. 438).[8] Even during this favourable period for worker participation, and certainly since 1965 when market forces became dominant, the tendency has been for the degree of participation to decline from top to bottom in the skill hierarchy, with professional personnel most actively involved, then skilled workers, and unskilled workers least involved. If anything, the situation appears to have been changing for the worse. Workers' Council control over the Director, via the Management Board, has become more of a formality, with the reality increasingly becoming Director management of the Workers' Council (Neuberger and James 1973; World Bank 1979).

In the mid-1970s a new institution was created, the basic organization of associated labour (BOAL). The intention was that every economic activity producing output capable of being separately sold should be organized into a separate BOAL. The hope was that the creation of smaller units would increase worker participation in decision-making, increase competition, and enable worker income to be more closely related to work performed. In fact, the degree of participation did not increase. The newly created BOALs were often previously independent enterprises that had been merged and whose management structures had remained largely in place. Workers appear to have regarded the reorganization as merely formal. Nor was the extent of competition increased significantly. BOALs are not entirely independent but agree on market sharing, accept mutual liability for debts and lend to one another for investment (Comisso 1979; Sacks 1984).

BOALs within an enterprise enter into contracts with one another for the quasi-sale of output at transfer prices which determine the internal distribution of enterprise income. Negotiation over transfer prices takes place within a constraint set by the market price of enterprise output, which is more or less given. Transfer prices bear some relation to external market prices since BOALs are in principle able to buy and sell externally and in the final analysis have the right to withdraw from the enterprise. However, 'within the firm both buyer and seller are required to make a complete disclosure of their costs and revenues, as well as of the incomes of their workers, so social pressure tends to push the transfer price to a level that yields a "fair" distribution of profit' (Sacks 1985, p. 162). The social pressure may come from the prevailing ideology of solidarity or more directly from the party, the Yugoslav League of Communists.

The evolution of the Yugoslav economic system can be divided into three periods. The first, 1950–65, was one of gradual decentralization, with greater autonomy for enterprises and a decentralization of the planning function to republics and regions. Annual plans with quantitative targets were abolished, as were enterprise output targets and input allocations, but most investment continued to be determined by the centre. The policy objective for most of this period was industrialization through import-substitution. Priority to basic heavy industry was ensured by the central control over investment. The corollary was that market criteria could not be used to determine the significance of sectors or the success of enterprises.

Although economic performance in the 1950s was impressive, agriculture was neglected, foreign trade problems became evident and there was a growing disenchantment with federal government intervention. The result was a change of policy from import-substituting industrialization to export-led growth, with the objective of exposing the economy to the discipline of world market forces. The culmination of this policy was the series of reforms which ushered in the second period, 1965–75, when market forces were predominent in shaping the development of the Yugoslav economy. The reforms had two aspects. On the one hand, the role of the government at all levels was greatly reduced, in particular over 80 per cent of investment was devolved to the enterprise level, although some indirect government influence on investment remained through the banking system. On the other hand, the economy was opened up to international competition by devaluation and the reduction or abolition of import restrictions and export subsidies.

The effects of these 'ill-considered' reforms (Horvat 1982, p. 206) were predictable, although not apparently predicted. Foreign competition led to enterprise failure but since closure was socially unacceptable the outcome was rescue operations, particularly merger. The greater role of market forces was associated with a marked deterioration in macroeconomic performance, with a lower growth rate, rising unemployment and labour migration, rapidly accelerating inflation, sharply increased overseas indebtedness and severe balance of payments problems. The government responded with stop–go policies and a policy cycle of decentralization, followed by instability, recentralization, also followed by instability, further decentralization, and so on, all around an underlying decentralizing trend. The economy had ceased to be planned in any meaningful sense: 'The cyclical shifts in policy in the years after reform reveal an inability on the part of policy-makers to incorporate into the reform programme a consistent set of goals and instruments of economic control' (Flaherty 1982, p. 129).

The intensification of market competition also increased inequality. Income inequality increased between skilled and unskilled workers, between workers in different enterprises, and between workers in different republics and regions. Inequality of power within the enterprise also increased, as the pressure of market forces placed a premium on financial and marketing skills at the expense of production. The already existing tendency towards a hierarchical structure and control by professional managers was reinforced. Symbolically, in 1969 a new provision was introduced enabling the elected Management Board to be replaced by a Business Board appointed by the Director. The effect on workers is summarized by Zimbalist and Sherman: 'Increasingly removed from basic enterprise decision-making, worker councils and workers began to relate to the enterprise in more instrumental ways. They progressively took up the concerns of traditional trade unionism (wages, benefits, grievances, etc.) to the relative detriment of participation in central management issues' (Zimbalist and Sherman 1984, p. 439).

It is possible that the deterioration in economic and social performance from 1965 onwards was not due to the enhanced role of market forces but to other influences, namely the worsening inter-national economic environment and the centrifugal tendency of republican and regional separatism. The international recession when it developed certainly did not help, but it did not set in until the 1970s by which time Yugoslavia's economic problems were well established. The separatist influence is more convincing, although as an expla-nation complementary rather than alternative to the role of market forces. As part of political decentralization, responsibility for fiscal and monetary policy was decentralized, which led to fragmentation and the uncoordinated operation of the available economic regulators. There were different centres attempting remote control; not all pulling in the same direction.

By the mid-1970s it was recognized that a new approach to planning was needed and the third period in the evolution of the Yugoslav system began. However, there was no return to central planning. Instead, a system of bottom-up planning was introduced based on the newly-created BOALs. BOALs within an enterprise were to negotiate with each other to agree on a five-year enterprise plan; enterprises in the same industry were to exchange information in order to promote consistency; and the same was to occur between industries to check on the feasibility of the aggregate outcome and to identify bottlenecks. The results of this bottom-to-top-and-down-again iterative process were then to be incorported in self-management agreements and, at the federal level, in the five-year social plan. At the same time, social compacts, covering sectoral priorities, targets for productivity increase, and income distribution, were to be negotiated between social (government) bodies, the enterprises and the trade unions.

Actual transactions are supposed to be influenced by the outcome of this planning process. The negotiation of transfer prices between BOALs within an enterprise has already been discussed. Transactions between enterprises take place on a commercial basis, influenced by certain price controls and fiscal and monetary policy. Investment is influenced by the terms on which credit is made available, although some investment in new industries and in less developed republics and regions is determined directly by the federal, republican or regional governments. However, respcnsibility for most regulators has been decentralized, sometimes as far down as commune level, and it has proved very difficult to obtain agreement on any coordinated policy implementation.

For the most part the system continues to operate in much the same way as before the mid-1970s. Formal procedures for bottom-up planning through self-management agreements and social compacts seem so far to be largely wishful thinking. Market forces remain the principal coordinating mechanism, to a qualitatively greater extent than in any of the other statist countries, including Hungary. Sacks concludes, 'It is difficult to argue that there is much *effective* planning in Yugoslavia beyond some thinking ahead by independent actors. In any market system, the participants plan their own future actions and negotiate some of their contracts in advance' (Sacks 1985, p. 156).

However, internal competition is limited by strong republican and regional protectionism. Inter-republican trade actually fell during the 1970s, as a proportion of total trade, and is less important than inter-country trade in Western Europe. Inter-republican capital mobility is also low, which partially explains why the less developed republics and regions are falling relatively further behind. Republics and regions subsidize their own enterprises in order to compete against each other for Western trade and technical agreements. Thus, 'Despite a sequence of market-oriented reforms, the competitive market pressure is still rather weak and the economy is yet highly politicised' (Gomulka and Ostojic 1986).

During the 1980s, Yugoslavia experienced acute economic crisis: living standards fell sharply and worker unrest developed; unemployment and inflation reached very high levels; balance of payments problems were severe, with mounting international indebtedness; regional disparities and tensions became explosive. Reviewing the evolution of the economic system of this small, relatively underdeveloped country, through all three periods, Flaherty argues: 'The market, domestic or international, cannot provide the institutional framework within which such a country can at the same time ensure domestic stability and growth and keep a payments deficit within manageable limits' (Flaherty 1982, p. 142). One consequence of the crisis has been a sharp fall in the popularity of the ruling Yugoslav League of Communists. Between 1974 and 1983 confidence in it, as expressed in opinion polls, fell from three-quarters to just over one third of the population (Myant 1984, p. 28).[9]

The Yugoslav objective of creating a self-governing society is an inspiration, even though it remains more of an ideal than a reality. For a society to proclaim its belief in the possibility of workers running their workplaces and people more generally running their communities is of immense historical significance. It holds out the promise of overcoming the age-old division of people into the doers and the done to. There are, I think, three factors which have limited the extent to which the project of moving towards a self-governing society has been achieved. The first is the relatively low level of material and cultural development that prevailed in Yugoslavia in 1945. Self-government requires resources – material resources but above all human, cultural, resources.

The second is the absence of political and economic democracy. Political democracy, political pluralism, have been explicitly precluded by the statist system. Worker management has been largely confined to the managerial and professional elite, with most workers having a status little different from that of wage labour and exhibiting the subaltern consciousness and behaviour associated with that status. Although the economy remains highly politicized, Yugoslav society is becoming less political, as memories of the war and the Partisans fade. Indeed, it may be that the statist character of the society, by confining political activity to the ruling group, has not only contributed to the privatization of behaviour but has also reinforced rather than undermined the nationalist and separatist tendencies that pose such a threat to the country's integrity.

The third factor inhibiting the development of a self-governing society has been the inability to devise an economic system that enables effective planning at the different levels at which it is needed. An effective combination of centralized and decentralized decision-making has not been achieved. The system of bottom-up planning introduced in the mid-1970s is extremely interesting as a framework for negotiation. However, at levels above the enterprise it appears to lack any means of introducing system-wide considerations into the negotiations. It is at best additive, with a check for consistency. Furthermore, with respect to implementation, it relies on the flawed logic of indicative planning, with minimal, if any, policy instrument back-up.

Within the enterprise, the process of negotiation between BOALS, not so much over the vague five-year intentions but over the actual annual production and inter-BOAL transfer plans, appears to work. This is not really surprising, since most transactions in established economies involve a large measure of institutionalized contact and continuity – the arm's length pure market model being very much an exception. Perhaps the most interesting aspect of the process is that it enables income differentials within the enterprise to be negotiated and agreed on. This is the one element in the system as it actually operates that may still be transformatory. It provides the possibility for people to assess their own situation, in the light of that of others, and seek an equitable agreement. Of course, to the extent that the negotiation is in fact between the managerial bureaucracies of the BOALs the transformatory potential is reduced.

Yugoslavia does not have a planned economy. Workers do not run their workplaces. Market forces have undermined the conditions for both. In Yugoslavia a regulated market mechanism cannot be said to have been used as an instrument of planning. Market socialism in that sense has either not been attempted or has failed. It certainly exists nowhere else. Yet market socialism remains the favoured third way for most Western socialists and Eastern reformers. What theoretical models have been offered?

4.4   Models of Market Socialism

Relatively few elaborated models of regulated market socialism have been developed and most of them have been by reformers from the East.[10] In this section I discuss the models of Brus (1972) and Nove (1983), one from the East, one from the West, one of the earliest and one of the most recent, concentrating mainly on the way in which they deal with investment and the reallocation of productive capacity between enterprises, industries and regions. The analysis will be conducted in terms of the definition of market forces adopted in chapter 1, section 5: 'a process whereby change occurs in the pattern of investment, in the structure of productive capacity . . . as a result of atomized decisions, independently taken, motivated solely by the individual decision-makers' perceptions of their individual self-interest, not consciously coordinated by them in advance.' It is to the social and personal consequences of this process that critics of the market mechanism refer when they speak of putting profits before people or of the coercion of impersonal market forces.[11]

Both Brus and Nove assume a democratic political system within which decisions about priorities and strategic direction are made. Both envisage a market and a non-market sector, with the boundary between the two being democratically decided. Brus envisages state-owned enterprises with worker participation; Nove assumes different legal forms of enterprise – state-owned and run, state-owned and worker-managed, cooperative, private (with an upper size limit), and one-person. Both assume that decisions on major investment would be the function of the centre, in order to determine the strategic direction of development of the economy and to deal with major externalities. Both envisage that most current economic decisions would be made by enterprises motivated by profit-maximization. Both insist on the need for regulation of the environment within which enterprises take their profit-maximizing decisions.[12]

Three questions arise. First, how much investment counts as major? Second, when is regulation appropriate, what forms would it take and what problems might arise? Third, how is differential success leading to income inequality and threatening job loss or closure dealt with? It is remarkable how little attention has been given to these questions and to their implications. If most investment is regarded as major and decided on centrally, then the scope for enterprises deciding independently, without reference elsewhere, on how to respond to changes in demand or technology is highly circumscribed. Enterprises will be concerned primarily with making decisions over the use of their existing capacity. However, such decisions, motivated by short-run profitability considerations, although not unimportant, involve at most a minor part of what is normally thought of as the resource allocation and coordination function of market forces or the invisible hand.

Brus appears close to this interpretation: the centre takes direct decisions 'In choosing main investment trends, which is accomplished by allocating the central investment fund among branches and by prescribing increments to capacity and saying specifically how they are to be achieved. Connected with this are direct decisions in the choice of the best method for achieving a desired capacity (methods of investment) without the necessity, however, of taking direct decisions about detailed problems in this field' (Brus 1972, p. 140). This is consistent with Brus's insistence on distinguishing the regulated market, as an instrument of planning, from the Yugoslav system and the models of Selucky and Sik, where the market is assigned a qualitatively different role and market forces are to a large extent the immediate determinants of investment. On this interpretation, my provisional conclusion is that Brus's model is not one of market socialism, in the sense that I am arguing against in this book. My difference with his position, rather, is that his centralized determination of the disposition of investment is too centralized and non-participative.

Nove's position is at first sight less easy to pin down. He distinguishes between investments 'of structural significance, usually involving either the creation of new production units or the very substantial expansion of existing ones, and those which represent an adjustment to changing demand (or to new techniques)' (Nove 1983, pp. 221–2). The former would be the responsibility of the centre, the latter would be decided on by the enterprise. Nove assumes that growth rates would be low and the need for rapid structural transformation limited. He continues:

> A large part of investments would therefore be of the 'adjustment-to-demand' sort. It is plainly essential, within a controlled market environment, that firms . . . have the means to make such adjustments, for otherwise the profits they make would serve no rational purpose . . . The function of this rise in . . . profits in a market economy is to stimulate additional production, which, unless there is already spare capacity, requires investments. If this result does not follow, the mechanism would be failing to work, and the existing enterprises would be making excess profits to no social or economic purpose. (Nove 1983, p. 222)

Unlike Brus's model, then, Nove's really does seem to be a model of market socialism. Decisions about most investment are taken atomistically by enterprises, in pursuit of profit, without reference to anywhere else in the system. This immediately raises the danger of the investment cycles characteristic of capitalist economies, as Nove recognizes. However, he points out that investment cycles also occur in centralized administrative command economies and, with a dismissive reference to fundamentalists, he continues:

> It will indeed be a difficult task for the centre to steer the rest of the economy by remote control, without detailed orders, avoiding mass unemployment and inflation – difficult, but surely not impossible. It will have at its disposal such weapons as credit policy, the setting-up (or the encouragement of setting-up) of production units, control over prices in the centrally managed sectors, the drawing-up and enforcement of ground-rules on profit disposal, income distribution and taxation. (Nove 1983, p. 223)

In Brus's model, regulation is required in two circumstances: when the pattern of prices generated by short-run competition on the basis of existing capacity diverges from that which corresponds to socially determined collective preferences; and when competition is absent due to a concentrated industrial structure. Prices have to be 'independent parameters for the enterprise' and they have to express 'the social scale of preferences' and 'the true ratios of social costs' (Brus 1972, pp. 146, 151, 152). Brus lists the usual instruments – fiscal and monetary policy, prices and incomes policy and controls – but does not discuss how these could achieve the regulated environment he regards as essential. However, he insists that it must be achieved in order to preserve *the principle of central plan primacy* (Brus 1972, p. 143) and it is this insistence that leads Gomulka to argue that Brus's model is not really decentralized at all. In Brus's model, Gomulka argues,

> consumers are not really active players, and producers operate within an environment (of prices and decision criteria, such as profit-maximization) carefully devised by the centre to deprive them of any effective counter-strategy . . . social preferences dominate. The market is merely an instrument for planners thought to be more effective than direct orders, if, as is usual, the centre has very poor knowledge about producers' production possibilities . . . the potential practical difficulties associated with translating those preferences, however imperfectly arrived at, into millions of 'socially optimal' prices are of course well known, and they are acknowledged by Brus to be serious. In any practical application of Brus's model, the planners would probably have to limit the control of prices to priority products and . . . rules similar to those advocated by Brus . . . may well be effective. However, his idea of full wage control seems both impractical and, in a democratic society, difficult to implement. Unfortunately, the potentially serious implications of these practical and political limits to parametric planning remain largely unexplored. (Gomulka 1986, pp. 7–8)

Nove's recognition that in his model remote control regulation would be needed to maintain macroeconomic stability has already been noted. He also recognizes other reasons for regulation or intervention. First, he adopts a distinction between 'benign and undesirable forms of competition' (Nove 1973, p. 203), with a need for rules to deal with the latter and for price control where monopoly power exists. Second, 'In those sectors where externalities are likely to be significant, intervention is essential; it can take the form of regulations (e.g. measures to protect the environment from pollution, ribbon development, ugliness), subsidies (e.g. to public transport, research), the correction of regional imbalances, and so on' (Nove 1983, p. 208). Third, 'the planners would endeavour to monitor decentralized investments, conscious of the need to avoid duplication and the financing of plainly unsound projects initiated locally' (Nove 1983, p. 207). Finally, 'there would be the vital task of setting the ground-rules for the autonomous and free sectors, with reserve powers of intervention when things got out of balance, or socially undesirable developments were seen to occur' (Nove 1983, pp. 207–8).

Of course, Nove can offer us only a 'sketch, a try-out of a few ideas' (Nove 1983, p. 197) in his 33 pages on 'feasible socialism'. Nevertheless, as the culmination of a sustained, effective and justified attack on fundamentalist, dogmatic, utopian socialists, we are asked to take pretty well everything on trust.[13] Macroeconomic stability has so far proved beyond the ability of macroeconomic management to deliver. The problem of developing an effective competition policy in capitalist economies has so far proved insuperable. While the control of pollution in capitalist economies is probably further advanced than in statist countries, that is primarily due to the activities of environmental protection groups operating through the more open democratic political process. Regional inequalities have proved unyielding to market-based regional policy. In an economy such as Nove's, where market forces have sufficient weight in determining resource allocation for the term market socialism, in my sense, to be appropriate, what reason is there to suppose that regulation could produce a socially acceptable performance?

It may be that a worry about this explains Nove's recognition of the need for central monitoring of decentralized investment and for reserve powers. However, as they stand these provisions raise more questions than they answer. What criteria are to be used to assess whether there is a danger of duplication or whether a project is unsound? Where is the information to come from? Suppose the danger or the unsoundness is established, what is to be done about it and by whom? Similar questions arise over the reserve powers to be used when things have got out of balance or undesirable developments are taking place. These are not minor issues. They lie at the heart of the discussion about decentralization, about the independence or otherwise of enterprises, about the extent to which they are allowed to exercise responsibility and take the consequences, for better or worse, of doing so.

Although Brus recognizes that there is no necessary connection between the use of profitability as an indicator of enterprise efficiency and its use as an incentive, as a basis for rewards and penalties, he assumes that the two will in practice be connected: 'when an enterprise obtains good results, it improves its prospects for expansion raising the level of employee incomes. Conversely, when results are unfavourable, and it loses a part of its funds, the employees' incomes decline (possibly to a legal minimum) and in extreme cases, it may even go bankrupt' (Brus 1972, p. 142). What happens then he does not discuss. However, as was noted at the end of the last section, he accepts that the Hungarian experience, particularly in this area, has 'exposed the difficulties of combining central planning with a regulated market mechanism' (Brus 1985, p. 61).

Nove, of course, also recognizes that 'competition implies not only winners but also losers' (Nove 1983, p. 209). He argues that a procedure for winding up failures or changing their management, as well as for facilitating new entry, would be needed. Cooperative and private enterprises would be expected to bear any costs of failure themselves and would in any case be exempt from the agreed wage levels and differentials arrived at in the course of bargaining over an incomes policy. Employees of state-run enterprises, with no worker management, could not be expected to gain or lose from enterprise success or failure and would receive the rates incorporated in the incomes policy. In the case of worker-managed enterprises, Nove discusses various ways of linking 'the worker's material incentives with the longer-term health of the enterprise' (Nove 1983, p. 220). He argues that this requires a specified wage to be counted as part of costs, so that profit can be calculated and incentives established that are related to long-term profitability performance.

What Nove does not discuss is the set of problems that have arisen in the Hungarian economy when individual enterprises claim special treatment. This may be either special pleading or the drawing of attention to legitimate, socially desirable, enterprise-specific reasons for special consideration. There are two alternative approaches. The first is to adopt a parametric policy, on the grounds that it is impossible to have the unbiased information, or the time for adequate consideration, on the basis of which to distinguish between deserving and specious cases – the logic of market socialism. The second approach is to recognize that the fortune or fate of enterprises affects people as subjects, and the communities in which they live, and that they will not be prepared, nor should they be, to accept an adverse outcome unless they have been consciously involved in deciding on it and are convinced of its justice.

Brus's model has the great virtue of insisting on the retention of the essence of planning – social determination at the level of the system as a whole of its overall priorities and direction of development, and *ex ante* coordination of investment. At the same time he recognizes that current decisions over the detailed use of existing productive capacity are in general best made by those involved in the production unit. His argument that prices and profitability are important means of conveying information about relative costs and benefits that is relevant when making decisions is obviously right. The need to link the two levels of decision-making, and the fact that prices and profitability have a part to play in doing this, seem to me incontrovertible.

The problems arise over Brus's view of how the centre discharges its functions and whether the information that can be conveyed by prices and profitability is by itself an adequate basis for making decisions at the enterprise level. The task Brus sets the centre is formidable. It has to decide not only the overall rate of investment, but also its disposition between industries and enterprises, with only minor exceptions. In addition, the centre has to regulate the price structure, so that it faces enterprises with hard budget constraints and they are left with little effective choice about what to decide. Of course, in Brus's model the centre stands for all levels above the enterprise, so some intermediate decentralization would be possible. Even so, the information condition required seems close to that of perfect knowledge.

Brus is insistent on the need for political democratization to enable genuine social involvement in decision-making at the national level, the centre. He rightly considers this to be a necessary condition for the full socialization of the means of production. However, I do not think it would be enough in itself to enable the information problem to be dealt with. For that to be possible, enterprises must be involved in the process of determining the disposition of investment, together with other enterprises and representatives of the centre. In this way, system-wide and local knowledge, overall social interests and local interests, can be brought together and a decision made in the light of all the relevant considerations. Although prices and profitability provide some relevant information, they do not and cannot provide all relevant information. That is why the quest for parametric regulation and hard budget constraints is theoretically misconceived.[14]

While Brus's model is not really one of market socialism, Nove's is. Unfortunately, it provides only the barest outline of such a system and does no more than nod towards some of the problems that would be likely to arise. The crucial question of *ex ante* coordination is not seriously considered. More generally, the possibility of effective regulation is asserted but not discussed. Procedures for rewarding and penalizing differential success are considered but not the underlying reasons for differential performance. Apart, that is, from a celebration of what Nove takes to be realism: 'An imperfect world cannot be rendered perfect because we wish it so, and the assumption of original sin is (alas) a more realistic basis for organizing society than the assumption of a noble savage deformed by the institutions of capitalism and the state' (Nove 1983, p. 229).

It is a sad end to a fascinating, if infuriating, book. Nove gives the impression of having been taunted beyond endurance by fundamentalists, dogmatists and utopians. Desperate to insist on realism, and fully justified in doing so, he has mistaken conservatism for realism. It is realistic to start from where people are. It is not realistic to deny them the possibility of changing. The basic problem with Nove's model, and market socialism generally, is their lack of a transformatory perspective, their lack of vision.

4.5 Conclusion

The Hungarian New Economic Mechanism is clearly not yet a form of market socialism, although it is widely regarded as such. It may possibly be moving in that direction, as discussion develops around the creation of an active capital market through which resources are shifted from one line of production into another. The corollary, acceptance of greater inequality and the discipline of unemployment, as the price to be paid for hardening the budget constraints facing enterprises, is also under discussion. So far, however, such developments remain on the periphery of the Hungarian economy, although bankruptcy laws have recently been introduced. The Yugoslav worker self-managed economy, perhaps, does qualify as a form of market socialism, but as it stands is not a very good advertisement for it. It is not really a planned economy and the sense in which it is self-managed is very limited. Of course, both Hungary and Yugoslavia are statist societies, lacking political and economic democracy, so whatever assessment were made of their economic system, neither could qualify as models for a third way.

The next chapter discusses the nature of the mode of production in the statist societies of Eastern Europe. In so far as they represent an alternative to capitalism as a way of developing the material and cultural preconditions for socialism, they share certain characteristics with it, as well as being fundamentally different from it in other respects. One interpretation of the Gorbachev emphasis on the need for democracy and openness, as preconditions for economic reform, is that it represents the interests of the technostructure, the stratum of able, educated, energetic experts. This is consistent with the stress on accountability, rewarding success, and cutting out corrupt and dead wood. It may also be consistent with the introduction of a greater role for elements of market forces, although there is little real sign of this yet. Thus, a move in the direction of market socialism in the statist countries might, given their exising characteristics, be associated with a stage in their transition towards democratic, self-governing societies.

However, despite this possibility and the growing interest in market socialism in the West (Hodgson 1984; Kellner 1984; Forbes 1986; Nolan and Paine 1986; *The New Statesman* 1987), very few models of market socialism have been elaborated. In those that do exist, with the notable exception of Brus's, planning appears to have effectively disappeared, although it is not easy to be sure, since they lack any coherence at the level of their economic *modus operandi*. My reasons for believing that market socialism, including regulated market socialism, is not likely to be the way forward can be summarized as follows.

First, the concept of market socialism, so far at least, is utopian in the bad sense of the word. It assumes that it would be possible to plan and regulate, primarily by remote control, an economy in which private ownership of the means of production had been abolished. However, there is no theoretical reason or historical evidence based on existing economic systems to support the assumption that an economy based on market forces can be planned and regulated to a degree that would produce a socially acceptable outcome. It could be argued that this is because historical experience so far has been primarily of capitalism, but no argument has been developed to show why the situation would be fundamentally changed by the abolition of private ownership. The Yugoslav experience is, *prima facie*, a counter-example.

This is a serious weakness since, even with the formal abolition of private property, in one form or another Nove's assumption of original sin is virtually always retained in discussions of market socialism. Yet why should state-run or worker-managed enterprises, pursuing their narrow self-interest within a regulated socialist market, aggregate to a system with fundamentally different characteristics from those of capitalist economies, in which privately owned enterprises pursue their narrow self-interest within a regulated capitalist market? It would presumably be a more just system, since there would be no unearned income, but why should it be more stable and more subject to overall social control?

Second, the logic of market socialism is for there to be parametric regulation. The reason for decentralization arising from the information problem is that the centre cannot in principle have access to local knowledge, unless the locals choose to provide it. Since the locals are assumed to be narrowly self-interested, they will always use their local knowledge to bend the centre's regulated environment to their own ends. The relative success of individual enterprises may be due to factors which they can do something about, or to factors beyond their control, but the centre is in general unable to distinguish between the two situations. To avoid regulation bargaining and the regulator game, which the centre cannot win, the best it can do is to engage in parametric regulation.

However, while parametric regulation may be the best that the centre can do, its outcome will inevitably appear arbitrary to some enterprises. People never accept the adverse outcome of impersonal market forces, if they can do anything about it, unless they are convinced that it is just, and sometimes not even then. They are no more likely to accept the outcome of impersonal parametric regulation. For the long run it is a non-starter.[15] Instead of this chimera what is needed is a cooperative system in which information is provided in good faith as a basis for participatory decision-making.

Third, for all that is said about harmonizing social and self-interest through a regulated market environment, with the regulators reflecting democratically agreed national priorities and values, the underlying structure of market socialism is necessarily non-transformatory. No less than the direct instructions of command economies, the coercion of market forces reinforces and reproduces alienation. In both cases, workers in enterprises experience powerlessness and non-involvement in relation to decisions that have major effects on them. In both systems, people are treated instrumentally, as objects to be manipulated by carrot and stick incentive systems that reinforce their narrowly self-interested consciousness, rather than being encouraged to transform themselves in the direction of self-activating subjects.

It is important not to be utopian. I am interested in how to encourage transformation, but I do not start from the assumption that it has already occurred. In this connection, it is necessary to distinguish between different aspects of what usually go together in the market mechanism. Differences in profitability, because they may indicate the need to reallocate resources, are an important part of the information on the basis of which investment decisions should be made. That does not necessarily mean that enterprises should take those decisions atomistically, nor that more profitable enterprises should automatically expand at the expense of less profitable ones. The information is relevant, but it could be used, together with other information, in a cooperative and coordinated way, rather than in the competitive and chaotic way that is the case with the market mechanism. Market forces are also a form of discipline, a means of exerting pressure on enterprises to adapt. To argue that market forces lack transformatory potential because they are impersonal, as I do, is not to deny the need for people to be accountable and in that sense to be under pressure. What is at issue is the most constructive form accountability and pressure could take.

Although consciousness in which narrow self-interest is the dominant motivation may gradually become transformed, so that broader social awareness and social concern predominate, there will always be different perceptions of the relative social importance of different activities. Leaving aside special pleading based on bad faith, people understandably tend to think that what they are doing and know about is particularly important, perhaps more important than what other people are doing. The coercion of market forces merely imposes an outcome on people, without addressing their perceptions that what they have been doing is being undervalued, possibly even reinforcing such perceptions. Negotiated coordination, a process of direct personal interaction, would help people to perceive the need for change, without appearing to undervalue their existing activities, and would therefore contribute to cooperative rather than antagonistic social adjustment.

Thus, market socialism is unlikely to provide a third way because it is utopian, parametric and non-transformatory. However, Nove's challenge must not be forgotten: 'There are horizontal links (market), there are vertical links (hierarchy). What other dimension is there?' (Nove 1983, p. 226). There is no other dimension – but vertical links do not have to be hierarchical, in any authoritarian sense, and horizontal links do not have to be market based, in the sense of being coordinated *ex post* by the invisible hand of market forces. Both can be based on negotiated coordination, the subject matter of Parts III and IV.

PART III

Objectives

5

The Socialization of Production

5.1 Historical Materialism and Statism

The overall objective of this book is to contribute to the historical process of movement towards a self-governing society. The next three chapters are concerned with different aspects of this process: the achievement of social control over production; participatory democracy; and the abolition of the social division of labour. This chapter considers the first of these. The analysis is within the historical materialist tradition which is first briefly summarized. The tradition is then drawn upon to suggest that the social formation and dominant mode of production in the Soviet Union are best characterized as statist. Section 5.2 then argues that in both the capitalist and statist social formations a contradiction has developed between the productive forces and the existing social relations of production, a contradiction that can only be resolved by the socialization of the means of production. Section 5.3 discusses Brus's concept of socialization as a process, focusing on the distinction between the public and the social, and section 5.4 then considers the conditions necessary for bringing the production process under social control. The chapter ends with some conclusions.

The historical materialist approach to understanding the structure and dynamic of a society starts from the relationship between the social forces and the social relations of production. Between them they define the mode of production. The forces of production consist of the means of production, that is, capital equipment and other material inputs, together with the workers who make use of them in the labour process. However, production requires social organization, which is what is meant by the social relations of production (Hobsbawm 1964, p. 17). Social organization encompasses division of labour within the labour process, exchange, and, in class-divided societies, the relationship between different classes. Since different classes are defined in terms of different relationships to the means of production, that is, different forms of ownership and non-ownership, class relations involve property relations. Thus, a mode of production is defined by the material forces of production and the social organization, or social relations of production, associated with them; and in class-divided societies the dominating social relationship is the prevailing property relationship.

There will typically be more than one mode of production present in any actual society and the specific form taken by each mode will be influenced by its relationship with the other modes present, in particular its relationship with the mode of production that is dominant in that society. Thus, within the historical materialist approach a mode of production is an abstract model while an actual society is referred to as a social formation. Capitalism, then, refers to those social formations in which the capitalist mode of production is dominant and statism to those in which the statist mode is dominant.

There is an immense literature discussing the different modes of production and social formations identified by Marx and Engels and by subsequent Marxist historians. There seems to be general agreement on three broad historical periods: primitive communal societies; pre-capitalist class-divided societies; and capitalist societies. Within each of these periods, which have overlapped chronologically, there is an almost infinite variety of particular forms. In the Preface to his *Critique of Political Economy*, Marx referred to the 'Asiatic, ancient, feudal, and modern bourgeois modes of production' (McLellan 1977, p. 390), with the first three coming between primitive communal society and capitalism. However, subsequent historical evidence has cast doubt on the generality of the ancient, or slave, mode. Thus, at a high level of abstraction, it is possible to think of capitalism as having been preceded by varieties of 'Asiatic' or of feudal society.[1]

Class-divided societies differ according to the way in which exploitation takes place:

> The specific economic form, in which unpaid surplus labour is pumped out of the direct producers, determines the relation of rulers and ruled . . . It is always the direct relation of the owners of the conditions of production to the direct producers, which reveals the innermost secret, the hidden foundation of the entire social construction, and with it of the political form of the relations between sovereignty and dependence, in short, of the corresponding form of the state. (Marx 1909, p. 919)

On the one hand, then, societies are defined according to the dominant relations of production through which exploitation occurs; on the other hand, there is also a correspondence between those relations of production and the character of the other central aspects of the society.

There has been endless discussion of whether Marx intended this correspondence to be the result of causal determination, as is suggested by the famous statement in the Preface: 'The sum total of these relations of production constitutes the economic structure of society, the real foundation, on which rises a legal and political superstructure and to which correspond definite forms of social consciousness. . . . With the change of the economic foundations the entire immense superstructure is more or less rapidly transformed' (McLellan 1977, p. 389). At issue is whether the metaphor of base and superstructure is misleading and, associated with that, whether Marx's approach amounts to technological or economic determinism.[2]

Within the historical materialist framework, the dynamic for societal change comes from the development of a contradiction, a lack of fit, between the forces and the relations of production. As Marx puts it in the Preface: 'At a certain stage of their development, the material productive forces of society come in conflict with the existing relations of production, or – what is but a legal expression for the same thing – with the property relations within which they have been at work hitherto. From forms of development of the productive forces these relations turn into their fetters. Then begins an epoch of social revolution' (McLellan 1977, p. 389). The historically progressive role of capitalism, despite its inhumanity, is to create the preconditions for classless communist society. By contrast with the relatively conservative character of pre-capitalist social formations, capitalism is revolutionary.

The preconditions for communism that capitalism creates are twofold. On the one hand, by developing the productive forces it increases labour productivity and so removes the objective need for most people to spend most of their time working merely in order to produce their subsistence. On the other hand, by socializing the labour process it creates the agents of revolutionary change, the working class. Eventually, 'The centralization of the means of production and the socialization of labour reach a point at which they become incompatible with their capitalist integument. This integument is burst asunder. The knell of capitalist private property sounds. The expropriators are expropriated' (Marx 1976, p. 929).

Marx envisaged that capitalism would be replaced by communism, with a first phase in which it remained 'stamped with the birth-marks of the old society from whose womb it has emerged' and then

a more advanced phase of communist society, when the enslaving subjugation of individuals to the division of labour, and thereby the antithesis between intellectual and physical labour have disappeared; when labour is no longer just a means of keeping alive but has itself become a vital need; when the all-round development of individuals has also increased their productive powers and all the springs of cooperative wealth flow more abundantly – only then can society wholly cross the narrow horizon of bourgeois right and inscribe on its banner: From each according to his [sic] abilities, to each according to his needs! (Marx 1974, pp. 346, 347)

Some time after Marx wrote this the first phase came to be called socialism, with the term communism being reserved for the more advanced phase, to be achieved only after a more or less lengthy transitional period.

Within this historical materialist framework, where do the Soviet Union, the other countries of Eastern Europe, China and Cuba come in? In the 1970s the system in the Soviet Union began to be referred to officially as developed, mature or real socialism, although this terminology appears to have been dropped since the advent of Gorbachev. The term actually or really existing socialism was coined by the authorities in the German Democratic Republic to defend their system from what they regarded as utopian Marxist criticism. It was taken over by Bahro and used to distinguish the existing system in the GDR from what he meant by socialism (Bahro 1978, p. 22). Nove, who is highly critical of the Soviet system, has subsequently adopted Bahro's term because of its transformation of official usage into a critical concept. However, he believes that 'Marxian socialism and "really existing socialism" diverge largely, but certainly not exclusively, because of the utopian-romantic aspects of Marx's vision' (Nove 1986, p. 4).

It is accepted by virtually everybody that the social formation of really existing socialism, or what I call the statist countries, is different from any envisaged by Marx. In my view, attempts to force it into the space defined by a historical movement from capitalism to communism are unconvincing. This applies to the Trotskyist or Maoist concepts of a degenerate workers' state, a transitional society and state capitalism. It also applies to official Soviet, orthodox communist and some independent analyses, which accept, explicitly or implicitly, that existing socialism differs from what was envisaged by Marx but argue that it is nevertheless socialism.

I believe, along with Bahro and Horvat, that actually existing socialism, or statism, is not socialism at all, but rather a social formation *sui generis*, unforeseen by Marx, and an alternative to capitalism as a means of creating the preconditions for socialism/communism. Although I have previously used the term actually existing socialism myself to refer to this new social formation (Devine 1981, p. 114), I now prefer the term statism. In my view retention of the word socialism gives too much away, above all by allowing the possibility of socialism without democracy.

Horvat states the argument clearly: 'etatism is not a successor of capitalism, not a more advanced social system. It is an alternative mode of social organization that has to achieve essentially the same task: the development of productive forces and socialist consciousness up to the point where socialism becomes possible' (Horvat 1982, p. 43). However, it is Bahro who has developed the argument most fully, even though he uses the term actually existing socialism and considers the countries concerned to be 'proto-socialist' (Bahro 1977, p. 22).

Bahro's thesis is that

> Actually existing socialism is the arrangement under which countries with a pre-capitalist formation work independently to produce the preconditions of socialism, and it is the pressure of the industrial productive forces created by capitalism that gives this process its decisive impulse . . . Its place in history is determined by the way that, just like capitalism, it brings the productive forces to the threshold of socialist restructuring, but in a completely different manner so far as the social formation is concerned. (Bahro 1977, pp. 9–10)

He points to continuities between the new, previously unknown, actually existing socialist social formation and the earlier Asiatic social formation, whose legacy, he argues, still dominated pre-revolutionary Russia. However, the Asiatic mode of production is characterized by relative stagnation, with no internal dynamic moving it in the direction of transition to a new, industrializing mode of production. For that, Bahro argues, the external impact of capitalism, in the form of imperialism, was necessary.[3]

Bahro's interpretation of the place of the new, non-capitalist social formation in the broad schema of historical evolution is represented in figure 5.1 (derived from Bahro 1978, Part One and pp. 125–8). Whereas feudal social formations, based on the feudal mode of production, contain a dynamic leading to the transition to capitalism (Dobb 1946; Hilton et al. 1976), Asiatic social formations, based on the Asiatic mode, do not. Accordingly, Bahro argues, Asiatic society

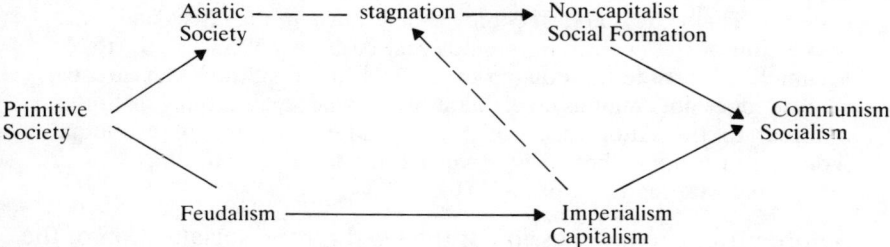

Figure 5.1 Bahro's alternative roads to socialism/communism

where it existed continued in relative stagnation until the disruptive impact of imperialism was felt. The Russian revolution, whatever the beliefs of the Bolsheviks, was not socialist but anti-imperialist and ushered in not socialism but a new non-capitalist social formation.

Although not necessarily agreeing with Bahro's account of its origins, there is widespread agreement, outside the orthodox communist, Maoist and Trotskyist traditions, that the Soviet Union and the other statist countries constitute a new social formation, with a new dominant mode of production, in its own right (Nove 1986, ch. 4).[4] What, then, are the defining characteristics of this new mode of production? These have already emerged, in an unsystematic way, in the discussion in Parts I and II. The overriding characteristic is the dominance of the political, in the form of the party/state and ultimately the party. Bahro identifies the politbureaucracy in particular, and the apparatus or bureaucracy in general, as the leading or ruling group (Bahro 1978, ch. 9). Nove considers those people on the *nomenklatura*, covering the leading positions in all officially recognized activities, to constitute the ruling group (Nove 1986, pp. 40–1).

What is the relationship between the political and the economic in the statist mode of production? According to Bahro,

> State property, as the domain of this politbureaucratic and administrative power of disposal, represents a relation of production *sui generis*. 'For the good of the people' . . . the oligarchy at the top of the pyramid decides the goals for which the surplus product should be used, and subjects the *entire* reproduction process of economic, social and cultural life to its regulation. As in the case of all earlier systems of domination, the steady reproduction of its own monopoly, and when possible its expanded reproduction, goes into the overall calculation of social development and has to be paid for by the masses. (Bahro 1978, p. 241)

Feher, Heller and Markus develop the point slightly further:

> the maximization of the volume of the material means (as use values) under the global disposition of the apparatus of power as a whole constitutes the goal-function governing the economic activities of the state . . . That is, in this society only expenditures of resources under the disposition of the apparatus count as real costs . . . What is effectively accumulated outside the domain over which the apparatus can directly dispose, does not count as an element of national wealth, but constitutes a threat to the latter, because it can confer a degree of economic independence upon those who own it formally or practically. (Feher, Heller and Markus 1983, pp. 65–7)

Before turning to a discussion of the need for the socialization of the means of production in both capitalist and statist societies, an implication of the argument that the political is dominant in the statist mode of production should be noted. If historical materialism is interpreted in terms of the economic base as the foundation for the political superstructure, then the social relations of production should be independent of and should determine the form of the state. However, in the statist mode of production the state, not a private group or class, owns and controls the means of production. Members of the party/state apparatus control the means of production by virtue of their position in the apparatus. They do not hold their positions in the apparatus because they own the means of production. Thus, it is the character of the political system that determines the character of the social relations of production, not the other way round.[5]

There is one further stage in the argument, which turns out to be crucial for the discussion, in chapter 7, of long-run transformatory possibilities. It can be approached from consideration of the two sides of the *nomenklatura*. All leading positions in society are on the *nomenklatura*; all those who fill these positions are also on the *nomenklatura*. How do people come to fill leading positions and therefore to be included on the *nomenklatura*? Political reliability is a key factor and in the early years of the Soviet Union was often paramount. Increasingly, however, education and expertise have become the dominant factors, with party membership frequently being sought for careerist reasons as a necessary condition for progress up the hierarchy of the bureaucratic apparatus.

Membership of the ruling group increasingly depends on position in the division of labour hierarchy: 'the general relation of production that gives actually existing socialism its character as a social formation . . . is the organization of the entire society on the basis of the traditional division of labour' (Bahro 1977, p. 12). Those who run the society, in the sense that they perform a functional role of organizing and directing activities, also run it in the sense of running, of directing, the subaltern 'masses'. Thus, a functional, or technical, vertical division of labour is fused with a social, or traditional, vertical division of labour, with those at the top end constituting the ruling group in society.

5.2 The Socialization of Production

The argument of the previous section was that capitalism and statism can be regarded as historical alternatives for the creation of the preconditions for socialism. Once these preconditions have been created, once the development of the productive forces has reached a certain stage, the traditional Marxist position is that socialism becomes necessary for their further development. The historical materialist approach focuses on the relationship between the characteristics of the production process and the social organization within which that process takes place. To say that socialism has become necessary for the further development of the productive forces is to say that a lack of fit has developed between actual or potential methods of production and the existing structure of social relationships. This lack of fit, or contradiction, means that the social organization is preventing the most effective use possible of existing productive capacity and is inhibiting innovation.

The classical Marxist argument is that capitalist social organization initially develops the forces of production but then begins to hold back their further development. Exactly the same argument applies to the social organization characteristic of the mode of production in the Soviet Union and the other statist countries. Having been the means for rapid primitive accumulation and forced industrialization during the Stalin period, the administrative command planning system and absence of political and economic democracy have become fetters, as discussed in chapter 3.[6] One of the most interesting aspects of the Gorbachev era has been recognition of the fact that the existing social organization in the Soviet Union, in particular the lack of openness and democracy, has for some time been preventing the efficient functioning of the Soviet economy and holding back its further development.

What is it about the productive forces today that makes a change of social organization necessary? In general terms, the argument is that methods of production and the production process as a whole are becoming ever more social in character, by contrast with their earlier, more individual, or fragmented, character. The production process is becoming more complex, both in its separate parts and as a whole. Interdependence is increasing within separate production units, between production units, and between the economy and the cultural, social and political spheres. High-quality motivation, knowledge, cooperation and creativity are becoming ever more essential for the effective operation and development of society's productive capacity and potential.

This increasing socialization of production underlies the principal changes in economic organization evident in modern capitalism: the ever-increasing size of the dominant corporations, internalizing the planning of production; new forms of corporate organization, notably the multidivisional firm; the internationalization of production through the transnational corporation; the development of flexible speciali-zation – a new method of organizing production which places a premium on coordination; a new impetus, largely under the impact of the revolution in information technology, to the penumbra of small firms, constantly changing in composition, which provides flexibility in the interstices of the dominant structure of large corporations.

Increasing socialization of production is also a major reason for the extensive role of the state in the economy in modern capitalism, covering the forms of intervention discussed in chapter 2 and also the provision of infrastructure, education and training, and other essential inputs (Gough 1979, chs 3–4).

However, even with these adaptations, capitalist property relations remain an obstacle to the effective use and development of the productive forces. They preclude the deployment of society's productive capacity, of the means of production and labour, as an integrated whole. Capitalist ownership necessarily involves the division of the means of production into separately owned capitals, with decisions over their use being taken independently of one another. These independently taken, atomistic, decisions can only be coordinated *ex post*, through the market mechanism, whereas, when production has become highly socialized, interdependent decisions need to be taken together, to be planned and coordinated *ex ante*. Socialists have traditionally argued for the common, or social, ownership of the means of production on the grounds that control, the power to decide on the use to be made of productive capacity, normally goes with ownership.

It is important to note that common, or social, ownership has traditionally been counterposed to private not capitalist ownership. Capitalist ownership is, of course, private, in the sense that control over the use of the means of production is fragmented and decision-making is atomized. However, an economy consisting of self-employed producers, worker cooperatives or labour-managed enterprises, whose independent decisions were coordinated by an unregulated market mechanism, would also be based on private, or sectional, ownership in this sense. The significance of private, or sectional, as opposed to common, or social, ownership is that the former precludes the possibility of consciously taking into account the interdependent, social character of production through planning and *ex ante* coordination. Some versions of market socialism are based on the assumption that this can be done through regulated market coordination. My reasons for doubting this have been discussed in chapter 4.

The specific significance of capitalist ownership is not that it is private ownership, although it is, but that capitalist property relations are relations between owners of the means of production and non-owners. They involve exploitation, unearned income, oppression and subalternity. Social ownership, as well as making possible the planned use of society's productive resources, would remove the conditions for the private appropriation of the surplus product, the product over and above that consumed by the direct producers, in the form of unearned income. At the same time, by ending competitive capitalist exploitation, it would remove the necessity for coercion in the production process. Social ownership is a necessary condition for the ending of alienated wage labour and the start of a qualitatively new historical era in which the instrumental manipulation of people treated as passive objects is gradually replaced by the self-transformatory possibilities of participation, leading towards a community of self-activating, self-governing subjects.

The socialization of production consists of increasing complexity and interdependence in the production and innovation processes of society, individually and as a whole, with an enhanced role for information, conscious coordination, flexible adaptation, cooperation and creativity. Increasingly, human knowledge, expertise and motivation are becoming central productive forces or factors of production. They will not be forthcoming from alienated wage labour, which is treated instrumentally and treats work in the same way. Social organization that depends on and reproduces subaltern consciousness and a narrowly self-interested motivation is therefore increasingly dysfunctional. The further development of the productive forces is inhibited not just by the private character of capitalist ownership but also by its specifically capitalist character.

The conclusion of the discussion so far is that, at a certain stage in the process of the increasing socialization of production, pressures develop for a change in social organization in the direction of the socialization of the means of production. This has two aspects. In relation to society as a whole, it involves collective decision-making about the overall disposition of productive resources, taking into account major interdependencies, which requires system-wide planning. In relation to individual production units, it involves decisions by those affected about what to produce in detail, where and how. Both planning and democratization are necessary: planning corresponds to the aspect of the socialization of production involving coordination and interdependence; democratic decision-making by those affected, at the level of society and locally, corresponds to the aspect of socialization involving information and motivation. The socialization of production has reached the stage at which the effective use of society's productive potential requires democratic planning.

Capitalist social organization does not correspond with the prevailing level of socialization of production because it is based on private ownership of the means of production and alienated wage labour. Nationalization, in capitalist economies, although sometimes discussed in terms of the traditional socialist objective of common ownership of the commanding heights of the economy, has normally come about for particular, partial reasons. It has not been extensive enough to enable the planned deployment of productive capacity in accordance with national priorities and objectives, nor has that ever been seen as its purpose in capitalist countries. Furthermore, labour relations within state-owned industries or enterprises have not, in general, been qualitatively different from those in privately-owned enterprises, apart from an unquestioned recognition of trade unions.

Nevertheless, state ownership in capitalist economies, because of its public character, is a different social relation of production from capitalist ownership. State ownership enables socially desirable but unprofitable activities to be undertaken, since loss-making activities are more readily subsidized from public funds when publicly-owned. Decisions of publicly-owned enterprises are potentially subject to more public and political scrutiny than are those of privately-owned enterprises and, in that sense, public enterprise is potentially more socially accountable. Since the state is a political institution, state ownership inevitably moves the means of production involved into the public domain, the sphere of politics. The extent to which this results in public enterprise being run on the basis of different principles from private enterprise depends on the balance of political and ideological forces in the society.

State ownership is the predominant form of ownership in the statist countries, with the frequent exception of the agricultural sector. The means of production are owned and controlled by the state, formally on behalf of the working class, or the people, or society as a whole. They are not legally owned by private individuals or groups and in this sense the relations of production are not capitalist property relations, since the latter involve private ownership. Of course, it is important to distinguish between legal ownership and *de facto* ownership, in the sense of control, as in the controversy over the managerial revolution in the context of the capitalist corporation. However, no one has seriously suggested that individuals or groups within the statist apparatus are able to dispose of the means of production whose current use they manage, nor that the surplus created by that use is predominantly at their private disposal. On the contrary, the absence of a capital market and the tenuous relationship between managerial efficiency and managerial income have been widely identified as central reasons for the unsatisfactory performance of the statist economies, as discussed in chapter 3.

Of course, the statist mode of production does distort the use of resources in favour of the apparatus, with individuals and groups within the apparatus frequently able to divert part of the surplus to their own use. In these respects, the position of the apparatus is to some extent comparable to that of managers in the capitalist corporation. However, statist enterprises are integrated into an administrative structure, the administrative command system, which constrains them in qualitatively different ways from the constraints exercised on capitalist corporations by market forces. State ownership is public ownership, with the crucial difference between public and private ownership being that the former enables the means of production to be deployed as a whole, in a consciously coordinated way, while the latter does not.

State ownership of the means of production in the Soviet Union was the legal basis for command planning and the rapid industrialization it was used to bring about. What that legal basis meant in fact was the ability of the party/state to mobilize and deploy the resources of the entire society to achieve its priorities. It had the power of decision, which it could more or less enforce, and so it was able to plan and coordinate *ex ante* the use of the available means of production and the labour force. The fact that the planning and implementation were rough and ready, with much arbitrariness and waste, does not mean that overall control was not exercised at the level of the system as a whole. State property, public ownership, was the relation of production which made that possible.

However, decisions about the use to be made of the means of production and the labour force were certainly not taken by those affected. The party decided on behalf of the masses and the party leadership decided on behalf of the party. This was so in relation to society-wide decisions and also in relation to decisions at the level of individual enterprises and workplaces. The principle of one person management, the absence of independent trade unions, the reality of ultimate control by the party leadership at each level, meant that workers had virtually no say in the decisions affecting them. As argued in chapter 3, their status was little different from that of wage labour in capitalist countries. It was better in that their ideologically privileged status as workers more or less guaranteed employment; it was worse in that they were atomized, devoid of trade union protection and liable to end up in a labour camp. Alienated labour was motivated by fear, material incentives, social and political pressure, residual revolutionary commitment, and, especially during the Second World War, nationalistic and patriotic sentiment.

State ownership, then, is public ownership, but not necessarily social ownership. If extensive enough, it enables integrated decisions about the overall use of the means of production to be made, but not necessarily by society as a whole. For it to become social ownership, decisions about both overall use and more detailed use of the means of production have to be made socially – political and economic democracy are necessary. In neither of the pre-socialist modes of production can the means of production be said to be socialized. In the capitalist countries, generalized public ownership, planning and economic democracy remain to be achieved, but there is political democracy.[7] In the statist countries, public ownership and planning have established the preconditions for the socialization of the means of production, but political and economic democracy are absent.

5.3 Socialization as a Process

Brus has developed the most convincing analysis to date of what is involved in the socialization of the means of production. He argues that social ownership must fulfil two criteria: '(1) the means of production must be employed in the interests of society, and (2) society must have effective disposition over the means of production it owns' (Brus 1975, p. 27). The two are interconnected, indeed inseparable, since the interests of society can only be defined by society:

> a definition of what is and is not in the social interest is impossible . . . without putting into operation some mechanism for revealing contradictions and reaching solutions which in the nature of things will contain an element of compromise; it is thus impossible without ensuring for society an active role in the process of taking economic decisions . . . of setting the aims of plans and the basic methods for their implementation. (Brus 1975, p. 30)

The basic criterion, therefore, is democracy, the extent to which control is exercised by society, which is discussed in chapter 6.

It follows that a legal change from capitalist to state ownership cannot be assessed unambiguously from the standpoint of socialization. As already noted in chapter 1, one approach is to say that it all depends on the character of the state. If it is a capitalist state then state ownership is public not social ownership; if it is a socialist state then state ownership is the form taken by social ownership. However, this merely pushes the analysis back one stage to an evaluation of the character of the state, which would itself have to be made largely in terms of the extent to which social control over the state and state property had been achieved. A further problem with this approach is its suggestion that socialization is an all or nothing phenomenon.

Brus's approach, conceiving of socialization as a process, is more fruitful:

> the socialisation of the means of production is a process and not a once-for-all act. For it is clear that both our criteria for the social character of ownership cannot be completely realized in one fell swoop. The nationalisation of the means of production in the course of a revolution is undoubtedly the critical step on the path to overcoming alienation but it is, none the less, only the first, and not the last, step in a long and complicated process in which the fundamental role is played by

the increasingly comprehensive influence of society on the way in which the nationalised means of production are deployed. (Brus 1973, p. 90)

Although not always put as clearly as by Brus, this approach has informed most Marxist attempts to make sense of the statist social formation, leaving aside the Stalinist and orthodox communist dogma that the Soviet state is unambiguously socialist. Bettelheim argues that the significance of state property depends on the real relations, the balance of power and control, between the state apparatus and the masses. As long as this remains effectively contested, the society is transitional. In the Soviet Union, he argues, this is no longer the case, the apparatus has triumphed and capitalism has been restored (Bettelheim 1976a; 1976b, pp. 98–9).

Hegedus adopts a similar analytic position on state property but draws a different empirical conclusion:

> Its total societal character can only be realised to the extent that the state administration, which exercises rights of property, is under actual and effective social control . . . state ownership in the socialist countries in its present form cannot be considered as bureaucratic state ownership without any further analysis, because the possibility exists for society, through various mechanisms, to exercise a certain control over the administrative institutions of possession, even under the present circumstances . . . the core of the problem of property in the European socialist countries is, with the exception of Yugoslavia, the replacement of possession by the state administration with ownership-exercise by society as a whole. (Hegedus 1976, p. 111)

Conceptualizing the socialization of the means of production, the achievement of social ownership, as a process has the consequence of focusing attention on analysis of what furthers and what retards that process. Such analysis is helped by a more detailed look at the concept of ownership. Ownership consists of a set of property rights, the exercise of which relates to different aspects of the property involved, specifically here the means of production. It is usual to distinguish between the rights of custody (decisions over current use), usufruct (income arising from current use), alienation (transfer of the set of ownership rights to another), and destruction. These rights may be specified in the form of a legal title to ownership or they may be based on accepted practice. They may be exercised by the nominal owners or by their agents. The complete set of rights may be owned as a whole or each distinct right may be separately owned. Each distinct right may be individually owned or jointly owned with its exercise shared and in either case its exercise may be constrained by some external, usually political, authority (Holesovsky 1977, pp. 41–2).

Most discussion of the process of the socialization of the means of production has been concerned with the relationship between state, or public, and social ownership. However, once the socialization of ownership is conceived of as a process, the process can be identified as already at work within capitalism, as Marx recognized: 'The capitalist stock companies as well as the co-operative factories may be considered as forms of transition from the capitalist mode of production to the associated one' (Marx 1909, p. 521). The joint stock company with limited liability enables capital to be deployed on a qualitatively larger scale than is possible on the basis of purely individual private ownership. Within the capitalist corporation operating decisions are the legal responsibility of the Board of Directors, whereas choice of Board members, decisions over the distribution of profit, and transfer of ownership, are legally vested in the voting shareholders. Different types of share carry with them different combinations of voting rights and rights to company income. Income rights may also be shared with employees through profit-sharing schemes.

Within capitalist societies private decisions over the current use of the means of production are constrained by the legal framework regulating health and safety at work, conditions of employment, the safety and sometimes quality of the product, pollution and other matters of social interest. Company behaviour is constrained by competition policy. The state influences the use made of the privately owned means of production by industrial policy and attempts at planning. Income arising from the use of means of production is subject to taxation. Procedures for the sale and purchase of companies are regulated. In these ways the objective pressures for the socialization of the means of production, for social control over their use, are reflected in capitalist society. However, private ownership remains an insuperable obstacle to the employment of the means of production as a whole in the interests of society, by society.

That is why Brus regards the nationalization of the means of production as the crucial, although only the first, step towards their socialization. He considers two arguments against the view that the socialization of the means of production is a process, both of which he rightly rejects (Brus 1973, pp, 92–4). The first of these, that state ownership already constitutes social ownership, has been discussed in the previous section. The second, that state ownership has no features in common with social ownership, has also been touched on, but the reasons why it is wrong are so important that they deserve further consideration.[8] The issues can be approached via analysis of the Yugoslav experience and the self-management model.

Self-management at the level of the enterprise is a necessary condition for those affected by the decisions of a given enterprise to be involved in taking those decisions. It is a necessary part of the exercise of real social control over the means of production and the overcoming of alienation. However, it can only ever be a part of the exercise of social control. For all round social control, enterprise self-management has to be exercised within an overall framework resulting from socially taken decisions at the level of the system, of society, as a whole. The broad disposition of the means of production has to be determined centrally, by society as a whole, and then given effect through planning. As argued in chapter 4, the predominant role of market forces in the Yugoslav economy, based on the self-management model, precludes effective system-wide planning. The result is that although legally the means of production in Yugoslavia are socially owned they are actually to a significant extent owned sectionally, by those who run them, at least with respect to the property rights covering decisions over current use and to a lesser extent income distribution.

Brus, as usual, puts the point very clearly: 'the self-management model comes into collision with the objective tendency towards growth of the role of central planning, or any active planning based on the supremacy of macrocriteria and long-term economic calculation extending far beyond market criteria and signals. It could be said that the self-management model – conceived as a consistent whole – is an attempt at solving the problem of socialization of the means of production *not by giving public ownership certain specific features which make it social ownership . . . but by limiting the public character of ownership*' (Brus 1975, p. 88; my emphasis). In effect, the direction of democratizing decision-making and thereby moving from public to social ownership has been rejected. Instead, market forces have been given the role of coordinating the decisions of self-managed enterprises and the public character of ownership has been undermined in the direction of sectional private ownership.

This is an important conclusion. The dangers of arbitrariness, irrationality and oppression inherent in a state not subject to social control are only too real. However, in both East and West, pessimism about the prospects for democratization gave rise in the 1970s and 1980s to a tendency towards escapism, a quest for ever more decentralization, in the futile hope of thus avoiding having to come to terms with how to bring the state under social control and eventually abolish its role as a force separate from, and above, society. There will always be decisions that need to be taken centrally, at the level of society as a whole, even when we have succeeded in decentralizing everything that can be decentralized to the most local level possible. Furthermore, at each level of decentralized decision-making the question of how to move towards real social control of decision-making at that level remains, not least within the Yugoslav self-managed enterprise.

Thus, as Brus concludes, 'it is not "depoliticisation of the economy" but "democratisation of politics" that is the correct direction for the process of socialization of nationalized means of production' (Brus 1975, p. 92). Brus places his main emphasis on political democracy at the level of national politics, stressing the importance of party political pluralism and parliamentary procedures, as is understandable given his focus on the experience of the statist countries. Because of his insistence that the socialization of the means of production requires overall planning, with as much enterprise level decision-making as possible within the framework set by it, political democracy is for him a necessary condition for economic democracy.

On this, I fully agree with Brus and disagree with Bahro and Horvat who, while totally committed to the socialization of the means of production, nevertheless both argue against party political pluralism (Bahro 1977, p. 22; 1978, pp. 350–1; Horvat 1982, pp. 316–22). However, I also get the impression that Brus, although he rarely omits to mention the importance of enterprise level democratization, none the less somehow tends to consider it less important than the democratization of national level decision-making. If true, this may reflect the 'perfectly indirectly centralized' aspect of his model (Ellman, quoted in Gomulka 1986, p. 7), discussed in chapter 4, which leaves enterprises with little effective discretion.

The socialization of the means of production, then, is a process, with state, or public, ownership constituting a crucial stage and subsequent progress in the direction of fully social ownership consisting of political and economic democratization. Such democratization needs to occur at the national, enterprise and intermediate levels. However, before considering this process further in the next section, the practical significance of conceiving of socialization as a process should be noted. It has important implications for political practice and intervention. Given a clear vision of what the objectives of the socialization process are, the forms of political practice and social intervention best calculated to advance that process at each stage can be debated. They are, of course, likely to differ according to the country in question and the stage of its political, economic and social evolution. The further along the process a society is, the greater will be the possibilities for adopting consciously transformatory policies.

5.4 Popular Control

Social ownership, or socialization, of the means of production is necessary to bring the social relations of production into correspondence with the increasingly social character of the social forces of production in modern society. The quality of motivation and information required in individual production processes and in the production process as a whole is only likely to be fully forthcoming when alienated labour is superseded by the self-determining activity of self-governing subjects. That is one side of the argument for the socialization of the means of production, but not the most important side. Its significance is that, if correct, it provides grounds for thinking that there is a historical momentum pushing in the direction of socialization, which is not to say, of course, that there is anything automatic or predetermined about the outcome. The obstacles may be too great, human society may destroy itself, the acts of imagination and will required may prove too much for us. Barbarism is always a possible alternative to socialism.

The most important side of the argument for the socialization of the means of production, however, is that it is necessary if people are to be in control of their lives. That is, if we are to be able, first, to play a real part in deciding on the overall structure and character of the world and the society in which we live, and, second, to participate with the other people involved in running the different communities and resources within which we live and which shape our daily lives. In a sense, this is tautological, since socialization, as I have used the term, is defined as the effective exercise of popular control. That is not accidental. The socialization of production, the achievement of popular control by self-activating, self-governing subjects, has been the principal, indeed at the most general level the only, objective of socialists and communists through the ages. It remains my objective and is what the model of democratic planning through negotiated coordination set out in Part IV is designed to further.

I have used the term popular control, in addition to social control and political and economic democracy, in an attempt to convey the overriding importance of the control being real, or substantive, rather than formal, and being generalized to all those affected, rather than restricted to the 'politically active'. The implications of this requirement are twofold, one familiar and relatively uncontroversial, the other less familiar, rarely discussed seriously these days and not widely accepted. The first implication is that the political and economic democratization involved in the process of socialization of the means of production must really be substantive and general not just formal and limited. The second implication is that the social division of labour, the division of people into leaders and led, those who are run and those who run them, those with hegemonic consciousness and those with subaltern consciousness, must be overcome.

What is required for substantive generalized political and economic democracy? A democratic political process, in the familiar liberal sense of a parliamentary-type system, with party political pluralism and regular elections, is, I believe, a necessary condition. The dismissal of this immensely important historical achievement on the grounds that it constitutes mere 'bourgeois' democracy is, at best, an unthought through legacy from an earlier historical period or, at worst, active dogmatic fundamentalism. Its counterpart, in the statist countries, has been 'the fetishisation of the state as the emanation of the will and interests of the working masses' (Brus 1975, p. 49) and, among fundamentalists in the West, retention of the concept of soviet type 'congresses of . . . workers' and popular councils' as the locus of the most general level of decision-making (Mandel 1986, p. 27).

Political democracy is, of course, absent in the statist countries. However, Western political democracy as it stands is itself far from fulfilling the requirements of substantive generalized democracy, although the importance of being able to change governments through elections at regular intervals cannot be overestimated. The form that representative democracy takes in the existing parliamentary democracies is premised on either a paternalistic or a policing view of the role of the state, or more accurately on a combination of both. The electorate elects a government which, on the one hand, does things for people and, on the other, holds the ring while they compete for individual or group success – or failure. The one thing governments in capitalist countries typically do not do is to play a facilitating role enabling people to do things for themselves.

As the economic boom and social consensus that followed the Second World War came to an end, so the welfare state came under pressure and the underlying cynicism about politics and politicians endemic in capitalist societies came to the surface. Low and in some countries falling participation rates in elections, together with falling membership of political parties, reflect a general sense of impotence in face of the felt divisions between 'us' and 'them', in the political as much as in the personal, social and economic spheres. Overall, the present form of parliamentary democracy in the West reinforces the combination of passivity and self-seeking, the subaltern consciousness, that people develop in the process of growing up, have confirmed in the workplace and/or experience as passive clients of the welfare or workfare state.

At the same time, there is a powerful tendency in the capitalist countries towards further centralization of political power. Three influences contribute to this tendency: the weight and dynamic of military and national security considerations; the need for political authority to parallel, however imperfectly, the growing socialization of the forces of production; and the diverse, uneven, but ever-renewed growth of popular movements and social practices which threaten to undermine the cohesion and legitimacy of the existing social order. This last set of pressures encompasses traditional institutions like trade unions, separatist national or regional movements, developing black consciousness, feminism, green politics, and movements against civil and military nuclear power.

The tendency for political power to become more centralized has taken the form of a transfer of authority from the local to the national, and to some extent the international, level and a growing autonomy of government in relation to representative assembly and of state apparatus in relation to government. Furthermore, the ideological hegemony and legitimation of the established order are assisted, although not fundamentally created, by the lack of social control over the media and a more general absence of openness of information. Thus, Western parliamentary democracy, although a necessary condition for political democracy, is very far from substantive generalized political democracy. At the moment its contribution to the socialization of the means of production is limited. It needs to be transformed in major respects before it can fulfil the role of enabling real social control over political decisions.

The process of achieving economic democracy in the capitalist countries is even less advanced and in the statist countries it has hardly started. As has already been argued, economic democracy has two aspects. It requires social control over the broad disposition of the means of production at the level of the society as a whole and also over their detailed use at the local or sub-system level. Fully developed political democracy is necessary to determine overall priorities and system wide planning is necessary to give them effect. Thus, two necessary conditions for economic democracy are political democracy and economic planning. A third necessary condition is the participation of workers in decision-making at the level of the workplace and the enterprise.

Worker involvement at these levels has taken many forms, in practice and in theoretical models. It has ranged from collective bargaining, through co-determination and other forms of industrial democracy, to workers' councils, worker self-management and producer cooperatives. For economic democracy to be real, the detailed use of socially-owned means of production at the local, or sub-system, level must be controlled by those most directly affected by their use at that level. This clearly includes those who work with the means of production in individual workplaces and enterprises. However, other categories of people also have an interest, including users of what is produced, the community in which the workplace is located, the society as a whole in the case of large scale enterprises, groupings concerned with equal opportunities and environmental effects, and possibly others. A way has to be found to enable all with an interest in how particular means of production are used to be involved in the decision.

Rather confusingly, the term social ownership has recently come to be used in two senses. The first is the sense in which I have used it, referring to ownership and control by society as a whole, as a basis for planning at the level of society as a whole, by contrast with fragmented private ownership and atomized decision-making. The second refers to any form of collective, non-exploitative ownership, by contrast with capitalist or individual ownership. In this second sense, state, local authority, worker self-managed and cooperative ownership are all by definition forms of social ownership. This is an attractive usage. It emphasizes the fact that different forms of production unit are likely to be needed for different types of productive activity and to reflect differences in people's preferences. However, there is also a problem with the use of the term social ownership in this second sense.

Strictly speaking, this second usage is referring to non-capitalist (and non-individual) ownership. Yet, as has already been argued, whether or not collective, non-exploitative ownership constitutes social ownership depends not only on whether the detailed use made of the means of production involved is decided by those most affected but also on whether that use is consciously integrated into the planned use of the means of production as a whole. Unless it is integrated into a framework determined by society-level decisions about the broad disposition of the means of production as a whole, such ownership is in effect sectional private ownership, whatever its legal form. This is the direction in which things have gone in the Yugoslav worker self-managed system. It is, in my opinion, the logic of market socialism when interpreted as a system in which significant deployment of the means of production, significant allocation and reallocation of resources, occurs as a result of autonomous enterprise-level decisions in response to market forces.

There is a real issue here. Much of the attempt to renew and modernize socialist theory and vision fails to come to terms with production and planning. There has been an understandable and necessary reaction against the adverse experience to date of state ownership, which for the most part has been subject to little effective social control. This has been associated with a tendency to replace the concept of public ownership with that of social ownership, interpreted, in the second sense of the term identified above, as collective, non-exploitative ownership. However, in the context of a retreat from serious discussion of planning, this represents a limiting of the public character of ownership, rather than a real shift towards social ownership proper, in the primary sense of the term identified above. With the loss of confidence in planning[9], all that remains to perform the necessary function of coordination is the market mechanism.

The popular control involved in the socialization of the means of production, then, requires substantive generalized political and economic democracy, which in turn requires planning. While there is plenty of scope for discussion of the institutional form most likely to further democratization in any particular context, the objective itself is relatively uncontroversial. This is not the case in relation to the objective of overcoming the social division of labour, the distinction between leaders and led, which is the second requirement for real popular control. Bahro is the principal theorist in modern times to have placed this objective at the top of the historical agenda. For the most part, however, the objective of overcoming the social division of labour is regarded as a utopian hangover, on the grounds, as Nove puts it, that 'there is bound to be a division between governors and governed' (Nove 1983, p. 197).

Bahro's argument is based on a restatement of the basic historical materialist schema. He distinguishes between what he calls the primary, secondary and tertiary formations. The first corresponds to primitive communal society; the second to the social, or traditional, division of labour, initially in the form of the state arising above and governing society, later generalized to a division between the directing and the directed in all human activity; the third formation corresponds to class society based on the private ownership of the means of production (Bahro 1977, pp. 13–14). Only this tertiary formation is removed with the abolition of private property. The secondary formation remains and with it 'the oldest historical layers of oppression and social inequality. . . . The exploitation and oppression of women. . . . The dominance of the town . . . over the country. . . . The exploitation and oppression of the manual worker (whoever has to perform principally physical, schematic, *executive* work) by the mental worker (whoever performs predominantly intellectual, creative, planning and managerial activity)' (Bahro 1978, pp. 46–7).

People who spend their lives performing partial tasks, determined for them by others who plan the activity as a whole, develop partial consciousness. People who spend all their time being told what to do, rather than learning how to decide what to do for themselves, develop subaltern consciousness. People with partial, subaltern consciousness cannot take an overall view and share the responsibility of running things. Thus, Bahro argues, the abolition of the social division of labour is a necessary condition for the full socialization of control over the means of production. Turning Lenin's adage on its head, he refers to 'the inherently illusory demand that every cook should learn to govern the state, which she simply cannot learn in the normal case if she is to remain a cook' (Bahro 1978, p. 152).

Bahro is in no doubt that the socialization of the means of production is a process: 'it needs several generations . . . to establish a new subjectivity as an average type . . . [it is] simply impossible that an oppressed and alienated class of immediate producers, subjected to the [traditional or social] division of labour, could "itself" become the ruling class and in this role exercize hegemony over the entire cultural process of its society' (Bahro 1978, p. 199). However, this is not a prescription for immobilism. On the contrary, it requires a transformatory perspective for 'the overthrow of the traditional division of labour – not of course as a violation of living generations who have already internalized their confined character, but rather as a planned process to be executed in historical time' (Bahro 1978, p. 278).

The theoretical conclusion of this argument is drawn by Williams: 'change in a mode of production can not occur only on the basis of a change in *relations* of production . . . but must also involve change in the *forces* of production' (Williams 1980, p. 7). The forces of production in question, of course, are people. Williams insists, rightly in my view, that Bahro's vision is not utopian: 'He thinks through, in unusually sustained detail, the processes of transformation of conditions and needs' (Williams 1980, p. 10). It is important to be realistic and Bahro is under no illusions about people's existing levels of consciousness. However, it is even more important not to be conservative, not to deny the possibility of change. What is needed is realistic thought about what changes now will assist the process of the present generation's self-transformation and therefore enable subsequent generations to start from a more emancipated consciousness. The overcoming of the social division of labour is discussed in detail in chapter 7.

5.5   Conclusion

Increasing socialization of production requires increasing socialization of the means of production. Social, as opposed to private or state, control over the use of the means of production is a necessary condition for a society in which self-activating, self-determining people have control over their lives. Movement towards communism, for that is what such a society amounts to, is today more urgently needed than ever. The spectre of nuclear annihilation, the destruction of the world's ecological balance, uncontrolled industrialization and unbridled consumerism, the persistence of global inequality, a resurgence of fundamentalism and irrationalism, the unending reproduction of oppression and subalternity – these are the challenges. If we are not to destroy one another we need to create the social relations and organization that enable us as aware and informed people to take control of our individual and collective destiny.[10]

Capitalism and statism are alternative modes of production developing the preconditions for socialism and communism in different ways. Neither can be considered a more advanced social formation than the other. Historically, capitalism has been associated with the achievement of political democracy, however limited, and statism with the achievement of generalized public, but not social, ownership. Both achievements need to be qualitatively transformed and each needs to be complemented by the other. That is what is involved in moving towards democratic planning, part of the continuing process of achieving social control over production.

In this chapter, I have argued that the socialization of the means of production requires society wide planning, political and economic democracy, and the abolition of the social, not functional, division of labour. The conditions for political and economic democracy are discussed in the next chapter, along with possible institutional forms. The case for abolition of the social division of labour, what it would mean and what it would not mean, how a society in which it had been achieved might be organized, are then discussed in chapter 7. Part IV develops a model of democratic planning based on negotiated coordination as an alternative to both command planning and market socialism. I believe that, unlike them, it is consistent with and necessary for a self-activating, self-determining society, while avoiding utopianism. It promotes and for its full development requires the fundamental human values for which socialists and communists have historically stood – cooperation between equals, mutual respect, a sense of community.

Three conclusions have emerged from this chapter's discussion of the socialization of the forces and relations of production that I should particularly like to emphasize. The first is that the long overdue attention to the centrality of democratisation in the process of socialization should not cause us to lose sight of the importance of the public or common aspect of social ownership. It is this aspect of social ownership that makes society-wide planning, conscious decisions about the overall use of resources, possible. Interestingly, it tends to be an older generation of socialists who are most acutely aware of the danger of throwing the baby out with the bathwater. Perhaps this is because of the continuous and at times painful process they have experienced of actively and creatively reworking a classical Marxist theoretical formation acquired in the first half of the twentieth century in the light of the changing reality of the second half.

Williams, for example, writes:

> the best democratic and socialist way of running organizations is through
> regular and informed collective decision-making . . . but this principle
> cannot be limited to specific enterprises and communities . . . there is

even some danger that the growing belief in existing and commonly foreseen forms of community politics and workers' control will actually hide from us the more difficult problems of the general framework within which, necessarily, they must be practised. (Williams 1980, p. 12)

Hobsbawm is equally unambiguous: 'what socialism is about is precisely taking the sort of decisions which cannot be taken if social resources are allocated by the market, that is, by a system whose basic mechanism is the reinforcement of inequality. For this, planning and public control, whatever they are called, are indispensable tools' (Hobsbawm 1987, p. 13).

The second conclusion is related to the first. There is a real danger that the chilling experience of Stalinism and the sobering experience of social democracy is producing a lowering of sights, a loss of focus on the priorities and values that make the socialist/communist project revolutionary and worthwhile. Ironically, a pessimism not only of the intellect but also of the will seems to have taken hold. It is as if the reactionary argument that you can't change human nature has triumphed after all, this time round in the guise of a hard headed, post-fundamentalist, post-utopian realism. I continue to believe that a society in which 'the antithesis between intellectual and physical labour have disappeared' (Marx 1974, p. 347) is possible. That is why I consider Bahro's project of abolishing the social division of labour to be of such fundamental historical importance.

Thirdly, however, it certainly is essential to be realistic. That is why I attach so much importance to process and transformatory practice. The appeal to realism can be either conservative or revolutionary. Conservative realism starts from the way people are at any particular time and assumes that that is how they always will be. Hence Nove's appeal to 'original sin' (Nove 1983, p. 229). Revolutionary realism displays pessimism of the intellect, in starting from an unromantic view of the way people are, and optimism of the will, in believing that people can change themselves: 'it all comes down to whether a realism of this kind is presented fatalistically and apologetically, or alternatively in a critical and hence revolutionary way. This realism can only be critical and revolutionary if it neither sees the domination of the traditional [social] division of labour as an unalterable fact, nor leaves the task of overcoming it to future generations' (Bahro 1978, p. 176).

The task of the present generation is to refuse the temptation of cosy incorporation in new rightist realism and assert an autonomous, historically situated revolutionary realism. Realism, to be revolutionary, in fact to be realism, must be transformatory. The challenge for the present generation is whether 'enough of us can reasonably believe that a new human order is seriously possible' (Williams 1980, p. 3).

6

Democracy

6.1 Introduction

In the last chapter I argued that political and economic democracy, along with planning and the abolition of the social division of labour, are necessary conditions for the socialization of the means of production. I also used the term popular control in order to emphasize the importance of democratic control being real, rather than merely formal, and involving everyone, rather than just the politically active. My objective is a society of self-activating, self-governing people individually and collectively in control of their lives. Such a society must by definition be democratic. The task of this chapter is to discuss what this means, to identify the conditions necessary for the achievement of a fully democratic society and consider the institutional form it might take.

It could be argued that at a very general level a certain convergence has been taking place in relation to the conditions thought necessary for a fully socialist or democratic society. From within the Marxist tradition the Eurocommunist trend has broken decisively with the classical Marxist concept of the dictatorship of the proletariat and unqualified hostility to 'bourgeois' democracy. As Poulantzas puts it, 'socialism will be democratic or it will not be at all' (Poulantzas 1978, p. 265). From within the liberal tradition there has been a growing realization that the fullest development of democracy is incompatible with the existence of capitalism and that economic democracy is necessary to complement political democracy.[1] Thus, socialism must be democratic and democracy requires socialism.

The concept of people individually and collectively in control of their lives has often been held to be incoherent, by socialists and anti-socialists alike, on the grounds that in the event of a conflict there is an unavoidable choice between the individual and the collective interest. Beetham's argument against this position seems to me conclusive:

> the only sustainable justification for democracy is one based on equal *rights* to share in determining the rules and policies under which one lives, and . . . this in turn has to be underpinned by a tough conception of personal autonomy as well as of equal human worth. . . . Personal autonomy in a political . . . context is a condition of being free to decide along with others the rules and policies of common life. Respect for the equal autonomy of others also means . . . accepting a majority verdict on matters where a collective decision is necessary. . . . Democratic rights thus have a dual character. They are rights which are guaranteed to individuals, but which can only be exercised collectively. They recognise together both the autonomy of the individual person as an unconditional value, and the interconnectedness of his or her life with others as a basic condition of existence. (Beetham 1981, pp. 198–9)

A society of autonomous, self-activating, self-governing people must be democratic, but democracy is a contested concept. Macpherson distinguishes three models of liberal democracy which, he argues, have prevailed at different times: protective democracy, designed to protect the governed from oppression by the government; developmental democracy, as a means of individual self-development; and equilibrium democracy, based on competition between elites with little popular participation. He also proposes, as a possible future model, participatory democracy (Macpherson 1977, p. 22). Held offers eight models of democracy, with some variations, ranging from classical democracy, through several liberal and Marxist versions, to the new right's legal democracy and the participatory democracy of Pateman, Macpherson and Poulantzas (Held 1987, chs 1–8). He, too, developing particularly the work of Beetham, proposes his own model, which he calls democratic autonomy or liberal socialism (Held 1987, pp. 289–90).

For democracy to be real, not just formal, people need to participate in taking and implementing the decisions that affect them. Wherever possible this participation should be direct. It is generally easier for people to acquire the knowledge and develop the capacities needed to participate effectively in relation to their immediate, small scale, local environment, as has long been argued by advocates of developmental democracy. This creates a presumption in favour of decentralization. However, decentralization is not always possible or desirable. Some decisions have to be taken and implemented at the level of the society as a whole, or at intermediate levels. The principle of participation remains valid, but in these cases it can only be indirect participation.

Thus, the longstanding antithesis between direct and representative democracy must be laid to rest. Both are needed. This has now become common ground among most theorists seeking a democratic socialism or a fully developed democracy.[2] The real issues are, first, the criteria for determining the appropriate balance of centralized and decentralized decision-making for each functional area of social activity and, second, how effective participation can be achieved at each level. This second issue requires particular attention at the level of society-wide decisions, since participation appears *prima facie* more difficult to achieve indirectly than directly.

Most discussion of the problems of achieving effective participatory democracy is concerned with decision-making. Equally important, however, indeed central to the reality of democratic control, is participation, direct or indirect, in the implementation, the carrying out, of decisions. For people to be self-activating and self-governing they need to run things themselves, not leave things to be run by others, otherwise they themselves also end up being run by others. This fundamental insight is what underlies the classical Marxist argument against the separation of the legislature and the executive. However, while the importance of people participating in the implementation of decisions cannot be overemphasized, abolition of the separation of powers is not the answer.

There are two reasons for this. The first is that implementation typically requires an administrative structure and specialist expertise. Since we cannot be experts in everything some technical division of labour is unavoidable. The challenge is to develop ways of ensuring that expertise does not convey social power, power over other people. The second reason for wishing to retain, indeed to increase, the separation of power in society follows from this. Arguing for 'a pluralism of power centres to ensure the liberties intrinsic to democracy', Beetham proposes 'a general law that the greater the concentration of decision-making authority, the more difficult it is to subject it to democratic control, and the greater the threat to the freedoms which are central to a democratic society' (Beetham 1981, p. 200).

Poulantzas poses the problem of how to move towards a fully democratic society as follows: '*how is it possible radically to transform the State in such a manner that the extension and deepening of political freedoms and the institutions of representative democracy . . . are combined with the unfurling of forms of direct democracy and the mushrooming of self-management bodies?*' (Poulantzas 1978, p. 256). Held makes essentially the same point in arguing for his model of democratic autonomy:

> for democracy to flourish today it has to be reconceived as a double-sided phenomenon: concerned, on the one hand, with the *re*-form of state power and, on the other hand, with the restructuring of civil society. . . .
> The principle of autonomy can only be enacted by recognizing the

indispensability of a process of 'double democratization': the interdependent transformation of both state and civil society. (Held 1987, p. 283)

Given the subject matter of this book – democratic economic planning – these issues of democratic theory cannot be avoided. On the other hand, neither can they be discussed exhaustively, let alone resolved. My principal concern in this chapter is to explore the possibilities for real popular control of society in general and the economy in particular, with an outline of possible enabling institutional forms where appropriate. Institutional forms can only be enabling since in the end what matters are the social relationships mediated by them and these depend ultimately on the extent of self-development and personal autonomy achieved by the people involved, to be considered in the next chapter.

The rest of this chapter discusses political democracy in relation to the national and local state, focusing particularly on ways in which representative democracy might be transformed to render it both more participatory and more effective in exercising control over the administrative structure. It then considers the conditions necessary for economic democracy and how they might be achieved. This leads on to an examination of how the diverse interests comprising civil society, separate from both the state and the economy, might make themselves felt in the traditional political and economic spheres. Civil society, the sphere of self-governing groups, is a particularly important site for participation in the form of direct democracy.[3]

6.2 Political Democracy

A self-governing society should operate on the principle that decisions and their implementation are the responsibility of and should be undertaken by those affected by them. This is the principle which should determine the governmental and administrative framework within which collective activities are carried out. A balance between centralization and decentralization has to be struck on two dimensions, functional and vertical (Beetham 1981, p. 203). Concentration of power may take the form of the responsibility for all functional activities being vested in a single representative system and administrative structure. It may also take the form of all authority within a given representative system and administrative structure being vested in the centre.

Thus, the separation of power, pluralism within the sphere of the state, involves, on the one hand, separating out responsibility for different functional activities and assigning it to those affected, and, on the other hand, within each functional activity decentralizing responsibility vertically downwards to the most local level consistent with efficiency and equity. The desired balance between centralized and decentralized powers will typically differ according to the functional activity concerned. In order to enable as much direct participation as possible and to safeguard personal freedom decentralization should normally be preferred in cases of doubt. What emerges is a network of representative bodies and administrative structures responsible for different functional activities with varying territorial extensions – local, regional, national, and perhaps eventually also international (Beetham 1983, p. 13).

As well as democratic bodies with particular functional responsibilities, however, there would continue to be democratic assemblies representing all citizens at the national, regional and local levels. The national assembly would remain responsible, as now, for determining overall priorities, the broad allocation of resources to different uses, redistribution, the constitution of functional bodies and the procedure for achieving coordination between them. Regional and local community representative assemblies would have similar responsibilities within the area of their jurisdiction. The independence of a democratized judicial system and media are also evident requirements of political pluralism.

Although outlined in rather general terms, the above structure displays clear continuity with, and yet would constitute a revolutionary transformation of, existing systems of representative democracy, not to mention the political systems of the statist countries. Within the capitalist democracies the actual trend is towards greater concentration of power along both dimensions. In Britain, the autonomy of local authorities is being steadily reduced and relatively autonomous functional activities like the health service and education are increasingly being brought under central government control. The notion that a general election every few years confers a democratic mandate on the central government for any policy, in any area of social life, is a major threat to democracy, not least because it undermines its legitimacy.

The next issue to consider is how the membership of the representative assemblies and functional bodies should be determined. I do not see how, in a self-governing society, this can be other than by democratic election.[4] A fundamental challenge to this view has recently been advanced by Burnheim, who rejects democracy in favour of what he calls demarchy. This is a system under which membership is determined by lot in such a way as to ensure that the composition of the decision-making body is statistically representative of the group of people on whose behalf it is acting. The advantages of this system are claimed to be the avoidance of endless elections for functional bodies, involving issues about which people are inadequately informed, and the dangers of mediocrity and corruption said to be inherent in party politics (Burnheim 1985, ch. 3).

However, demarchy is incompatible with generalized participation and it therefore lacks the self-transformatory potential claimed for developmental and participatory democracy. Under demarchy, people would not be responsible, directly or indirectly, for the decisions that affected them. They would be under no obligation to assume responsibility for running anything. This is undesirable for two reasons. On the one hand, people who have not been involved in taking the decisions that affect them typically feel no particular obligation to cooperate in their effective implementation. On the other hand, people who have no experience of running things, of having to make difficult decisions and assume responsibility for them, retain a partial, subaltern, consciousness. They are denied, or deny themselves, the experience that would enable them to appreciate situations, or systems, as a whole and to develop a hegemonic consciousness.

The more familiar objection to the principle of election relates not to representative assemblies but to the election of those responsible for running the many functional activities organized by the state, ranging from education, health and welfare, through transport and cultural activities, to local services and the police. Although formally the responsibility of national or local government, these functional activities are largely run by wholly or partially appointed bodies and professionals. The standard justification for this has two, contradictory, aspects: that functional services should be professionally run, with politics kept out; and that any attempt to influence the way in which the service is run, other than through the elected national or local government, is a sectionally-based attack on democracy. The effect is to render the functional activities organized by the state largely immune to any form of popular control or accountability.

The possibilities for popular participation, direct and indirect, by users and others with a legitimate interest, would be greatly increased by the introduction of pluralism within the sphere of the state. The existence of an extensive network of democratically elected functional bodies and administrative structures, responsible for taking and implementing decisions, would greatly increase the scope for participation. If there were limits on the period for which any person could hold a particular office and also, perhaps, on the number of public offices people could hold in the course of their lives, the scope for participation would be increased still further. Part of the process of overcoming the social division of labour, to be discussed in the next chapter, involves spreading the experience of serving as a representative on behalf of others as widely as possible.

Democratically elected bodies making decisions in relation to the functional activities for which they were responsible would constitute a major reform and deepening of representative democracy. However, the relationship between these bodies and the administrative structures through which policy decisions would be implemented remains to be considered, as does the related issue of the way in which popular participation might occur.

The problem of how to control the state machine, the bureaucracy, the administration, remains unsolved. Legal and institutional changes can help, but in the end the social power of the state rests on its hegemonic role in being responsible for organizing and running central aspects of social life and its relative monopoly of the resources, particularly the knowledge, involved in doing so. This can be illustrated, negatively, by the relationship between the state and the economy in capitalist societies, in which the state plays a subordinate role. The state depends on privately owned enterprises for economic performance but, because of their autonomy from it, cannot in general compel them and must therefore obtain their cooperation (Lindblom 1977, ch. 13). The dominant position of the capitalist enterprise also gives it a relative monopoly of essential information and specialist knowledge.

It is for these reasons that the detailed planning apparatus of wartime Britain was largely staffed by people seconded from the bigger firms and that the crucial non-state personnel involved in industrial policy in France, Japan and the UK have been leading businessmen. These are just instances of the continuing, day-to-day, corporate capitalist involvement in the detailed determination of state policy and its implementation. In the UK each major industry has a sponsoring ministry, a government department responsible for mediating the relationship between the industry and the state. New legislation affecting the industry, proposed changes in safety or pollution control regulations, recommendations of the Monopolies and Mergers Commission, all are discussed with representatives of the industry and the key firms and typically an agreement is negotiated. However, because of the privileged position of business and its relative monopoly of knowledge the negotiation is not between equals.

For the social power of the state, of the administrative structure, to be controlled, reduced and eventually abolished, requires the development of self-government in all aspects of civil society as the norm. On the one hand, it would result in the creation of autonomous centres of power with which the administrative structure would have to cooperate in the implementation of policy. On the other hand, it would provide the basis for independent expertise informed by alternative values. Thus, within civil society people would increasingly take responsibility for all aspects of their lives, directly by involvement in running their immediate communities and local services, indirectly by making demands on the various levels of government for resources and desired policy changes. At each level of the administrative structure consultation and negotiation would involve representatives of all groups with a legitimate interest in the policy under consideration, not just business as is typically the case at the moment.

Once again, there are clear continuities with the present, but the flourishing of self-government in civil society would be a revolutionary transformation in social relations and is the only way that the social power of the state can be addressed. Quoting Gramsci on the transition from socialism to communism, 'it is possible to imagine the coercive element of the state withering away by degrees, as ever more conspicuous elements of civil society make their appearance' (Gramsci 1971, p. 263), Simon argues that, 'The evolution towards communism consists, then, in the continual extension of civil society and its relations of autonomy, self-government and self-discipline' (Simon 1982, p. 77).

Whatever the eventual outcome of this process, it will take a very long time. Nevertheless, a long-term perspective provides guidance for the direction of present struggles for change and also helps to ensure that a transformatory element is included. For the foreseeable future the crucial issue will be the precise articulation of the relationship between the varying levels of the state's administrative structure and the developing forms of self-government. It is important to avoid any suggestion of dual power, since state administrative structures and self-governing organizations have distinct roles to play. The key question is rather the character of the relationship between them. This is bound to be contradictory, combining cooperation and antagonism, partnership and struggle. The relationship is perhaps best summed up by the phrase 'in and against the state' [5] and is considered further in section 6.4.

What is involved is, in fact, a three-way relationship between representative bodies, administrative structures and self-governing groups within civil society. Since those elected to representative bodies come from the community, they are likely to have pre-existing relationships with the self-governing groups. Thus, it is possible to envisage cooperation between elected representatives, with whom formal legal power and responsibility reside, and self-governing groups, with an interest in and knowledge of the services provided by the administrative structures. In this way, the social power of the state can be contested by parliamentary and extra-parliamentary pressure, and similarly at the local level. Both forms of pressure are needed, but in the end the development of self-governing groups in the sphere of civil society will be decisive.

Elected representatives by themselves are relatively powerless, lacking access to the resources of the administrative structure and detailed knowledge of its activities. Open government, freedom of information, departmental select committees, new forms of social performance indicator, other measures to achieve greater accountability and responsiveness, all would increase the ability of elected representatives to fulfil their responsibilities. However, they are no substitute for the active involvement of the people affected by and making use of the services organized by the state. In the end it is only they, organized on a self-governing basis, who can make demands on the state for what they want and by becoming involved in running things ensure that things are run as they want them to be.

In doing so, self-governing groups will find themselves working with state employees possessing specialist expertise. In the long run, the position of the state's administrative structures as outside and above society can only be overcome as the social, but not of course the functional, division of labour is abolished. However, in the shorter term the composition of state employees needs to be and can be brought more into line with that of the population as a whole. Openness of recruitment and equal opportunities policies, backed up by carefully planned and targeted education and training programmes, could greatly increase the representation of women and ethnic minorities. Indeed, if there is a place for statistical representativeness as an operational policy in a democratic society it is probably in the public service.

The discussion so far has centred on the relationship between the state and civil society, without, however, considering the role of political parties and the way in which economic interests would make themselves felt. Party political pluralism and self-government have frequently been considered incompatible with one another. If the people affected by a particular functional activity are running that activity themselves, either directly or through a combination of representative and direct participation, the presence of political parties may understandably appear as an external intrusion. There may be a conflict between loyalty to the group and to the party.

While this argument has some force when applied to the organization of functional activities, it certainly cannot be carried over to the responsibilities of representative assemblies. Choices about the overall allocation of resources between different activities have to be made at the level of society as a whole. General principles applicable to society as a whole have to be decided. Such choices and principles determine the ethos, the feel, the character of the social relationships of a society, what is meant by citizenship. They reflect particular values and priorities. Since it cannot be assumed that everyone in a fully democratic society will somehow agree on values and priorities an essential role for political parties will remain.

The classical Marxist position was that since parties represent classes they will eventually disappear, as a classless society is achieved, and in the transitional period only one party, representing the ruling working class, will be needed. However, there is no reason to suppose that interests and differences arising from cultural formation, gender, race, and regional and national identity will disappear. I find it difficult to envisage the end of politics, in the sense of contested decisions about, first, the distribution of resources, rights and responsibilities and, second, strategic, non-marginal choices concerning the general direction of development of society. Political parties offering alternative unified and coherent perspectives on these issues, for which they seek to win hegemonic support, seem to me an essential part of a fully democratic society.

These issues, Beetham's 'rules and policies under which one lives' (Beetham 1981, p. 198), affect everyone, directly, as with redistributive policies, or indirectly, by determining both the framework within which particular exercises of self-government take place and the externally provided resources available for them. For this reason, decisions about these issues can only be taken democratically by a representative assembly elected by all citizens, and similarly at the regional and local level. Elections, as now, would typically involve a choice between the candidates of political parties, although with proportional representation, at least with some forms of it, there would be greater scope for differentiating between individuals, and independents would stand a greater chance.

Of course, existing political parties in capitalist societies developed as a response to the extension of the franchise in order to reconcile formal political equality with real social and economic inequality. The models of equilibrium democracy, identified by Macpherson, and competitive elitist democracy, classic pluralism and neo-pluralism, identified by Held, capture in different ways the reality of the elite political leaders of non-participatory parties competing for the votes of a passive electorate (Macpherson 1977, pp. 64–92; Held 1987, chs 5–6). However, given the weight envisaged for self-government in civil society, and progress towards abolition of the social division of labour, 'the real possibility of genuinely participatory parties' (Macpherson 1977, p. 114) opens up.

The remaining issue to be discussed in this section on political democracy is the question of how economic interests would be represented in the decision-making process. The question arises because of a tendency, observable in widely differing contexts, for economic interests to be independently represented in some way, alongside bodies elected on the basis of universal suffrage representing citizens as a whole. Thus, Middlemas has drawn attention to the development of a 'corporate bias' in Britain in the fifty years following the First World War (Middlemas 1979, ch. 13), typified by the tripartite character of the National Economic Development Council discussed in chapter 2; while Horvat, building on the Yugoslav experience, envisages a Chamber of Trade 'to harmonize the interests of industries' and an Assembly, consisting of Houses of Citizens and Producers, to resolve more general conflicts (Horvat 1982, pp. 361, 366).

The idea of an economic council of some sort has a long history, summarized in the British context by Smith (1979, Preface, chs 1–2). It reflects the centrality of the economy in social life. The privileged position of business and at times in some countries, notably Britain, the strength of organized labour have meant that without the broad agreement and cooperation of these economic interests government has been relatively powerless. However, a necessary condition for a democratic society is the abolition of the privileged position of business and there is no reason why this should be replaced by a privileged position for the interests of people as producers, as opposed to their interests in other aspects of their lives.[6] In line with this argument, I have previously advocated an 'interest chamber' to complement the representative assembly. In the British context it could replace the House of Lords alongside the House of Commons with, however, an advisory role only (Devine 1981, p. 116).

The House of Interests could be a development from the National Economic Development Council but on a much broader basis. To the existing representatives of central government, major industries, major enterprises and trade unions would be added representatives of other interests. These would include: regional and local government; autonomous self-governing organizations like consumer groups, users of publicly provided services, community groups, environmental and recreational groups, women's groups, ethnic groups; and any other interests around which people chose to organize themselves. Criteria would need to be agreed to determine which interests should be represented and on what basis. As with political parties, the interest groups themselves would have to be genuinely participatory.

The purpose of such an interest chamber would be to face squarely the fact that conflicts of interest cannot be disposed of merely by invoking a general social or public, let alone national, interest. Different interests need to be involved from the beginning in the process of working out a broad set of priorities, a broad distribution of resources, at the level of society as a whole. It would be an important innovation for the various interests to negotiate in an attempt to arrive at what they could agree on as a fair, or at least an acceptable, outcome. Interests would find themselves having to take an overall view and evaluating their priorities in relation to those of others. In this way, sectionalism would be challenged and people would be given the opportunity to change their consciousness if persuaded of the need to do so.

Of course, complete agreement is unlikely always, or indeed ever, to be reached. In the end, the representative assembly, the body representative of all citizens, would decide. Interest groups would be free to campaign for their position and seek to bring pressure to bear. They would typically include people who were also active in political parties. Thus, there would be a two-way traffic of ideas and influence between interest groups and parties. If persuasive enough in their advocacy, interest groups would succeed in changing opinion within all parties and throughout the society as a whole. The process envisaged is a complex one, combining actively negotiated consent and social stability with openness to innovation and the potential for dynamic change.

6.3   Economic Democracy

Economic democracy has been placed on the historical agenda with increasing urgency by two related developments. First, there is the historical experience of workers demanding and achieving more say in their conditions of work and the decisions that affect them. This occurred initially within the workplace or enterprise and is usually referred to as industrial democracy (Kiloh 1986) and/or worker participation in management (Walker 1977). More recently workers have raised their sights and the concept of industrial democracy has expanded to include worker involvement, through their trade unions, in decisions at the level of the economy as a whole (Elliott 1978). Second, there is a growing awareness among political theorists that full political democracy and capitalism are incompatible.[7] The requirement of equal access to the resources needed for effective participation in a self-governing society rules out minority private ownership of the means of production and a privileged position for business.

In the previous chapter, following Brus, I argued that socialization of the means of production involves a combination of social control over the broad disposition of society's productive resources at the level of society as a whole and social control over the detailed use of productive resources at the level where production actually takes place. This is what I mean by economic democracy. However, the concept of economic democracy has sometimes been confined to the level of the enterprise and identified with an economy consisting of self-governing enterprises, run exclusively by those working in them (Horvat 1982, ch. 8; Dahl 1985, ch. 3). This usage is normally associated with a market socialist model of the economy in which coordination between worker self-governing enterprises is achieved by regulated market forces.

There are two reasons why the historical significance of the concept of economic democracy is diminished if it is limited in this way. On the one hand, it then has nothing to say about the deployment of economic resources at the level of the economy as a whole. Since the overall economic context constrains what happens at the level of the enterprise, economic self-government confined to that level is inevitably partial. On the other hand, the identification of economic democracy at the level of the enterprise with self-government by those working in the enterprise is itself mistaken. It confuses sectional control with social control. Those who work in an enterprise are obviously affected by its activities but so are those who make use of what it produces and those who live in the community within which it is located.

A necessary condition for economic democracy at the level of society as a whole is the public element in the social relationship constituting ownership of the means of production. It is this public element that enables overall planning of the economy. For public ownership to be then transformed into social ownership at this level requires that planning priorities and the decisions derived from them are arrived at through political democracy. Fully developed participatory democracy, as discussed in the previous section, would enable decisions about overall priorities and the associated allocation of resources to be determined by society as a whole. Self-government by society as a whole in the economic sphere involves economic planning and political democracy.

A corollary of economic democracy at this level is that people would be more likely to be committed to macro-level decisions and to the need to cooperate with one another in order to implement them. The significance of this can be illustrated from the problem of inflation. In so far as inflation is due to a conflict over the distribution of resources, of real output (Devine 1974; Rowthorn 1980, chs 5–6), it can only be dealt with in a non-coercive way if the conflicting interests reach some agreement on how available resources should be distributed between different uses and different people. Such agreement, passive or active, must underlie any negotiated incomes policy or social contract which people voluntarily abide by. The coercive alternative solutions to the problem of inflation are mass unemployment or state imposition, the market or statist solutions.

Possible ways in which real social determination of a plan for the economy as a whole might be achieved, based on choices between alternative values, priorities and strategic decisions, are outlined in chapter 8. The rest of this section is concerned with the second aspect of economic democracy, the determination of the detailed use of productive resources at the level of enterprises or production units. Since I have argued that the achievement of a self-governing society is the fundamental objective of socialism and democracy, my rejection of worker self-governing enterprises as the institutional form for economic democracy at the level of the enterprise needs further discussion.

The basic principle of self-government is that decisions in relation to any activity and responsibility for their implementation should rest with those affected. The identification of those affected, and therefore the definition of the self-governing group, is clearly a major problem (Dahl 1985, p. 148). It is equally clear, however, that in the case of economic enterprises the relevant group is wider than those who work in the enterprise. This is, in fact, recognized by advocates of the worker self-governing enterprise. In exceptional cases of particular social or national importance they typically allow that enterprises should be owned and managed by the central government, or at least have external social interests represented at the summit of their decision-making structure (Horvat 1982, p. 248; Nove 1983, pp. 200–1; Held 1987, p. 290).

Yet, once it is recognized that others besides its workers have an interest in the activities of an enterprise, the general case for self-government exclusively by workers within the enterprise disappears. While not all enterprises are of society-wide, national importance, all are of at least regional or local significance. Furthermore, all have users of what they produce. It is true that advocates of the worker self-governed enterprise rely on competition and the coercive pressure of market forces to safeguard the interests of users. However, the problems associated with the coordination of resource allocation through the market mechanism have already been discussed in Parts I and II. User choice is an important source of information as a check on the effectiveness with which enterprises are fulfilling their social function of supplying what users want. However it is not the only information relevant for decisions at the level of the enterprise. Social control over such decisions requires a cooperative decision-making procedure involving all the interests affected.

It follows that at the level of the enterprise economic democracy, self-government in the sense of social control, cannot be self-government solely by those who work in the enterprise. In the end, decision-making has to be vested in a body representative of all the interests affected. This basic principle of self-government, of course, has to be tailored to the particular circumstances of each enterprise. An enterprise's workers will always be involved. What other interests are represented and with what weight will depend on the activity involved, the size of the enterprise and its location. It will also depend on prevailing social values, on the relative importance attached by society to different interests. The social interest in each case has to be socially constructed.

I think that this conclusion is inescapable. Nevertheless, the virtues claimed for worker self-government remain very real. Direct democracy, direct participation in the organization of work, is an essential part of the process of overcoming alienation and contributing to the transformation of subaltern into hegemonic consciousness. It is also likely to increase efficiency as changed consciousness and motivation result in a more constructive use of local knowledge. Some way is needed to combine social control with worker self-management. The obvious way is for the overall government of the enterprise to be vested in a body representative of all affected interests, including its workers, and for the enterprise to be organized and run internally on the basis of self-management by its workers. This is discussed in more detail in chapter 9.

This suggestion about how to combine social self-government at the level of actual production with self-management by the workers actually undertaking the production is similar to Held's proposals for state administrative services and community services.[8] He suggests that both should be internally organized on the principle of direct participation but with coordination of user demand in the former and priorities set by users in the latter (Held 1987, p. 290). This is because in both cases society's resources are being used to provide a service for society and hence users' interests must ultimately be paramount.

What has emerged from this discussion, I think, is an important clarification of the concept of self-government. The concept of self-government is relevant within civil society. It consists of autonomous, self-activating, voluntary activity and organization. It is not relevant within the state's administrative structures, nor within economic enterprises, in relation to both of which self-management is the relevant concept. At the moment, state structures and economic enterprises have a dual role: the administration of things to provide what people use in their collective and personal lives; and the administration of people through the exercise of social power. The first is a necessary role that will endure and will become increasingly subject to social control as the second is overcome by the development of self-government within civil society. Whatever form the administration of things eventually takes, it will presumably be organized on the basis of self-management within a framework set by a self-governing society.

6.4   Interests

Civil society, not the state and not the economic enterprise, is where self-government takes place. The process of achieving social control of the polity and the economy consists of ever more developed and extensive forms of self-government asserting themselves in relation to the state and to production. Self-government is necessarily based on voluntary association for particular purposes. People typically belong to several self-governing groups. They constitute themselves as a group when they perceive themselves as sharing a common concern and decide to act collectively in relation to it. Groups are more or less permanent or temporary according to the purpose for which they constitute themselves and they differ in the degree of formality or informality of their organizational structure. However, while direct participation seems inseparable from self-government, some sort of indirect participation through a representative structure is also in general necessary.

Three types of self-governing group, or association, can be distinguished, at least in principle: interest groups, ranging from trade unions and professional bodies, through community-based groups concerned with specific functional activities or single issues, to groups concerned with cultural and recreational activities; cause groups, such as the feminist, environmentalist, anti-racist and anti-nuclear movements; and political parties.[9] Of course, in practice groups may be based on interests and yet also embrace causes and/or form links with political parties, as in the case of community groups affiliated to the anti-nuclear movement or trade unions allied to socialist parties. The different types of group are likely to have qualitatively different characteristics that may be of relevance when it comes to decisions about which of the self-governing groups of civil society have a legitimate interest in which activities of the state and of economic enterprises.[10]

In both capitalist and statist societies, though to differing extents, the passivity of alienated consciousness, contributed to by a sense of powerlessness, is a formidable obstacle to the development of participation. However, although there are similarities, the differences between the situation in capitalist and statist societies are of great importance. In the statist countries the dominance of the party/state means that civil society remains very underdeveloped, with the only fully autonomous self-governing groups being dissident. In capitalist democracies, by contrast, there tends to be a proliferation of voluntary associations and this vitality of civil society is an important factor in the long-run viability of the system. Of course, these voluntary associations are typically oligarchic and elitist, rather than fully self-governing, and atomization and privatization inhibit the development of self-governing activity in many areas where it would greatly improve the quality of life. Nevertheless, autonomous voluntary groups exist and civil society is relatively developed.[11]

During the last two decades in the West there has been an upsurge of attempts to create new forms of democratic involvement and to inject a new democratic impulse into the existing institutions of civil society (Held and Pollitt 1986). These have not all been successful and have had a reactionary as well as a forward looking aspect to them (Hall and Jacques 1983, Parts I and II). Much experience has been accumulated of relevance to the prospects for the development of self-governing activity and participatory democracy, not least the identification of unresolved problems. Two issues in particular stand out: the relationships of self-governing groups with representative bodies and the state's administrative structures; and internal relationships within the potentially self-governing groups themselves – their internal democracy, or lack of it.

A distinction needs to be drawn between political parties, on the one hand, and interest and cause groups, on the other. Political parties belong to civil society, unless, that is, they are fused with the state as in the statist countries. To the extent that they are themselves participatory, are genuinely self-governing, they are part of the process through which a self-governing society collectively decides on those matters identified in section 6.2 as the responsibility of the representative assembly. In this, political parties differ from interest and cause groups, in that they are multi-issue, seeking to integrate the concerns of all such groups on the basis of alternative sets of values, traditions and visions. The distinction is not of course absolute. In some cases an interest group may establish a political party, as in the case of the Labour Party in Britain, or what was initially a cause group may enter the domain of the political parties, as when environmentalists constitute themselves as a Green Party.

The interest chamber proposed in section 6.2 embraces what I have in this section subdivided into interests and causes. That is because both types of self-governing group should be involved in the process of the social construction of the social interest. However, the reason for the subdivision is that there are differences as well as things in common between the two types of group. In particular, community-based interest groups concerned with specific functional activities often require resources on a scale that can only be provided collectively by society as a whole, through the representative assembly. This applies in particular to nurturing and caring activities like child care, education, and care of the handicapped, the ill and the elderly. In these activities a

combination of collective provision and community involvement is likely
to be shape of the future.

Such a partnership, fraught though it will be, is probably also
applicable to other functional activities to varying degrees. Even if it
turns out that there is no scope for direct community participation in
some functional activities there will always be a need for indirect
participation by those affected. That is the only way in which effective
social control can be exercised over the use made of collectively provided
resources. In addition, there may be a case for collectively provided
resources to be made available to certain interest and cause groups on an
enabling basis. The record of the Greater London Council in this
respect, particularly in relation to minority groups and the arts, was
inspiringly prefigurative and the quality of life in London has been the
poorer since the GLC's abolition.

Assessing the experience of attempts to operate community control of
services that made use of local authority-provided resources,
Rowbotham discusses some of the problems that arose and continues:
'Community control can thus be a complicated extension of democracy.
Between competing interests within the community, or between workers
and users in a community nursery, who decides? Increasingly it tends to
be the sovereign body of the local council. It is representative democracy
that holds the purse strings' (Rowbotham 1986, p. 102). In the end, of
course, that is how it should be. Yet there are ways of helping to reduce
conflicts by promoting dialogue and helping people to transcend their
sectional interests, to move from subaltern to hegemonic consciousness.

In the case of conflicts between competing interests a local equivalent
of a national chamber of interests might be one such way. Thinking
about it at the local level, incidentally, helps to clarify the issue of which
interests and causes should be represented in such interest chambers.
The principle should be that any group of people who choose to organize
themselves around an issue and wish to be involved in decisions over the
distribution of collective resources should have the right to representation. Criteria would be needed to identify the extent of involvement in
a group in order to assess its weight in the community, with particular
care taken to allow for minority interests and innovation. The principle
would apply at all levels of society, although the precise form of its
application would obviously differ between national, regional and local
chambers of interest. In the case of conflicts between workers and users
the appropriate way to reach decisions would be through a governing
body on which both were represented, together with other legitimate
interests and the local representative assembly.

As long as the state exercises coercive social power, as long, that is, as
self-government in civil society is not fully developed, in other words for
the foreseeable future, the relationship will be one of in and against the

state, as already mentioned in section 6.2. Agreement will not always be reached, conflict and struggle will continue. Yet there is no other way. Only by participating, by seeking to run things, do we learn how to participate, how to run things, and in the course of doing so slowly transform ourselves and take control of our lives.

What can be said about the internal structure of self-governing groups, about their internal democracy? The most far-reaching experience has come from the feminist movement. It has had a transforming influence on perceptions and, to a lesser extent, on practice. Its insistence on challenging existing definitions and distributions of power and on asserting the importance of caring personal relationships has been a revolutionary contribution to thinking about what a self-governing society might look like. Rowbotham identifies three 'extended meanings of democracy', already present in earlier movements, that are now associated with feminism: 'the idea that "the personal is political", which involves challenging the boundaries of concepts of politics, the assumption that democratic control has to be extended not only to the workplace but to the circumstances of everyday life, and the conviction that the *forms* of action chosen contribute to the result, and should consequently seek to prefigure an alternative' (Rowbotham 1986, p. 86).

There are three aspects of this experience which emerge as having general relevance for self-governing practice: the need for adequate material and personal resources; the need for an organizational structure combining direct and indirect participation and democracy; and the need to address the issue of leadership and expertise. Progress in relation to all three has been uneven and has involved struggle – against the existing unequal distribution of power in all its complexity, for theoretical and conceptual clarity, and for personal change.[12] The fact that attempts at prefigurative practice and hard thinking about the unresolved issues associated with it are now firmly on the agenda is a major source of optimism.

Without adequate resources effective participation is impossible. That is why capitalism and statism are incompatible with fully developed democracy. However, it is important to recognize that the resources involved are not just material, although adequate material resources are obviously essential. Participation takes time, as feminists have insisted in their demands both for a redistribution of domestic labour and for the collective services and facilities needed to minimize the unrewarding side of caring and housekeeping. Time is also needed for personal development, for the acquisition of the experience and skills – the confidence, expertise and sensitivity – needed to participate effectively in social life.

The fundamental significance of this personal dimension is why so much weight attaches to small-scale, directly participatory forms of activity, based on relationships between people consciously, almost self-consciously, recognizing one another as being of equal importance, with equally valuable things to contribute. The direct democracy associated with this has typically been characterized by informality, by a conscious rejection of formal structures and a prioritization of consensus. Subsequent reflection and the identification of the problem of the tyranny of structurelessness (Rowbotham 1986, p. 89) has done nothing to diminish the crucial significance of directly participatory activity. However, it can only be one aspect of participatory democracy and self-government. Forms of representative democracy are also needed, not least within the self-governing associations themselves. How else can they carry out their role as the vehicle for self-government within civil society, other than at the most local level?

An unresolved problem for participatory democracy and the concept of self-government more generally is how to think about leadership and expertise. The problem arises because prefigurative practice requires that personal and social relationships are conducted on the basis of equality, whereas capitalism and statism generate and reproduce inequality, not just material inequality but also human inequality. In fact, practice which does not recognize this inequality is not actually prefigurative in any desirable sense. It results in a denial of individual differences and undervalues some people's experience and knowledge – certainly not part of any desirable future. Only by creating the possibilities for everyone to develop their capacities to the full will it be possible for everyone to participate on an equal basis. This will require the fullest possible use of people's existing experience and skills, including their capacity for leadership and their expertise.[13]

The objective is to separate out the technical functions of leadership and expertise from the social status and power associated with being leaders and experts, to retain the former and abolish the latter. The corollary of abolishing the social status and power of leaders and experts is the abolition also of the lack of social status and power associated with being followers and non-experts. Only when everyone has the experience and skill involved in exercizing leadership in some area of activity, only when everyone is expert at something, will the social distinction between leaders and followers, between experts and non-experts, be abolished. This is what Bahro means by the abolition of the social, as opposed to the functional, division of labour. It is discussed further in the next chapter.

6.5 The Desire and Ability to Participate

Since most people in capitalist and statist societies do not participate to any significant extent in running their own lives, the objective of a self-governing society run by self-activating subjects has appeared to many as a utopian illusion. This position is often advanced in bad faith, as a convenient rationalization for the status quo, by those who possess social power as part of the minority that currently runs society. Yet there is more to it than that. The power of hegemonic ideology should not be underestimated, particularly since it captures a central fact of people's lives, of the reality that they actually experience. The distinction between 'us' and 'them' is not an illusion. Lively comments on one aspect of this: 'the less educated (who are also in all likelihood the poorer) may *feel* less able to influence government because they *are* less able' (Lively 1979, p. 74). The minority who run society in all its different aspects in general genuinely regret the apathy of the majority. What they fail to recognize is that the alienation they regard as apathy is at one level a rational choice by people whose experience suggests that their power to have any real influence over the determinants of their lives is small.

'Apathy is not an independent datum' (Macpherson 1977, p. 88). This is the starting point for those committed to the desirability of fully developed democracy, of a self-governing society. The challenge is to be realistic about the existing characteristics of people, associated with the existing unequal distribution of power and opportunities for self-development, while being equally realistic about the potentialities of people to develop the capacity for self-activation and self-government and about what is needed if those potentialities are to be realized. As Held puts it: 'The position that emerges . . . is that people are able to *learn* to participate by participating and are more likely to seek participation *if* they can be confident that their input into decision-making will actually count; that is, will actually be weighted equitably with others and will not simply be side-stepped or ignored by those who wield greater power' (Held 1986, p. 12).

The desire to participate and the ability to participate are in a symbiotic relationship. As developmental and participatory democrats have argued from Rousseau, Wollstonecraft and Mill to Macpherson and Pateman (Held 1987, chs 4, 8), participation feeds on itself. As people increasingly take control of their lives, so their ability to do so also increases. The challenge of having to take responsibility for decisions that make a difference is at the same time an opportunity for personal development. It is part of the process of becoming fully human. The feminist concept of empowering has a general relevance.

To begin to feel powerful, having previously felt powerless, to win access to the resources required for effective participation and learn how to use them, is a liberating experience. Once people become active subjects, making things happen, in one aspect of their lives, they are less likely to remain passive objects, allowing things to happen to them, in other aspects.

Thus, a capacity for participation acquired initially through direct democratic participation in the immediate context of daily life is likely to be associated with enhanced desire and ability to participate, directly or indirectly, at levels of social organization not susceptible to direct democracy. There are two sides to this. First, participation involves working together voluntarily with others. Although this may be painful and frustrating it nevertheless tends to foster collective values, mutual respect and a democratic ethos. Second, in order to run a particular aspect of social life efficiently it is necessary to understand it – how it works, how the different parts interact with one another to form a whole, how it relates to other aspects of social life. This capacity to think in terms of systems as a whole and their interaction with other systems is necessary for an understanding of how society works. It is an essential precondition for effective participation and self-government.

If the desire to participate is associated with the ability to do so effectively, then it may be expected to increase as the conditions necessary for effective participation are achieved by ever more people and eventually by everybody. This process involves complementing the formal political equality of liberal democracy with the real economic and social equality associated with the socialist, particularly the Marxist, tradition. Only with real economic and social equality can there be real political equality. The redistribution of economic resources and social power remains as urgently needed as ever and the struggle to achieve it has a long way to go. However, the experience of attempts to develop and theorise new forms of democratic practice suggests that this traditional socialist programme by itself is not enough.

Unequal distribution of material resources is associated with social relationships of exploitation and oppression. These social relationships are between people and are associated with unequal access to the activities through which personal growth and development occur. Unequal social relationships produce unequal people, people whose underlying potentialities have been developed to different degrees. This is a problematic issue. On the one hand, it is an obvious fact of present reality and everybody recognizes it. On the other hand, to say that people, as opposed to the distribution of material resources or social relationships, are not equal can easily be interpreted as saying that people have innately unequal potentialities or do not have equal validity and rights as human beings. The problem can be particularly acute in the context of attempts to develop prefigurative forms of practice, as discussed in the previous section.

However, failure to think clearly in this area, refusal to face explicitly the fact of unequal personal development and the reasons for it, make it impossible to identify the forms of social organization that are most enabling for personal growth and development. The argument of the next chapter is that the most important inequality from the standpoint of the development of autonomous, self-activating people is the unequal distribution of time spent on rewarding, emancipatory, psychologically productive activities. Sharing out the time available for rewarding activities means also sharing out the time spent on unrewarding activities. As with all forms of redistribution, this will be resisted, perhaps more determinedly than any other form of redistribution. It is remarkable how frequently this issue is avoided by assuming some felicitous distribution of personal preferences broadly corresponding to the existing division of labour, to the existing distribution of the social tasks that need to be performed and the time spent in performing them.

Fully developed democracy, a self-governing society, will be achieved to the extent that people participate on a basis of equality with one another. How does this proposition relate to Beetham's concept of 'personal autonomy' (Beetham 1981, p. 198) and Held's model of 'democratic autonomy' (Held 1987, p. 290)? Both envisage autonomy in the form of equal rights to participate in public affairs, in Held's case enshrined in a constitution and a bill of rights. However, Held argues, 'it is one thing to recognize a right, quite another to say it follows that everyone must, irrespective of choice, actually participate in public life. Participation is not a necessity' (Held 1987, p. 291). While recognizing that within a model of democratic autonomy citizens would have obligations, Held's position is that there would be no legal obligation to participate in public life. Although he does not say so explicitly, he seems also to hold that there would be no moral obligation to participate either.

I agree with Beetham and Held that the concept of personal autonomy, together with a robust set of rights defining and safeguarding it, are an essential part of a democratic society. People can only be self-activating subjects if they are autonomous. There can therefore be no question of compelling people to participate.[14] For the same reason, it is likely that a self-governing society would not compel people to work, making this possible, perhaps, by paying everyone an unconditional basic income by virtue solely of their status as citizens (Purdy forthcoming). However, the absence of legal and economic compulsion does not necessarily mean an absence of social expectation and moral obligation.

There are two reasons why people should be expected to participate in running the society in which they live. First, as has already been argued, such participation contributes to personal development, with beneficial consequences for society as a whole, as well as for the individual. Second, if some people participate less, or not at all, in the running of society, others have to participate more. Apart from the danger of perpetuating the division of people into the governed and the governing, and thus inhibiting movement towards a self-governing society, this also has adverse effects on those who end up spending more of their time running things. There are other rewarding and emancipatory activities as well as participation in public affairs. Of course, a moral obligation to undertake a fair share of public responsibilities would not mean 'an obligation to get involved in all aspects of public life' (Held 1987, p. 292); and the distinction between moral and legal obligation is crucial. Yet there should be some obligation.

Like the socialization of the means of production, the democratization of society is a process. Lively suggests

> three criteria by which the degree of democracy in any community may be tested – firstly the extent to which all constituent groups are incorporated into the decision-making processes, or negatively the extent to which some groups are excluded from or under-endowed with political influence; secondly, the extent to which governmental decisions are subject to popular control, the extent that is of responsible government; thirdly, the degree to which ordinary citizens are involved in public administration, the extent that is of the experience of ruling and being ruled. (Lively 1979, p. 51)

With the provisos, first, that public administration is interpreted to include all organized collective activity and, second, that the involvement of all citizens in their fair share of such activity would in fact end the distinction between ordinary and other citizens, the application of Lively's criteria gives a good indication of the extent to which a society has become self-governing.

7

Abolition of the Social Division of Labour

7.1   Introduction

Division of labour is a ubiquitous feature of social life. It makes possible specialization and with it increased efficiency in the performance of certain types of work. It allows some people to concentrate on work that they prefer. At the same time, division of labour and specialization also produce narrowness and historically have always been associated with inequality. The classical Marxist objective of abolishing the division of labour, in particular the distinction between mental and manual labour, arose from recognition of the alienating and distorting consequences of narrow specialisation and the inequality inherent in a hierarchical ordering of people within the labour process. It was an objective to be achieved gradually, in the long run, as one of the central characteristics of a fully communist society.[1]

This classical Marxist approach to the division of labour has long been objected to as at best naively utopian and at worst menacingly illiberal: utopian on the grounds that not everyone is capable of doing everything; illiberal because of a supposed implication of imposed collectivist uniformity. There is also the objection that abolition of the division of labour is just impractical, since modern society is built on complex cooperative activity with each person involved playing her or his part. For most Marxists, as well as non-Marxists, abolition of the division of labour is today not a live issue. Instead, emphasis is placed on an uneasy combination of equality of opportunity in the competition to enter different occupations and equality of status between occupations.

The major exception in recent years has been Bahro, on whose work the argument of this chapter is largely based. His guiding principle, which I share, is that society has now reached the level of development at which it is possible to separate the functional hierarchy necessary for organizing central aspects of social life from the hierarchical social structure with which it has historically been associated. The essential distinction is between the functional, or technical, and the social, or traditional, division of labour. The argument is that it is now possible to abolish the social division of labour while retaining the functional division of labour, with people sharing between them the different levels of functional activity that are necessary (Bahro 1978, pp. 436–7).

The functional division of labour refers to the different kinds of specific work, the different detailed tasks, that have to be carried out in any given society, whereas the social division of labour consists of the social stratification of people into groups possessing differential social power based on relationships of domination and subordination. Historically the two have been fused together. The activities making up social life have to be organized. This involves functional activities, specific work, detailed tasks, at the levels of planning, direction, regulation and execution. Since most people spend the whole of their working lives performing functional tasks at the same level, frequently the same detailed task, the characteristics of the tasks and of the people undertaking them become indistinguishable. A minority of people spend their lives planning, directing and regulating the work of others, who spend their lives being planned, directed and regulated. A technical hierarchy of functional tasks is paralleled by a social hierarchy of people with differential power and status.

Bahro's argument, following Marx, is that while there was in the past an objective necessity for the two hierarchies to be fused together today this is no longer the case: a technical hierarchy of functional tasks remains an objective necessity of organized social life; the social hierarchy historically associated with it is today increasingly anachronistic. The possibility exists for the planning, direction and regulation of social life to cease to be the possession of a distinct social group and to become the property of everyone, of self-activating people in a self-governing society. Thus, Bahro argues, 'everyone should perform an equal share in activities at the various functional levels' (Bahro 1978, p. 274), in the planning, running and regulation of social life as well as in the subordinate functions that are necessary.[2]

Abolition of the social division of labour is necessary for people to become self-activating and self-governing. It is possible because in the advanced capitalist and statist countries productive potential has developed to such an extent that the social surplus in excess of the requirements of basic subsistence is now sufficient to provide everyone with the resources necessary for the self-development needed to become self-activating. The subversive and revolutionary twist that Bahro gives to this classical Marxist precondition for socialism/communism is to conduct the discussion in terms not of surplus labour or product but of surplus consciousness. He insists that it is the characteristics of the activities that people engage in, what they spend their time doing, that retards or advances their development towards becoming self-activating subjects. That is why he describes the process of overcoming the social division of labour as involving a cultural revolution.

The emphasis of this chapter is on abolition of the social division of labour interpreted as the stratification of people into those who perform functions and exercise social power at the level of systems and sub-systems as a whole and those who perform partial functions and are the objects of the exercise of social power by others. The chapter also considers abolition of the social division of labour in the sense of an end to the division of labour between those who nurture and those who are nurtured. Abolition in both senses would inevitably involve major changes in personal, intra-extended family and intra-living group relationships. It would, therefore, have far-reaching effects on the experience of infancy and early childhood and would thus influence people's early psychological characteristics, their young personalities. This in turn would have important consequences for people's potential for becoming self-activating and self-determining. However, discussion of these very early formative influences is beyond the scope of this book.

Bahro's analysis starts from an abstract analysis of the concept of social consciousness, which he divides into absorbed, or necessary, consciousness and surplus consciousness. Absorbed consciousness is that part of social consciousness used up in producing the basic requirements of human existence. This covers routine production and reproduction and also the hierarchy of knowledge associated with it. Surplus consciousness is what remains. It is free consciousness, not required for the organization and production of the conditions of daily life but available to us to use for good or ill according to the possibilities offered by the way in which society is structured.[3]

Surplus consciousness is used in two ways, for compensatory activity and for emancipatory activity:

> *compensatory* interests, first of all, are the unavoidable reaction to the way that society restricts and stunts the growth, development, and confirmation of innumerable people at an early age. The corresponding needs are met with substitute satisfactions. People have to be indemnified, by possession and consumption of as many things and services as possible . . . for the fact that they have an inadequate share in the proper human needs . . . *emancipatory* interests, on the other hand are oriented to the growth, differentiation and self-realization of the personality in all dimensions of human activity. (Bahro 1978, p. 272)

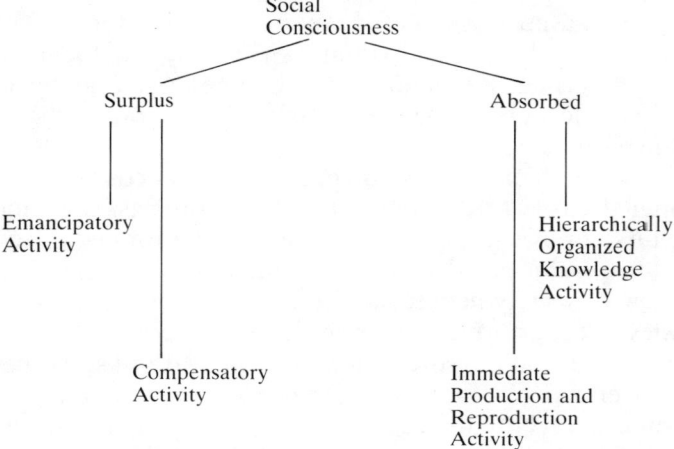

Figure 7.1   Bahro's taxonomy of social consciousness

Bahro's taxonomy of social consciousness is represented in figure 7.1 (derived from Bahro 1978, table 3, p. 315). As the educational and cultural level of society rises, so surplus consciousness becomes relatively more important and absorbed consciousness relatively less. However, the existing social division of labour prevents this growing surplus consciousness from taking the form of emancipatory activity. Instead, surplus consciousness is channelled into compensatory activity, especially privatized consumption. Since compensatory activity tends to be psychologically unproductive, discontent accumulates and this constitutes an ever increasing potential for change. At the same time, the pressure for economic growth associated with increased compensatory consumption poses a major ecological threat. Thus, abolition of the social division of labour is not only possible but also necessary. It cannot be postponed until sometime in the distant, utopian communist future but must be started now.

Absorbed and surplus consciousness are present in everybody, although in differing proportions. What characterizes absorbed consciousness in both capitalist and statist societies is that it is primarily subaltern. There are two aspects to activity that gives rise to subaltern consciousness – functional and social. First, functional activity confined to the execution of partial tasks, the performance of which does not require conceptualizing and operating at the level of a system or sub-system as a whole, on its own produces only a partial or sectional consciousness, devoid of an overall view. Second, experience wholly confined to activity that is directed by others produces consciousness that is simultaneously deferential, because of permanent subordination to others, and oppositional, because of resistance to that subordination. In both aspects, subaltern experience consists in activity that is determined at higher levels within a hierarchy, in the one case a hierarchy of technical function, in the other a hierarchy of social power. If people's entire experience is of this character they develop subaltern consciousness.[4]

What this amounts to is that subalternity consists in people performing the role of and being treated as objects, precluded from deciding on their own activities. The alternative is for people to become self-activating subjects, deciding for themselves on the basis of an overall view of society how social life should be organized and, within that framework, performing their share of the necessary planning and directing activities and also the necessary partial tasks. To be able to participate effectively in society's planning and directing activities requires in general both the expertise gained from higher education and the experience gained from actually participating. Hence, to overcome subalternity the social division of labour must be abolished.

Within existing societies, routine activities concerned with immediate production and reproduction are unambiguously subaltern and give rise to the general phenomena of alienation, instrumentalism and apathy. Activities concerned with planning and direction within the hierarchy of organized knowledge are also largely subaltern, because in existing societies they are inseparable from a position within the hierarchy of social power. Except at the very highest levels, this involves relationships of subordination with superiors and superordination with inferiors. However, the situation is contradictory. Activities at higher levels within the hierarchy of technical function increasingly require the ability to conceptualize and operate systems or sub-systems as a whole. They therefore carry with them the possibility of transcending subaltern consciousness. Yet to gain access to such activities involves competing for and occupying positions within the hierarchy of social power, which tends to produce subaltern consciousness.

People whose absorbed consciousness has been used in ways that produce subalternity will tend to be unable to use their surplus consciousness in emancipatory activities, since these require autonomy and self-activation. Instead, they will tend to seek compensatory activities. Bahro, correctly I think, emphasizes privatized consumption as the principal form of compensatory activity. However, he perhaps fails to recognize the element of contradiction potentially present. Although not involving participation in the planning and direction of social life, some forms of reaction to alienation, particularly those informed by a conscious alternative philosophy of life, do seem to be associated with a large measure of autonomy and self-activation, for example, local trade union activism or hippy communes. Consciousness is still subaltern, in that it is oppositional or disaffected, but at the level of subjectivity it is largely self-activating.

Nevertheless, to the extent that privatized consumption of goods and services is the main source of compensatory satisfaction it is self-defeating and the continued existence of the social division of labour that gives rise to it is a major threat to the ecology of the planet. As surplus consciousness increases there is an unending demand for more compensatory consumption, a revolution of rising expectations. This is what underlies the still predominant view that continuous, preferably faster, economic growth is necessary. It is what allows conservative realists to argue that there will always be scarcity, that the communist vision of abundance is utopian nonsense. It threatens the earth's ecological balance and with it the conditions of existence of the human species itself.

As long as the social division of labour and alienation persist, and demand for compensatory consumption continues to increase, so long will there be pressure for continued quantitative accumulation. If the concept of abundance is defined solely from the supply side, in terms of ever more material output to satisfy ever rising demand, it will certainly never be achieved. Only if it is approached increasingly from the side of demand is it a useful concept for thinking about the future.[5] Whereas subaltern consciousness emphasizes quantity, emancipated consciousness is more concerned with quality, since it is the quality of life that is central to personal growth and development. The crucial inequality in modern society is in the distribution not of output but of access to emancipatory activities, activities that contribute to personal growth and development.

In Bahro's view this is a major, perhaps the major, source of optimism: 'Precisely because the nature of inequality in our society no longer hangs on the private appropriation of material goods (although there still is this), but rather on the privileged appropriation of culture as determined by the division of labour, a culture whose sources today are no longer inherently scarce, the cultural revolution need not on the whole take away from some people what it gives to others' (Bahro 1978, pp. 364–5). I think Bahro is correct to stress this public good aspect of culture, the fact that the acquisition of culture by those who are at present culturally underprivileged does not require culture to be taken away from those already possessing it. What the generalization of culture will involve, however, is an end to its character as a positional good, to the complacent snobbery of those whose sense of identity and self-importance derives from the fact that they possess something that others do not.[6]

7.2   The Functional Division of Labour

The objection that it is impractical to abolish the division of labour because modern society is built on complex cooperative activity is clearly valid if it refers to the fact that many different functional tasks have to be performed. A functional division of labour is a necessary part of any developed form of social organization. What is not necessary is the social division of labour, with people spending their entire lives performing tasks at the same level in the technical hierarchy of functional tasks. That is the central theme of this chapter. However, the social division of labour exists not only within the sphere of production in the conventional economic sense. It is also present within the domestic sphere. Abolition of the social division of labour involves abolition of the sexual division of labour as much as of the division between mental and manual labour.

The functional division of labour can be analysed initially in terms of two dimensions, horizontal and vertical. Thus, at one horizontal level there are many different types of, say, skilled manual labour, and at another horizontal level many different types of, say, professional skill; yet in the vertical dimension the former skills are normally thought of as being at a lower level than the latter. Within the vertical dimension, unskilled manual labour is typically considered to be the lowest level of activity and perhaps planning and directing, or possibly some professional or artistic activities, the highest level. The actual vertical ranking of different horizontal levels of activity in existing societies reflects both the intrinsic characteristics of different sorts of activity and the values of the society, which in turn reflect history and the distribution of social power in the society.

Both the horizontal and the vertical functional division of labour are necessary. It is clearly impossible for people to perform every type of task at every level. Within the horizontal dimension, say at the level of skilled crafts or of professional skills, people cannot be equally skilled at everything. With respect to the vertical dimension, in any organized activity of any complexity people cannot operate simultaneously at each vertical level at which tasks have to be undertaken. However, it is possible to envisage people in the course of their lives performing at least one task, possibly more than one, at each level of functional activity. If the objective is to abolish the social division of labour, to share out the different tasks that have to be performed at each functional level, it is necessary to classify different sorts of activity according to their intrinsic characteristics, that is, the characteristics that determine their scope for contributing to personal development.

Bahro identifies five vertical levels of functional activity within overall social labour: simple and schematic work demanding particularized experiential knowledge; complex specialist work involving generalized vocational experiential knowledge; work involving the application of established scientific and technological principles; creative scientific work; and work concerned with understanding and taking decisions at the level of the economy or society as a whole (Bahro 1978, table 1, p. 164). Hegedus classifies work according to the demands made on human skills and the degree of control people exercize over their own and/or other people's work. He identifies three categories of manual work on the basis of the first consideration, and five categories of non-manual work on the basis of both considerations. He then draws a distinction between relationships of technical and of personal dependence, corresponding to that between the functional and the social division of labour (Hegedus 1977, pp. 49–54).

The general case for the abolition of the social division of labour is that different levels of activity within the functional hierarchy make different demands on people's capabilities. They are intrinsically more and less rewarding in terms of their potential for human development, in the extent to which they are psychologically productive. It follows that, if people spend their whole lives working at the same functional level, the activities conducive to self-development will be monopolized by some people, while others will be confined to psychologically and intellectually unrewarding activities and their development as human beings will be stunted. This is what is meant by the vivid references to the 'intellectual pauperism' (Deutscher 1972, p. 204) of the masses that are so characteristic of classical Marxist writing.

However, it is not just those confined to intrinsically unrewarding activities who lose out. Those who monopolize such activities are themselves ghettoized in enclaves of privilege, cut off from experience of the different levels of functional activity and from the people confined to them. In both respects their practical knowledge of functional and social systems is limited. This lack of practical experiential knowledge is personally restricting. It also prevents those who currently plan and run functional activities from doing so as effectively as would be possible if they had personal experience of activity at the different functional levels involved. Abolition of the social division of labour would thus increase the effectiveness of social organization and hence the possibilities for collective as well as individual self-determination.

Within this general case for the abolition of the social division of labour, Bahro's particular emphasis, with which I agree, is on the necessity for everyone to have access to and experience of activity at the level of a totality, that is, activity involved in planning and running a system as a whole. There is no substitute for such experience if people are to transcend subaltern consciousness, to become self-activating and self-governing. This, ultimately, is what is meant by overcoming the division between mental and manual labour. Nevertheless, the insights of feminism have added a new and crucial dimension to the analysis of the functional division of labour by insisting on the centrality of domestic labour, caring work and interpersonal skills.

One way of incorporating this new dimension into the framework used so far would be to divide each horizontal level grouping of functional activities into two. Thus, the functional level covering skilled manual work, or professional work, would be subdivided into work concerned primarily with nurturing people and work primarily of an impersonal character. In one sense the same level of skill would be required in both subdivisions, in another sense the quality of the demands made on human potentialities and the sort of self-development offered would differ. However, for the argument of this chapter there is no need to attempt a definitive classification of different categories of social activity. All that is required is agreement that the multiplicity of functional tasks that have to be undertaken in society can in principle be grouped into categories which have significantly different characteristics. Abolition of the social division of labour then consists in moving towards a situation in which everybody does their fair share of each category of functional activity.

I shall illustrate what this might mean in terms of the five categories of social activity that it seems to me desirable for everyone to participate in. These are planning and running, creative activity, nurturing, skilled activity, and unskilled and repetitive activity. The first four categories, freed from the relationships of domination and subordination arising from the hierarchy of social power, are in different ways psychologically productive and contribute to the realization of human potentiality. The fifth category is psychologically unproductive and an important objective of planning should be to reduce the amount of such activity that has to be undertaken. However, it is unlikely that it will ever be completely abolished and what remains should be shared.

Nothing turns on the particular categories I have chosen and I am certainly not suggesting that any particular task can be assigned unambiguously to any one category. For instance, much nurturing activity is both skilled and creative. The categories actually found to be most meaningful will be determined democratically as the struggle for an equal distribution of culture proceeds. Within each category there is a wide variety of different specific activities from which people would choose. There is no suggestion that everyone should do everything. Similarly, there is no suggestion that people would necessarily undertake activities from more than one category at the same time, although they might. What is being suggested is that there should be an expectation that, in the course of a lifetime, people would undertake activities within each category roughly corresponding to their share of the activities socially necessary or available within each category. The categories, and samples of options within them, are represented schematically in figure 7.2.

Category of Social Activity	*Illustrative Examples within Category*
Planning and Running	Running bodies responsible for functional services Running production units and other workplaces Running voluntary, self-governing groups Serving on representative bodies
Creative	Artistic, scientific Design Some higher education and research Some professional
Nurturing	Care of the young, the ill, the disabled, the old Personal support Primary education
Skilled	Secondary education Skilled craft and technical Skilled non-manual Some higher education and research Some professional
Unskilled and Repetitive	Assembly-line Cleaning and housework Copytyping Driving Labouring Refuse collection

Figure 7.2   Categories of social activity

The order in which the different categories of social labour are listed is not necessarily intended to convey an order of desirability or worthwhileness. In a way, the first as well as the last category might be regarded as consisting of tasks that people would prefer not to get involved in. The first category, planning and running, covers both the administration of systems and participation in the representative aspects of a self-governing society. It may be that the administration of systems will become so routinized as to become boring, although it seems unlikely. It may be that people would prefer to concentrate on creative, nurturing, skilled activities, rather than participate in the process of self-government, although to the extent that we become self-activating this is also unlikely. Whatever the outcome, somebody has to undertake these tasks, so it seems reasonable that everyone should be expected to do their share. Furthermore, as argued in the previous section, participation at the level of a totality is a necessary experience for the overcoming of subaltern consciousness and its transformation into the consciousness of an autonomous, self-activating subject.

The last category is less problematic. Unskilled and repetitive drudgery has nothing to recommend it. It is a measure of the power of ideology that the inhumanity of people spending their entire working lives on such activities should for so long, and still today, be regarded as natural, normal or, however regrettable, necessary. Even so, provided it is not part of a life sentence, there may sometimes be a positive aspect to work within this category. There are times in most people's lives when a period of undemanding routine activity, without responsibility, is what they need. Similarly, hard physical activity, for limited periods, has its own satisfactions. What is destructive of the human spirit is the prospect and reality of a lifetime spent on such work. Social life needs to be restructured so that people are able to realize their potentialities, to develop their individuality, by spending most of their time cooperating with others in creative, nurturing, skilled activities.

The abolition of the social division of labour, the restructuring of social life to enable everyone to engage in their fair share of activities within each category of social labour, has implications for the organization of education, work and domestic life.

In both capitalist and statist societies the educational system is structured to perpetuate the existing social division of labour. People are educated to the level appropriate for the category of social labour they are expected to perform throughout their lives. This is what underlies the concept of 'manpower' planning. There is formal equality of opportunity in the competition to enter the higher levels of education but the proportions in which different levels of education are available broadly correspond to the pyramidic structure of the existing fused hierarchies of the social and functional divisions of labour. By contrast, Markus and Hegedus have proposed the aim of overeducation. By this they mean two things: first, that people should receive more general education than is needed for any specific role in the functional division of labour; and, second, that more people should be trained for each functional role than are actually needed (Markus and Hegedus 1976, p. 121). Overeducation in these two senses would make it possible for people to retrain for more than one specific role and to learn to participate at each functional level.

Within the workplace it is possible to envisage the sharing of activities at different levels. Responsibility for running a department, an enterprise or a service can rotate. Much unskilled or repetitive work, like cleaning or copytyping, can be undertaken by people alongside their creative, nurturing, skilled activities. More broadly, the concept of one full-time job for life is no longer appropriate. Shorter, more flexible working weeks, years, lives, will make it possible for people to change jobs, retrain for different functional roles, combine paid work with unpaid activities, and take time out of paid work altogether. People tend to have different preoccupations and to be better suited to different types of activity at different stages in their lives. Real responsibility for and involvement in bringing up young children is difficult to combine with a conventionally defined full-time career. Heavy manual labour and long or unsocial hours are perhaps best undertaken when young.

The sexual, or gender, division of labour is evident in the workplace, where women are concentrated in low-paid, servicing, part-time jobs, and in domestic life, where women service men and care for the young, the ill and the old. The restructuring of education and paid work will make possible the redistribution of domestic labour, both the drudgery and the nurturing, and at the same time cannot be achieved without it. Changes within the home will be involved, without prejudice to the way in which the concept of the home may alter in the future, and there will also need to be changes outside the home, with the development of new forms of community or state care, probably a partnership between the two. In the sphere of paid work, abolition of the sexual division of labour requires, among other things, moving beyond the situation in which nurturing others is effectively women's work. Within both the home and the community it will require continuing struggle to end the double burden borne by women by ensuring that men do their fair share.

Although a long way off, the abolition of the social division of labour, the division between people who perform mental and those who perform manual labour, between men's and women's work, is an entirely realistic objective. In a society in which it had been achieved, socially necessary labour would be organized so that people in the course of their lives would have access to, and would be expected to undertake, their fair share of each category of social activity. The discussion in this section has outlined how socially necessary labour might be organized in such a society. The next section considers the major objections that might be made to this revolutionary proposal.

7.3   The Social Division of Labour

If abolition of the social division of labour is as realistic an objective as I have claimed in the previous section, why is it so widely regarded as utopian, even from within the Marxist tradition? For instance, Selucky writes, 'The nature of modern production requires a division of labour among those who manage and those who are managed – a difference between mental and physical labour' (Selucky 1972, p. 44) and he refers to, 'the conditions of social division of labour and scarcity which, as one may reasonably expect, will prevail in any foreseeable future' (Selucky 1979, p. 83). Similarly, Sik argues that, 'At the socialist stage of development *labour is still relatively onerous* (long hours) *and intensive*. There is a *relative lack of variety*, work is monotonous and, for most people, offers little creative scope. There is still a *fairly rigid division of labour*, binding the majority to *one occupation for life*' (Sik 1967, p. 139). From a somewhat different tradition, Nove takes it for granted that 'The state cannot be run meaningfully by all its citizens, and so there is bound to be a division between governors and governed. Also ships will have captains, newspapers will have editors, factories will have managers, planning offices will have chiefs' (Nove 1983, p. 197).

It could be that the problem is one of terminology, stemmimg from a failure to distinguish clearly between the functional and the social division of labour. References to a division between the managers and the managed or the governors and the governed may be intended as statements about the different functional roles being performed at any given time, rather than about a more or less permanent, lifetime division between those who run and those who are run. It could also be that the problem is one of timing, of different judgements about whether the objective circumstances for an end to the lifetime division of people into the runners and the run are yet ripe. After all, Sik refers to the socialist stage of development in terms which suggest that there is something beyond it and Nove is referring to 'feasible' socialism – 'a state of affairs which could exist in some major part of the developed world within the lifetime of a child already conceived' (Nove 1983, p. 197).

Nevertheless, whatever the position of these writers, and I get a distinct sense of 'The wisdom of resignation' (Bahro 1978, p. 375), there are some real questions that have to be faced. First, is everyone capable of functioning at each level? Perhaps those currently operating at the top of the functional hierarchy could do their own copytyping, empty dustbins and work on assembly-lines, but is the opposite true? Second, even if in principle everyone could perform functions at each level, is the skill and experience required for some functional tasks, or some levels of artistic and scientific excellence, such that they can only be attained through a lifetime's specialization, with no time left over for other categories of social labour? Third, is society's productive potential sufficiently developed, is labour productivity high enough, for everyone to be educated and trained to the level necessary for them to operate at each functional level, even if we were all capable of it? Can society afford it? Fourth, even if we could all undertake tasks in each category of social labour and resources were available to make this possible, perhaps people are relatively better at some things than others, perhaps they would prefer to concentrate on what they are best at or like best?

Explicit or implicit answers to these questions underlie the prevailing assumption in present socialist and democratic discussion that the social division of labour, in the sense of people spending their working lives primarily at one functional level, will be with us for the foreseeable future. Rather than seeking the abolition of the social division of labour, emphasis is placed on ways of moving towards greater social equality within its framework and of achieving greater control by the governed over the governors. The strength of this approach is that it starts from present reality. Its concerns are an essential part of the process of moving towards the abolition of the social division of labour and the creation of a self-governing society. However, its potential weakness is that, by assuming a permanent division between people and seeking to devise a more humane way of living with that division, it runs the danger of confirming and perpetuating inequality instead of confronting it and contributing to its erosion and eventual abolition.

Movement towards greater social equality within a framework of continued social as well as functional division of labour is seen as having two aspects to it. The first is greater equality of opportunity – ideally the creation of the economic, social and personal conditions that would transform the existing formal situation into one of real equality of opportunity. This could mean one of two things. It is usually taken to mean that people enter the race of life on equal terms with each other. Society's functional requirements determine the number of slots available in each functional role. People compete for one of the limited number of slots in their preferred functional role, with no handicaps due to their class or social background, ethnic status, sex or gender formation. With equal life-chances their success, or failure, would be entirely due to their individual characteristics. In the absence of reasons to suppose the existence of differential innate ability or preferences between groups, evidence that equality of opportunity had been achieved would be equal statistical representation of any definable group in each functional role. If there were such reasons, then the expected statistical distribution would have to be weighted accordingly.

Alternatively, equality of opportunity could mean that people had equal access to the resources required to develop their potentialities to the full. If these resources are not only material but also, and primarily, cultural and if their appropriation involves the active engagement by people, learning by doing, in activities within each category of social labour, then this interpretation of equality of opportunity is compatible with, possibly equivalent to, the abolition of the social division of labour. Its realization would require a society organized with the explicit objective of providing people with access to activities in each category – all people if they turned out all to have the ability and the inclination. Instead of shaping people's education, training and work experience to the requirements of social labour, social labour would have to be shaped to the requirements of people's self-development.

The second aspect to the achievement of greater social equality in the context of the continued social division of labour is seen as movement towards greater equality of status between different categories of activity. The fact that people do different things is not seen as being a problem. What constitutes a problem, it is argued, is that society values different activities differently and accords them differential status. Thus, there are many high status, highly paid jobs that many people, perhaps most, would regard as socially useless or even damaging. More generally, the argument is that all categories of activity, although not all activities within each category, are socially necessary and should therefore be equally regarded, equally valued. What is needed, then, is a change in perceptions, perhaps assisted by an inverse relationship between pay and the intrinsically rewarding characteristics of different jobs in order to equalize the combination of monetary and non-monetary benefits from each job. People would then be able to choose, according to their abilities and preferences, between equally valued functional roles equally rewarded with different combinations of extrinsic and intrinsic satisfaction.[7]

The problem with this argument is that while there is obviously something in it there is not much. It is true that what comes to be regarded as women's work is systematically undervalued in all societies. However, with this major exception of the undervaluation of nurturing activities, the status attached to most activities, the social valuation they enjoy, reflects to a significant extent their intrinsic characteristics, their potential for self-development. The reason why unskilled and repetitive activities have a low status is because they deserve it. There is nothing to be said for a life spent in drudgery, however socially necessary the work itself may be.

Within the skilled category the situation is more complicated. High status skilled manual or professional activities in existing societies reflect as often as not history and the social power of particular sectional interests, usually buttressed by trade union organization or the influence of professional associations. Similar considerations apply also within the creative and the planning and running categories, as defined in existing societies. Nevertheless, there clearly are differences in the intrinsic characteristics of different categories of activity, with different implications for personal development. It is unconvincing to suggest that the present distribution of people between different occupations reflects the personal preferences and real choices of autonomous, self-activating people and that all that is needed is a change in social perceptions.

Policies to increase social equality by increasing equality of opportunity and altering the social evaluation of different sorts of work are likely to be contradictory. On the one hand, they are subversive of the existing distribution of resources and power. On the other hand, in the absence of a transformatory element, they are consistent with a conservative vision of a meritocratic society in which the monopolization of cultural resources and the continued exercise of social power by the successful are obscured by a spurious ideology of equal worth. A transformatory element can be imparted by interpreting equality of opportunity not as equal chances in a competition for limited places but as equal access to the resources required for self-development. If the view that this involves access to all the different categories of social activity is correct, then this means consciously moving towards the abolition of the social division of labour.

A similar objection applies to the argument that the objective should be to devise ways of enabling the ruled to exercise more effective control over the rulers, rather than seeking to abolish the distinction between the two. Policies for more information and greater accountability are essential as part of a process of moving towards a self-governing society. However, their effectiveness is necessarily limited. In the context of a perspective of the permanent division of people into rulers and ruled, they are consistent with the perpetuation of political passivity and subalternity on the part of the ruled, with the social power of the rulers again obscured, this time by an ideology of non-participatory democratic control. A sketch of how an actively self-governing society might organize itself was attempted in the previous chapter.

The case for consciously seeking to build into present policies, designed to deal with existing reality, a transformatory tension, designed to change existing reality by moving towards the abolition of the social division of labour, does not require a definitive answer to the four questions posed at the beginning of this section. The way to discover whether everyone is capable of undertaking activities in each category is to ensure that everyone has the possibility of doing so. This means planning social activity in such a way that everyone has access to all categories of activity, without thereby depriving others of access to them.

The question of whether the skill and experience involved in some types of work, or in the highest levels of artistic and scientific excellence, require a lifetime of specialization is at first sight more difficult. Time, above all, is what is needed for all worthwhile activity, perhaps especially for creative activity. Is it impossible to achieve excellence in one activity and yet in the course of a lifetime also do a fair share of activities in other categories? I doubt it. I suspect that the crucial determinant is the social ethos. However, since compulsion is not envisaged, this is something that will be worked out in practice. Given a social expectation that people should undertake their share of each category of activity, in order to enable others to do the same, and a society planned to make that possible, I would expect that in general people would find ways of doing so, although it is possible that socially recognized and morally acceptable exceptions would emerge.

Resource availability is perhaps the most serious issue. Those who discount the possibility of abolishing the social division of labour frequently do so on the grounds that scarcity will always be with us, that a state of abundance is a pipe dream. The argument has two strands. First, it is claimed that the resources required to provide, say, higher education for everyone are just not available. Second, the standard argument that there is a trade-off between efficiency and equality, and that inequality is justifiable if it results in increased output that makes everyone better off (Meade 1964), is extended to the social division of labour. It is argued that if people are relatively better at doing some things than others it is inefficient to take turns since output would then be less than it could be and some people would be worse off than they need be.

However, following Bahro, I have already argued that, in the more advanced societies at least, the problem is primarily one of cultural not material resources. The problem of resource availability in these countries has to be tackled primarily from the demand side. As long as the social division of labour, alienation and subaltern consciousness are justified on the grounds of scarcity, and therefore persist, the prophecy of limitless material wants will be self-fulfilling. Competition and alienation generate discontent and a demand for ever more compensatory consumption. At issue are society's values and priorities and in existing societies these are determined within a social structure in which some people have social power and others do not.

The argument for the social division of labour on the grounds of efficiency is an application of the theory of comparative advantage and is vulnerable to the same objection. The comparative advantage argument for specialization in international trade is a short-run argument which assumes that each country's endowment of factors of production is given independently of the pattern of specialization. The comparable argument for the social division of labour assumes that people's endowments, their abilities, are independent of what they do. In this sense it is also a short-run argument, based on people as they perhaps are but with no transformatory element incorporating a dynamic towards what they might become. Of course, even if abolition of the social division of labour did turn out to be less efficient, in a narrow economic sense, which is unlikely, it might still be preferred on the basis of values that gave priority to the fullest possible personal self-development for everyone.

Finally, there is the question of whether people might prefer some activities to others. We may all be better at some things than others and might prefer to concentrate on them, irrespective of any efficiency considerations. In any case, would not a society in which everyone did the same things be monochrome and boring? Although frequently encountered, this argument is based on a misunderstanding. Within each category of activity there is scope for variety and choice – between different skilled work, between caring for the young and the old, between different forms of creative activity, between the planning and running of different social activities. Even unskilled work is of different types between which people may not be indifferent, for instance outdoor or indoor, manual or non-manual. Abolition of the social division of labour carries with it no implication that in the course of a lifetime everyone would have done exactly the same things.

However, this should not be taken as an argument in support of specialization between categories. Such specialization is self-evidently bad for those confined to drudgery. It is also bad for those who confine themselves to only one of the psychologically productive categories of activity. It seems unlikely that human potentialities are confined to any one category. Their fullest possible development is likely to require a combination of activities across categories rather than specialization within one category only. Variety between people will increase as the existing specialization within one category of activity becomes a combination of specializations drawn from each of five categories. Personal and social life are likely both to become infinitely richer.

7.4 Experts and Citizens

It has sometimes been suggested that the achievement of a self-governing society would require the simplification of the functional tasks of planning and running social activities so that anyone, and everyone, could undertake them at any time. However, it seems more likely that the expertise involved in political, economic and social life will increase rather than decrease. If so, effective participation in self-government is likely to require more expertise not less. Since we cannot all be experts in everything, does this mean that the project of moving towards self-government is doomed? This view, once again, stems from a failure to distinguish between the functional and the social division of labour. At issue is not the abolition of the functional division of labour between people who are experts in different things but the abolition of the social division of labour between experts and non-experts. We cannot all be experts in everything but we can all be experts in something.

Social activities of any degree of complexity involve administrative structures within which are brought together different types of functional expertise. For these administrative structures to be part of the institutions of a self-governing society they need to be at the service of society rather than, as at present, in a position of dominance above it. In the previous chapter the process of self-government was envisaged as one in which representative bodies and self-governing groups between them construct the social interest in relation to each social activity and work with the administrative structure involved to ensure its implementation. This development of civil society to the stage at which it has become self-governing cannot take place without overcoming the tyranny of the expert. However, far from abolishing expertise what is required is its generalization.

Horvat, in the context of a discussion of how economic enterprises should be run, draws a very clear distinction between what he calls

> the interest sphere and the professional sphere. . . . The former consists of policy decisions, the latter of professional work and administrative routine. Policy decisions are legitimised by political authority; executive and administrative work, by professional authority. The former represent value judgements; the latter, technical implementation. In the interest sphere, the rule of one man [sic], one vote applies; in the professional sphere, vote is weighted by professional competence. (Horvat 1982, p. 241)

The problem with this approach as it stands is that the professional sphere is conceptualized in terms of positivism, it is premised on an unproblematic view of professional authority.

I prefer the approach of the anarchist Bakunin:

> In the matter of boots, I refer to the authority of the bootmaker; concerning houses, canals or railroads, I consult that of the architect or the engineer. For such and such special knowledge I apply to such and such a *savant*. But I allow neither the bootmaker nor the architect nor the *savant* to impose his [sic] authority upon me. I listen to them freely and with all the respect merited by their intelligence, their character, their knowledge, reserving always my incontestable right of criticism and censure. I do not content myself with consulting a single authority in any special branch; I consult several; I compare their opinion, and choose that which seems to me the soundest. But I recognize no infallible authority, even in special questions. (Bakunin 1977, pp. 312–13)

There are two ways in which the tyranny of the expert can be overcome. First, it is essential that there is a pluralism of expert opinion available in each professional area. There is virtually never a complete consensus of expert opinion on any issue of significance. In existing societies, however, this fact is frequently obscured. There is a tendency for professionals to stick together. While they may disagree privately among themselves, there is a reluctance to engage in public disagreement, most noticeably perhaps in the case of the medical profession. A further source of foreclosed public discussion is the situation in which experts in a particular area are concentrated in a single enterprise or industry, as in the case of nuclear power. In the statist countries the situation has been made worse by the general absence of pluralism, the fetishization of science and the ideology of the 'correct' solution to a problem.

The demystification of professional expertise requires openness of information and opinion. It also requires alternative expert opinion to be available to people and to self-governing groups. In embryonic form this is already happening. Universities and other publicly funded institutions where research and expertise are concentrated are slowly becoming more accessible, although their external contacts are still overwhelmingly with state bodies or economic enterprises. Trade unions and other interest and cause groups are beginning to employ their own experts and research workers. Independent research groups, information centres and advice groups have also sprung up. In some cases decentralized units of political power, such as the Greater London Council before its abolition, finance sources of expertise independent of the central state and economic enterprises. Nevertheless, access to expertise is still largely monopolized by the state and economic management. Movement towards self-government requires that people in their capacity as citizens, within their self-governing groups, have access to multiple independent sources of expertise.

However, that by itself is not enough. The ability to make use of expert opinion is itself a skill, an expertise, which is acquired in part in the course of becoming and operating as an expert. In relation to most areas of expertise people will be citizens, with no specialist knowledge. On their own account, as members of self-governing groups, as representatives, they will frequently need to rely on expert opinion. They will need to know when expert opinion or help is needed, how to obtain it, how to evaluate different expert opinions and how to make effective use of the expertise available to them by forming a judgement about its overall implications for the purpose in hand. If the monopolization of expertise by the intelligentsia and the social power that goes with it are to be overcome then everyone needs to become an expert in something.

Professionals, experts, tend to treat each other as equals even though their areas of expertise are different. In this respect they are no different from any other group of people who spend their lives working at the same functional level. Skilled manual workers, for instance electricians and engineers, tend to be more at home with one another, irrespective of their trade, than they are with people in the same functional area but at a different functional level, for instance professional electrical and mechanical engineers. In existing societies there are two reasons for this. Given the fusion of the functional and social hierarchies, people whose activities are primarily within one category, who work primarily at one functional level, tend to belong to the same social class, with comparable backgrounds, income levels and lifestyles. They feel more comfortable with one another than with people from other social classes.

However, the hierarchy of knowledge also makes itself felt. A professional electrical or mechanical engineer is more likely to be able to assess the work of a skilled craftsperson in the same functional area than the other way round. The extent and degree of functional responsibility of the professional are also likely to be greater. The higher level of generality of the knowledge and expertise involved is what makes the difference. Of course, the competence of professionals who lack practical experience of the different functional levels of activity is likely to be less than that of professionals who have such experience. Nevertheless, within any complex social activity there is a hierarchy of function which involves Hegedus's relations of technical dependence. The crucial question is whether these relations of technical dependence are associated with relations of personal dependence. In part, this will depend on whether the technical relations are between experts and non-experts or between experts in that particular functional area and other experts, either in the same area, but currently performing a non-expert function, or in another functional area.

The abolition of the social division of labour would not involve a downgrading of expertise. Quite the opposite is the case. In existing societies the attitude of non-experts towards expertise is contradictory. On the one hand, it is revered as something mysterious and placed on a pedestal. On the other hand, it is treated with suspicion, even contempt, as expressed in the phrase blinding with science. These two attitudes, usually both present, reflect existing reality. Expertise is valuable but, for most people, it is alien and mysterious. It is also a source of social power and domination and is experienced as such by most people. The abolition of the social division of labour involves, among other things, all citizens becoming experts in something. Only as this occurs will the sense of awe and fear on the part of non-experts and the tendency towards arrogance and a sense of self-importance on the part of experts give way to a proper appreciation of the value of expertise. Only as everyone becomes an expert and develops the ability to form sensible judgements about areas in which they are not expert will the full potentialities of human beings for personal and collective self-development be realized.

7.5   Production, Planning and People

Socialization of the means of production, discussed in chapter 5, fully developed political and economic democracy and self-government, discussed in chapter 6, and abolition of the social division of labour, discussed in this chapter, are three different aspects of the same objective – self-determination by self-activating subjects in a self-governing society. Each aspect is envisaged as a part of the process in the course of which people, individually and collectively, gain increasing control over their lives, become increasingly able to make conscious, informed and effective decisions about how they want to live. Self-determination has both an objective and a subjective aspect to it or, perhaps more accurately, an external and an internal aspect. It involves the ability to make effective decisions about the determinants of the external framework within which we live. It also involves our being aware of the determinants of our internal lives, our subjectivity, so that we can, collectively and individually, shape the external framework to enable us to develop our human potentialities to the full.

In both capitalist and statist societies the second of these considerations is universally ignored. Discussion of economic organization is concerned with the production of goods and services. Controversy rages over whether production should be for profit or for use, whether coordination should take place *ex post* through the market mechanism or *ex ante* through planning, over which form of economic organization is most efficient at achieving macroeconomic stability, economic growth, innovation and consumer satisfaction. These are, of course, important questions but they are not the most important question. In the end, what matters is the relationship between economic activity and the sort of people we are, or become. The production of goods and services is also, and more importantly, the production of people.

If the social division of labour is to be abolished, production will have to be organized to enable everyone to participate at some stage in their lives in all categories of social activity, at all levels in the functional hierarchy. What is required is an economy planned to enable everyone to spend as much time as possible in psychologically productive, emancipatory activity that contributes to personal growth and self-development. Bahro, discussing socialism-communism, argues that '*the economy of individual time schedules* proves in fact to be *the decisive transition point in planning*' (Bahro 1978, p. 427). His claim, with which I agree, is that society's productive potential, the level of labour productivity, is now such as to make it possible for us, if we choose, to give increasing priority to the development of human potential, to the needs of personal development.

This would mean that economic planning would become progressively more and more concerned with the way people spend their time in the productive process, that is, with arriving at the matrix of productive activities that maximizes the amount of psychologically productive time available. Giving priority to the requirements for human development has implications for what is produced, how much is produced and how it is produced. The composition of output will differ according to whether it is for compensatory or emancipatory use. Higher levels of labour productivity can be used to produce more output or to reduce the amount of time spent in psychologically unproductive activities. The sort of technology we choose to develop and the way in which work is organized will change radically if human development becomes the primary objective.

Bahro proposes an economy of time made up of the time budgets of individuals. The objective is to structure social life so that the amount of time that has to be spent on psychologically unproductive activities is minimized and the amount available for psychologically productive activities is maximized. This is not the same thing as the reduction of socially necessary work to a minimum. Some work is psychologically productive and contributes to personal development. Indeed, in existing societies people who enjoy and get satisfaction from their work are highly privileged and, of course, a minority. What is required is '*priority for the shortening of psychologically unproductive labour-time within necessary labour-time*' (Bahro 1978, p. 415) and the sharing of both the necessary unproductive time that remains and the time then available for psychologically productive activities.

It should be evident, but may nevertheless be worth stressing, that a society in which the time available to people for psychologically productive activities is maximized, at work and in life as a whole, does not mean that people would be compelled to undertake activities according to a prescribed pattern. It means that we would all have the opportunity to dispose of the maximum possible amount of time in psychologically productive activities chosen by us. For that to be possible means that we must all have access to the necessary resources, which requires planning. The inner resource is our subjectivity, an autonomous, self-activating consciousness. The external resource is access to the different categories of psychologically productive activity. If together we plan society to ensure that these resources are available for each of us to make use of when we choose to do so, the rest is up to us.

Although this appears a long way off, the principle of collective responsibility for ensuring that the resources needed for people's self-development are available has long been accepted. The structure of education and training, provision for continuing and further education and for retraining, the concept of career development – all are recognition of this. In existing societies, however, the principle and its application are bedevilled by unquestioned acceptance of the social division of labour. Social provision, and people, are shaped to the demands of the economy, rather than the economy and social provision being shaped to the needs of people. The economy is organized on the basis of coercion by market forces or state direction, with people treated as objects to be manipulated in the process of producing other objects – the goods and services comprising economic output.

What is needed instead is an economic system that promotes the objective of self-determination by self-activating subjects in a self-governing society. Part IV develops a model of democratic planning that is consistent with this objective. The model is constructed around the concept of negotiated coordination. Unlike coordination through the coercion of market forces or state direction, negotiated coordination requires people to engage consciously with their interdependence and the consequences of their actions for others. It encourages people to transcend their sectional interests and take account also of the situation of others. It promotes cooperation on the basis of equality, mutual respect and a sense of community. In this sense, the process of negotiated coordination is potentially transformatory. It incorporates a dynamic, a momentum, towards a situation in which people take responsibility for the decisions that affect them. I believe that democratic planning through negotiated coordination is the form of economic organization most compatible with a society in which 'the human subjects of decision making are identical with its objects' (Holesovsky 1977, p. 59) – in other words, a self-governing society, communism.

PART IV

Democratic Planning

8

National Priorities and Planning

8.1 Democratic Planning: An Outline

The model of democratic planning developed in the next three chapters is one in which planning takes the form of a political process of negotiated coordination, with decisions being made and implemented, directly or indirectly, by those who are affected by them. Coercive coordination, whether through direction from above or the pressure of market forces, is replaced by conscious interaction and negotiation. This offers the possibility to those involved of modifying their perceptions and behaviour in the light of a detailed awareness of the way in which their own interests are interdependent with those of others. Thus, while conflicts of interest are not wished away, the process incorporates a transformatory dynamic in which particular interests are viewed in relation to one another and are integrated into a socially constructed general interest at each level of decision-making.

It is important to distinguish between the transformatory dynamic contained within the model and the process of transition from existing capitalist and statist societies to a society based on the model. The next three chapters are concerned with the model itself, offered as the form of economic organization appropriate to a self-governing society. The political process of transition, which of course also involves transformation, is considered in chapter 11.

The model is now briefly outlined before being developed in detail in the rest of Part IV. It assumes a democratic society, in which people participate through a variety of self-governing and representative bodies, with decision-making decentralized as much as possible, both functionally and vertically. National, regional and local representative assemblies, democratically elected in a context of political party pluralism, are vested with ultimate political power. Civil society is populated with autonomous, self-governing interest and cause groups coming together in chambers of interests. Collectively provided services are organized by functional social bodies, as vertically decentralized as possible, which coordinate their activities through negotiation. Economic activity of all types is undertaken by production units whose governing bodies consist of representatives of all those affected by their activities. Production units are organized internally on the basis of self-management.

Broad social priorities and changes in strategic direction are decided through the democratic political process on the basis of alternative plan variants prepared by the national planning commission. These priorities and strategic decisions determine the planned overall allocation of available resources between different uses and hence the planned distribution of purchasing power in the economy. They are also the basis for the determination of the primary input prices that are used by production units in setting their prices equal to long-run costs. The planning commission is responsible for major investment, sectoral coordination and regional distribution. A similar process occurs at the regional and local levels.

Production units meet demand from customers who in general have a choice of supplier. It is at this stage above all that the model of negotiated coordination differs from coordination through the atomistic response of autarchic production units to market forces, whether regulated or not. The pattern of demand reflects the desired structure of productive capacity, as determined by the decisions about overall distribution between alternative uses and the detailed decisions of social bodies and individuals. Desired structure and existing structure will only correspond in a steady state. In reality, some branches of production will need to contract and others will need to expand. Furthermore, within a particular branch of production the output of some production units may be preferred to that of others and there may, therefore, be a *prima facie* case for some units to expand and others to contract. The coordination of economic decisions only really becomes an issue when things are changing, when resources need to be reallocated, and capacity needs to be expanded or contracted through investment or disinvestment.

To reiterate the argument of chapter 1, 'economic planning essentially consists of an attempt to secure a co-ordinated set of investment-decisions *ex ante* – in advance of any commitment of resources to particular constructional projects or installations' (Dobb 1960, p. 5). In the model of negotiated coordination a distinction is drawn between the use of existing capacity, which is decided by production units in response to current demand, and changes in capacity, which are decided by negotiated coordination bodies covering all production units in a particular branch of production. Changes in productive capacity affect those who work in the production units concerned, and in interdependent production units, those who live in the communities where these units are located, customers, and usually also the concerns of some interest and cause groups. All would participate in the decision-making.

Negotiated coordination bodies for each branch of production, representing all those affected by the activities of the production units covered, would seek to arrive at an agreed set of investment decisions for their branch of production. They would take into account both the changing pattern of demand and the particular circumstances and interests of the production units, communities and other groups involved. Their activities would thus be a central part of the social construction of what is to count as socially useful productive activity. In this connection, they would pay particular attention to the implications of their decisions for the distribution of psychologically productive activities. A comparable process would be required for the coordination of investment decisions within sectors, where interdependence between branches of production is likely to be especially marked.

The institutional framework for the process of democratic planning through negotiated coordination at the national level is set out in figure 8.1. The national and regional planning commissions, negotiated coordination bodies and production units interact with one another to negotiate the coordinated set of investment decisions that constitutes economic planning. The constituent parts of the model, so far only sketched, are developed in the rest of Part IV.

The centrality of negotiation in the model may raise in some people's minds the potential problems of institutional sclerosis, stalemate and paralysis. There is also the related issue of sanctions. These questions are referred to in the exposition of the model but they are not its focus. The emphasis is rather on the development of a model in which the necessary information for effective centralized and decentralized decision-making in the social interest is generated without recourse to market forces. It is important to establish that this is possible in view of a widespread and growing belief to the contrary. The argument is that the necessary information can be obtained from a combination of socially shaped demand- and cost-based prices, on the one hand, and interest-based decision-making on the other. Once this has been established the issue of motivation can be addressed more fully. Of course, information and motivation cannot in the end be separated. Assumptions about motivation depend on a view about human beings and their potentialities. Market forces generate information through a process that reinforces narrowly self-interested motivation. The model of negotiated coordination, by contrast, generates information through

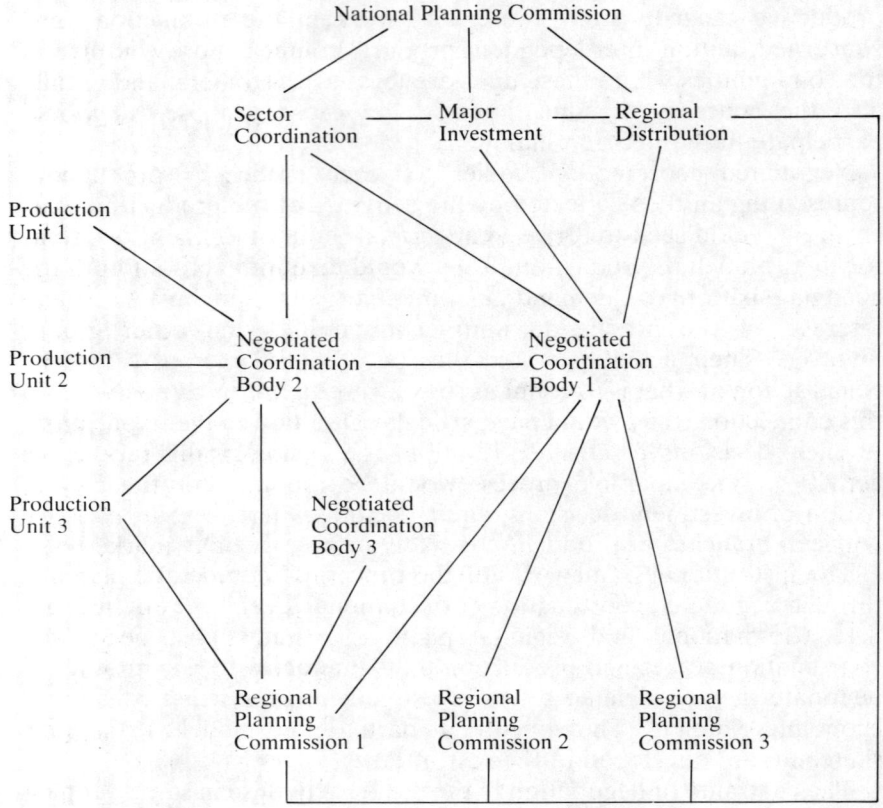

Figure 8.1   Outline framework for national negotiated coordination

Note   Not all linkages are shown. Interest and cause groups in particular are
omitted. The figure is an illustrative representation only. The constituent parts of
the model and their interrelationships are developed in detail as Part IV proceeds.

a transformatory process in which concern for others as well as for oneself
is encouraged and reinforced.

The rest of this chapter is concerned with the national level, with the
determination of the framework within which decentralized decision-
making takes place. An important omission is any explicit discussion of
the international dimension, although I believe that the basic principles of
negotiated coordination could be applied at that level and the model could
be adapted to take account of it. Chapter 9 deals with the regional and
local levels, with how the definition of what constitutes the social interest
is refined and how it is represented in the process of detailed economic
decision-making. Chapter 10 discusses the way in which decision-making

in the production units and negotiated coordination bodies would work and then considers the consistency of the model with macroeconomic balance. It ends with an assessment of the model as a whole.

8.2   Priorities and Allocation

Decisions about social priorities are inevitably political decisions. In a planned economy these decisions determine the desired structure of the overall allocation of resources and the desired strategic direction of development of the economy. At the national level only very broad priorities can be decided. National-level decisions would probably include: the desired macroeconomic distribution of resources between individual consumption, collective consumption, social investment and economic investment; desired developments in social policy and provision, for example education and health, and in the infrastructure, for example the energy, transport and communications sectors; policy towards pollution control, environmental protection and resource conservation; science and technology policy; and policy towards regional and personal income distribution. Decisions on these issues are likely to have implications for the expansion and contraction of existing branches of production, and the establishment of new branches. The timescale involved, the planning period, would of course differ according to the issue.

For choice at this level to be real, the democratic process needs to focus around a limited number of alternatives, each consisting of a realizable set of objectives but informed by different values, or values differently weighted. Such plan variants would be drawn up by the national planning commission on the basis of guidelines from the national chamber of interests, knowledge of the major issues of discussion and disagreement in the society at the time, and estimates of available productive capacity. Thus, plan variants would be based on the principal positions present in public discussion, while public discussion would be sharpened by an awareness of what was possible and of the implications of different priorities, as set out in the plan variants.

The discussion about the relationship between citizenship and expertise in chapter 7 is particularly relevant here. To participate effectively in taking decisions about the overall allocation of resources people need to understand the issues involved and form judgements about the implications and economic viability of the different plan variants. The higher the general level of expertise in society, the more informed will be discussion about social priorities and the desired direction of change in different aspects of social life. The existence of alternative centres of specifically economic expertise would also be of great importance, not least as a check on the work of the planning commission.

The participatory democratic process through which overall priorities and the broad allocation of resources would be decided can be thought of as a political process of negotiated coordination. Interest and cause groups would argue and campaign for their concerns to receive priority. Political parties would propose programmes, weighting the different concerns according to their values and visions, but also taking into account the strength of support the different groups appeared to have. The different interests and causes would come together in the chamber of interests to try to reach agreement on what they would regard as a reasonable outcome, given the way the public discussion had gone and the extent and strength of the feelings that had been revealed. On the basis of the report from the chamber of interests, covering areas of both agreement and disagreement, the representative assembly would in the end decide.

The political parties represented in the assembly would act in accordance with their values and in the spirit of the programmes they had proposed. Given an electoral system based on proportional representation, and a respect for minority opinion, the eventual outcome would probably reflect as closely as is possible the collective view of society. Once overall priorities and allocations to different heads had been decided the detailed decisions about resource utilization within each head would for the most part be decentralized, both functionally and vertically. Regional and local representative assemblies, and national, regional and local social bodies with functional responsibilities, would have resources at their disposal. The use made of these resources would be decided by a comparable process to that at the overall national level. Thus, participation in decisions about social priorities would become successively more concrete, although it would be real at all levels.

The productive resources available to society consist of people, with their knowledge and skills, natural resources, and the stock of produced means of production (capital goods). The broad structure of the output that can be produced by these productive resources is relatively fixed in the short run, although most of the output will have alternative uses. The longer the planning period envisaged, the more flexibility there is in the structure of output, since it takes time to expand capacity in existing branches of production or to establish new ones. Interdependent choices have to be made about the use of existing productive capacity and the ways in which it is desired to change productive capacity for the future.

If qualitative structural change is desired, rather than merely incremental or marginal adjustment, then major investment will be necessary. For reasons discussed in chapter 1, decisions on major investment cannot be decentralized. They are significantly interdependent and need to be taken by the planning commission directly. The interdependence arises from the fact that capacity expansion requires inputs from other branches of production and increases the availability of the output of the expanding branch in relation to that of other branches. This means that potential major investments should be considered together so that decisions about them can be coordinated. Thus, the planning commission would be responsible for arriving at a set of consistent major investments that took account of their interdependence. This question is considered further in the next section.

Although decisions about major investment would be taken centrally they would not be implemented centrally. In arriving at a decision that major investment in an existing branch of production was needed the planning commission would have interacted with the negotiated coordination body for that branch. Once the decision had been made the negotiated coordination body would then be responsible for implementing it. In the case of major investment to establish a new branch of production the process of arriving at the decision would have involved the negotiated coordination bodies for the most closely related existing branches. An embryonic negotiated coordination body would be set up, with the relevant existing branches represented, and would be responsible for creating the new branch. In both cases the central government would make available the resources, in the form of purchasing power, and the negotiated coordination body would decide where the major investment should be located and how it should be organized, whether through existing or newly established production units.

Thus, the planning commission would be responsible for deciding that major new capacity was needed, reflecting overall social priorities, and the government would be responsible for making the resources available. However, the location of the new capacity would be decided by the relevant negotiated coordination body, which would include representatives of those most likely to be affected – existing production units and their communities, other communities with suitable sites, and any other interested groups. The regional distribution of economic activity, and therefore of the different categories of social activity, would be an important consideration in making such decisions. Similarly, the objective of maximizing the availability of psychologically productive activities would be one of the considerations influencing the choice between alternative methods of production, existing and potential.

Negotiated coordination bodies would themselves be responsible for deciding on minor investment and allocating it between the production units in their branch of production, taking account of the interdependence between them. Sectoral coordination would be required to deal with interdependence between different branches of production in the same sector. This would be the responsibility of the planning commission, although if no major changes were envisaged in a sector it might delegate responsibility to the sectoral equivalent of a negotiated coordination body.

This section has outlined a process of arriving at a broad allocation of resources between different heads that reflects social priorities. It has also anticipated various ways of disaggregating these broad heads, to be discussed in detail in the next chapter. The result would be a pattern of specific claims on resources, that is, a distribution of purchasing power or demand, that had been shaped by overall social priorities and yet reflected group and individual preferences. Demand would be from government and functional social bodies for social consumption and investment; from government bodies, but channelled through negotiated coordination bodies and production units, for major economic investment; from production units for minor new investment, as agreed by their negotiated coordination bodies; and from individuals and households for personal consumption. In addition to this final demand there would be the derived demand from production units for intermediate inputs into their production processes. This derived demand, involving transactions between production units, would in fact probably be the largest component in total demand, although its extent would depend on the degree to which production units were vertically integrated.

Customers would in general be able to choose their suppliers, with exceptions such as when conditions of natural monopoly existed. Production units would therefore know whether they were producing what their customers wanted, whether they were meeting social need as expressed through demand. If they were not, then customers would go elsewhere, to other production units within the same branch of production. However, the response to this would not be left to the individual production units acting in isolation but would be the responsibility of the relevant negotiated coordination body. Decisions on whether individual production units should be run down or expanded would be taken in the negotiated coordination body by representatives of all those affected by the decision. They would be aware of the reasons for the differential performance of different production units and of the social consequences of alternative courses of action. They would thus be able to mesh the general interest of responding to socially-shaped demand with the specific interests of more immediately or locally affected groups. The result would be a negotiated definition of what was to count as the social interest in each particular case.

The model combines planning with decentralization, without relying on market forces. The overall allocation of resources is planned at the level of society as a whole. Major investment is coordinated centrally but implemented on a decentralized basis. Production units know what to produce with their existing capacity in order to meet society's collectively and individually determined demand. Changes in the capacity of production units are decided in negotiated coordination bodies by those affected by them. The social interest is defined in each case by the general and specific interests involved. Production units are under informed public scrutiny which encourages them to operate efficiently. Since people participate at all levels in taking the economic decisions that affect them, they are likely to be committed to the effective implementation of those decisions.

8.3 Primary Input Prices

The determination of overall social priorities and their disaggregation results in a distribution of claims on gross output, in the form of purchasing power, among government and functional social bodies, individuals and households, and production units. This process presupposes the existence of prices. Prices are needed to aggregate the physical output that can be produced with the existing productive capacity into a measure of the total output available for allocation between broad macroeconomic categories. Prices are also important determinants of the specific use that those possessing purchasing power make of their claims on output. Government and social bodies, individuals and households, are influenced in their decisions on how to make the most effective use of their purchasing power by the relative prices of the different goods and services that would meet their requirements. Similarly, functional social bodies and production units are influenced in their choice of the most efficient method of production by the relative prices of different intermediate inputs, the cost of capital in relation to the average wage, and the pattern of wage differentials.

In the model of negotiated coordination the prices of goods and services would be determined by the production units. The general principle would be that they should be set equal to the social cost of production. Costs of production at the level of the economy as a whole are the costs of the primary inputs used: labour, natural resources, and, although there are conceptual problems here, use of part of society's accumulated stock of productive capacity. Costs at the level of the production unit include use of these primary inputs but also the cost of bought-in intermediate inputs produced by other production units.

These intermediate inputs cover materials, energy, services and fixed assets. Since fixed assets are only partially used up in the production of individual units of output, a principle of depreciation is needed to spread their cost.[1]

The distinction between primary and intermediate inputs underlies that between net and gross output, with the former consisting of value added only and the latter including also the value of pre-existing output. It also underlies the distinction between primary, or factor, income and gross revenue. Primary income represents the output available for use after the intermediate inputs used up in production have been replaced. The determination of prices at the level of the production unit is discussed in chapter 10, in the context of their role as partial indicators of social cost in the process of relating productive capacity to need. The rest of this section is concerned with the determination of primary input prices: wages, rental on the use of natural resources, and rate of return on the use of society's stock of fixed assets.

Primary input prices must be determined at the national level since they are a central influence on the way in which society's productive resources are used and on the overall allocation of available output according to social priorities. The broad priorities arrived at through the political process will have implications for policy towards primary input prices. As outlined in the previous section, what is involved in the determination of broad priorities is an interaction between the national planning commission and the society-wide decision-making process. The implications for primary input prices of alternative decisions about priorities would be set out by the commission in the plan variants and would inform the eventual decision taken.

National decisions about the distribution of available output between personal or household consumption, on the one hand, and social consumption and social and economic investment, on the other, have implications for the average level of real wages. At a formal level, abstracting from rent, once the real wage is determined, the rate of return and the structure of relative prices are also determined; alternatively, once the rate of return is determined, the pattern of relative prices and the real wage are also determined (Sraffa 1960).[2] Workers are paid money, not real, wages. The real wage is determined by the relationship between the level of money wages and the money price level of the consumer goods and services bought. Given the prevailing money price level and an assumption about the personal saving rate, the planned share of personal consumption in total output implies a given level of money wages. If that level is exceeded the result is unemployment or inflation and the disruption of the planned distribution of potentially available output.

Thus, a planned economy requires an incomes policy to render effective the planned allocation of resources according to socially agreed priorities. An incomes policy, integrated with tax and transfer policy, is also needed to give effect to the nationally agreed distribution of personal income between individuals and households. To fulfil these two functions there needs to be agreement on: first, the overall sum for additional money wage payments that would be consistent with stable money prices; and, second, how that sum should be distributed between different functional tasks, or occupations, different branches of production, and different localities. An agreed incomes policy embracing these two aspects is the only alternative to coercion, either the coercion of unemployment as the incomes policy of market forces or the coercion of a state imposed incomes policy, if inflation is to be avoided and a planned allocation of resources achieved.

The planning of changes in the average level and distribution of money wages would take place through a process of negotiated coordination, seeking to arrive at an agreed incomes policy. Representatives of the national government, the planning commission, trade unions, other workers' organizations, and consumers, would meet under the auspices of the chamber of interests. They would have before them the views of the interests they were representing and of other interested groups, the planning commission's estimates of society's total productive potential, the preliminary views of the chamber of interests about the socially desirable allocation of total productive potential between different priorities, and the opinions of independent experts. Their task would be to negotiate an agreed overall sum available for money wage increases and therefore an average increase, or norm, taking account of the claims on available resources from other priorities.[3]

They might then be joined by representatives of the negotiated coordination bodies and the regions for negotiations over any differential distribution of the overall sum that might be thought economically or socially desirable. At this stage the relevant information would include the social priority currently being given to movement towards greater income equality, the results of a national job evaluation exercise, differential projections for the growth rates of different branches of industry, reflecting socially agreed strategic decisions, and regional differences in the availability of different categories of activity. The objective would be to agree on socially desirable changes in the structure of functional, branch of production or regional differentials, given the agreed overall norm for wage increases. In practice, this would probably take the form of agreement on a limited number of exceptions to the norm.

Since labour costs depend not only on the level and structure of wages but also on the prevailing level of labour productivity, wages and productivity would need to be considered together. Labour productivity depends on the methods of production used, the organization of the production process, the safety standards operated, and the work rate in the labour process. In relation to all these, broad guidelines would be adopted in the process of determining national priorities, reflecting the objective of minimizing the amount of psychologically unproductive labour that has to be performed and sharing the psychologically productive activities available. The guidelines would cover, in particular, the priority to be given to increasing the proportion of psychologically productive labour when developing new methods of production or choosing between existing ones. There might also be guidelines on the implementation of positive discrimination in favour of those people whose personal time budgets showed a deficit in relation to particular categories of social activity, by comparison with the norm for people at a comparable stage in their life history.

For an incomes policy arrived at by this process of negotiated coordination to be effective, for the policy agreed to work, it would be essential that those taking part in the negotiation were really representative of the interests they were supposed to be representing. In particular, the trade unions would have to be fully participatory, democratic bodies so that any agreement reached had the support of the workers affected. In capitalist countries, with the possible exceptions of Australia and Sweden, incomes policies imposed from above, whether by the government based on legislation or by the trade union centre based on agreement with the government, have had only short-term success. In Yugoslavia, where an absence of political democracy coexists with economic pluralism, incomes policies have lacked popular support and inflation has been a major problem. In the statist countries it has been possible to enforce incomes policies lacking general support due to the absence of both political democracy and economic pluralism.

If it were not possible to reach agreement on a non-inflationary incomes policy, or if agreement were reached but not accepted and implemented, inflation would result and agreed overall priorities would be frustrated. The consequences of this and the reason for them would be known, understood and publicly discussed. Those responsible for failure to agree or implement would be under moral pressure to account for their actions. Thus, the process of negotiation, experience of the consequences of any failure to agree or implement, and the ensuing discussion, would together constitute a learning process. It would be a transformatory process because all involved would be faced with the need to think about their position and perceptions, in the light of those of others, and to work towards the creation from below of an integrated and harmonious definition of agreed common social interest.

This is a good example of one of the central features of the model of planning through negotiated coordination. If agreement cannot be reached, if the negotiation fails, there will be adverse consequences. There will be what may be called social crises, major or minor. If the interests are equally matched, equally powerful, there is likely to be inflation (Devine 1974) or institutional impasse (Olson 1982). However, it is precisely the experience of such crises that contributes to the social learning process. The alternative is the imposition of a solution by the most powerful, which requires inequality and is imcompatible with self-government. The potentially creative role of social crises is discussed further in chapter 11.

The use of a natural resource, as opposed to the production process involved in that use, is not in itself a social cost in the same sense as the use of labour, since human activity has by definition not contributed to its existence. Nevertheless, natural resources are not infinitely available and their use has an opportunity cost, in that if they are used for one purpose they cannot be used for another. This is true at any particular time and also, in the case of exhaustible, non-renewable resources, through time. A rental on the use of natural resources, over and above the cost of making use of them, is therefore socially desirable so that production units are aware of the fact that the resources are scarce and their use has to be weighed against the social usefulness of what they help to produce. The rental for the use of each natural resource would reflect the socially determined evaluation of its relative scarcity with respect to potential current use and, in the case of exhaustible resources, of its desired rate of depletion.

The rate of return, or capital charge, on the use of society's stock of fixed assets would also reflect socially determined priorities at the national level. These priorities would determine the planned allocation of total output between personal consumption, social consumption and investment, and economic investment. Abstracting from rent, social expenditure and saving, the planned division between personal consumption and economic investment would imply both a rate of return on assets employed and a total value for the stock of assets. The rate of return applied to the value of the stock of assets would, if realized, generate a surplus equal to the value of the planned allocation of output for investment.

This surplus, this purchasing power available for investment, would in principle be equal to the value of the output not consumed, that is, the output available for investment. Hence, the required rate of return would equate the demand for with the supply of investment goods. The available purchasing power for investment would derive from two sources, corresponding to the distinction between major and minor investment. Decisions about major investment would be taken centrally, in order to enable them to be coordinated *ex ante*, and the purchasing power for them would be provided by the government out of taxation. Decisions about minor investment would be made by negotiated coordination bodies and the purchasing power for them would come from the retained surplus, or profit, of the production units they covered, after the share of the surplus planned for major investment had been taxed away. The way this would work is discussed in more detail in the next section.

This method of determining the target rate of return on assets employed, or the capital charge that production units would have to meet, would be an important part of the way in which planning at the level of the economy as a whole would be combined with decentralized decision-making. At a formal level there is a problem of indeterminacy. Relative prices reflecting scarcity ratios depend on the prevailing technical coefficients, that is, on the set of production techniques employed, yet the choice of the most efficient technique itself depends on relative prices. However, this vicious circularity of formal indeterminacy is broken by the central determination of the share of investment in output at the macroeconomic level and the consequential determination of the rate of return and the structure of relative prices.

These relative prices would reflect relative scarcities given social priorities, the current structure of productive capacity, and the existing methods of production in use. They would therefore be a reasonable guide for negotiated coordination bodies and production units contemplating routine replacement or minor new investment. On the one hand, the rate of return calculated in terms of these current prices provides an indication, no more, of whether the maintenance or expansion of capacity in a particular branch of production is socially desirable. On the other hand, they provide a starting point for deciding on the choice of the most appropriate technique for any such minor investment. In both cases they are no more than initial guides. Major investment underway or planned may change the pattern of relative scarcities, and therefore relative prices, expected to prevail during the life of the minor investment. Social considerations not captured by the structure of relative prices will normally need to be taken into account. The importance of any such additional factors would be assessed, alongside the rate of return calculated in current prices, when the negotiated coordination bodies were making their decisions.

However, while the structure of relative prices generated by the socially determined rate of return, the current structure of productive capacity, and existing methods of production, provides a reasonable initial basis for minor investment decisions by negotiated coordination bodies, it will not do for major investment decisions by the planning commission. These need to be made on the basis of the set of future relative scarcities and prices that will exist when the relevant set of *ex ante* coordinated major investments with comparable construction periods comes into operation. Since there may be more than one such set of major investments, each with a different construction period, there may be more than one set of future prices relevant for major investment decision-making.[4]

Thus, major investment decisions would be taken centrally, guided by one or more sets of accounting prices. Major innovations in the techniques of production to be embodied in these major investments would also be decided centrally. Once these decisions had been taken, responsibility for their implementation would be given to existing or new negotiated coordination bodies, in the form of specifications of what was required, with the necessary resources made available in the form of purchasing power. Purchases of the inputs needed to carry through these major investments would be made by existing or new production units. Since these inputs would be part of current production, their prices would be those arrived at by the supplying production units on the basis of primary input prices that had been determined by the overall priorities of society, as discussed in this section.

It is perhaps worth ending this discussion of the social determination of wages, natural resource rentals, and rate of return on assets employed, by emphasizing that the use of centrally determined primary input prices for decentralized decision-making by production units does not imply the operation of market forces. In the model of negotiated coordination, decisions on changes in capacity are not made atomistically but are coordinated in advance – by negotiated coordination bodies for minor investment and by the planning commission for major investment.

8.4 Policy Implementation

This section is concerned primarily with how the people making up a society of self-activating, self-governing subjects could implement the decisions they had taken. How would people who wished to use their local knowledge to further the social interest know what they should do? The discussion assumes that people who have been involved in the construction of the collectively determined social interest would actively want to implement it. Implementation is therefore seen primarily as a process of ensuring that the information people need to decide what best contributes to the social interest in any situation is available to them. It is not seen as a problem of devising a set of policy instruments designed to induce people through a combination of incentives and penalties to behave in predetermined ways, deemed by someone else to be in the social interest. Thus, the primary problem to be addressed is that of information not that of motivation.

To assign a secondary status to the problem of motivation might be considered utopian, in the bad sense, but I prefer to think of it as prefigurative. Of course, the problem of motivation and the need for back-up sanctions is likely to remain for the foreseeable future, in all spheres of life. The state, with its coercive power, will only wither away, the need for sanctions in the economic sphere will only recede, to the extent that civil society develops, as people become fully self-activating and self-governing. However, the economic system can hinder or help this process, can work against the grain of self-transformation by reinforcing subaltern consciousness and narrow self-interest or with the grain by seeking to anticipate and thus create the future. The model of negotiated coordination is prefigurative but it includes back-up sanctions and could accommodate more.

The first means of implementing nationally agreed social priorities is to ensure that both the macroeconomic distribution and the disaggregated pattern of purchasing power, of demand, correspond to those priorities. At the macro-level this requires the condition that aggregate effective demand, arising from the socially agreed allocation of claims on national output, should equal the full employment level of output, defined socially as well as technically, at the prevailing level of prices, with prices determined by social cost calculated on the basis of socially determined primary input prices. Abstracting from taxes on wages, transfers and saving, the share of wages in national income would determine the surplus available for social expenditure and economic investment; alternatively, the required surplus would determine the share of wages.

The purchasing power available to government and social bodies would come from taxes on production units, again abstracting from taxes on wages. The gross revenue of production units would cover the cost of intermediate and primary inputs. After intermediate inputs, including depreciation, had been paid for and wages had been paid there would remain a surplus representing the rental on any natural resources used and the return on the assets employed. The tax on production units would be set at a rate that would leave production units in the aggregate with a residual surplus equal to the value of the minor investment allocated in the plan for decentralized decision-making at the level of the negotiated coordination bodies. The way in which the negotiated coordination bodies would use this purchasing power, earmarked for minor investment, and decide on its allocation between production units, is discussed in detail in chapter 10.

Thus, the tax on production units in aggregate would equal the rental on natural resource use, plus the return on assets employed, minus the value of minor investment. The revenue raised in this way would be for social expenditure and major economic investment. In the previous section the determination of the rate of return was discussed abstracting from rent and social expenditure. Now that these have been reintroduced, the principle becomes that rentals and rate of return should be set at levels that, between them, generate a surplus equal to planned social consumption and investment, plus planned economic investment, major and minor. This would mean that, provided the tax on surplus was set at the appropriate rate, production units would be left with just enough purchasing power in aggregate to cover planned minor investment, while the revenue raised would be just enough to cover planned social expenditure and major investment.

An alternative way of raising part of the revenue required for social expenditure and major investment might be through a turnover tax and/or a tax on wages. In real terms, the aggregate effect ought in principle to be the same, since the broad macroeconomic allocation, between consumption, social expenditure and investment, is assumed to have been previously decided on the basis of social priorities. At first sight, what is at issue are alternative ways of implementing that allocation. Thus, if the combined rental and rate of return, and thereby prices, are lower, that would be offset by either a turnover tax, which would raise prices again, or a tax on wages, which would reduce nominal but, due to the lower prices, not real purchasing power. In fact, things are more complicated, since alternative ways of seeking to implement the agreed broad macroeconomic allocation would have different consequences for relative prices and the method chosen would therefore need to reflect social priorities.

Social priorities are equally relevant when it comes to the disaggregation of the broad macroeconomic allocations discussed so far. Decisions over the detailed use of the revenue available for social expenditure would be decentralized horizontally, between social bodies responsible for different functional activities, and vertically, within the bodies responsible for each functional activity. The revenue earmarked for major investment would be made available to existing or newly established negotiated coordination bodies and through them to production units. Negotiated coordination bodies, and social bodies responsible for functional activities, would decide on the regional distribution of their activities. Revenue would be made available to regional and local government to supplement the resources they raised themselves. The central government would retain some revenue itself for the residual activities for which it remained responsible and as a contingency reserve. This process of disaggregating the broad macroeconomic allocations would be informed at each stage by the social priorities determined at the national level, with the ever more detailed decisions being made by the successively smaller and more focused groups of people affected by them.

The disaggregation of that part of total output planned for personal consumption would also be informed by social priorities, incorporated in a nationally agreed target distribution of personal income between individuals and households. One part of the process of implementing this would be the incomes policy discussed in the previous section, which would determine the structure of differentials applying to payment for the performance of different functional tasks. However, since people during their lives would normally undertake activities in each category of social labour, as discussed in chapter 7, the structure of job-related differentials would not determine the structure of lifetime income distribution in the way that it does in capitalist and statist societies. Furthermore, although there would be an expectation that all those able to do so would undertake their fair share of social labour, both overall and in each category, the objective is that people should choose to do this and not be coerced, administratively or economically.

The possibility of an unconditional basic income received by everyone has already been mentioned in chapter 6. This would enable people who wished, and felt they could justify it to themselves, to live without undertaking paid work. A basic income scheme could also be designed to take account of the differing needs of all who would be entitled to a transfer income – the young, the ill, the disabled, the old, and those looking after them in the home or the community (Purdy forthcoming). Alternatively, there could be a system of separate transfer incomes for different purposes. In either case, there would probably need to be taxation of wages to finance it, although in principle a turnover tax would do equally well. However, progressive personal income taxation would be necessary if the structure of differentials that emerged from the negotiations over incomes policy produced a personal distribution of income more unequal than was thought socially desirable.

The outcome of all this would be a pattern of demand, disaggregated to the level of government and functional social bodies, production units, households and individuals, that would reflect as closely as seems possible a first approximation to a collectively and individually defined common social interest. As a first approximation, therefore, people would know that making the most effective use of society's productive resources to produce what people collectively and individually wished to use, that is, to supply what was demanded, would best contribute to the social interest. It is, however, only a first approximation. In addition to interests as users and consumers, people have interests as producers and members of communities and are affected by and care about a wider set of issues, which demand and relative prices cannot represent.

To arrive at a second approximation, the process of change and adjustment has to be taken into consideration. New branches of production have to be created, old branches disappear, existing branches expand or contract. The process of reallocating society's productive resources in accordance with changes in technology and what people want affects people's lives through their work and their communities as much as through the change in the pattern of what is produced. Central to the process of implementing broad nationally agreed social priorities in a way that involves people themselves defining in detail what those priorities mean for them is the work of the negotiated coordination bodies, discussed in detail in chapter 10. They have the task of meshing together the collectively and individually determined definition of the social interest, as reflected in the pattern of demand, and the specific local interests of people as producers, as members of communities, as human beings with diverse interests and causes dear to them.

The negotiation of adjustment within and between negotiated coordination bodies, which include representatives of affected regions and communities and also other interests and causes, represents the second approximation to the social construction of the social interest. The first approximation can be thought of as the social interest on the quantitative demand side. The second approximation is arrived at by meshing the demand side with the social interest on the qualitative supply side, the side involving human productive activity, and therefore of central importance if we are to become autonomous, self-activating and self-governing people. For implementation at this second level to be equitable, a framework of nationally agreed procedures and standards is required.

The establishment of new production units would be the responsibility of existing or newly established negotiated coordination bodies in consultation with the relevant level of government. The relationship between government bodies, functional social bodies, negotiated coordination bodies, self-governing interest and cause groups, and production units, is discussed in the next chapter. Legislation would set minimum standards for hours of work, health and safety at work, pollution control, quality and safety of output, and other issues on which it was felt some uniformity of practice was desirable. Guidelines would indicate the social priorities to be taken into account when developing new methods of production and when practising positive discrimination on the basis of people's lifetime budgets.

The banking system would facilitate transactions, savings and credit. The principle operated would be the one advocated in the course of planning in the UK during the Second World War: nothing that is desirable, is possible in real terms, and would otherwise be undertaken, should be prevented by lack of finance. Since prices would be determined on the basis of social cost, calculated in terms of socially agreed primary input prices, the only source of inflation, abstracting from import prices, would be money wages – if it proved impossible to agree on an incomes policy or an agreement was not observed. Excess demand, arising from dissaving or mistakes in credit policy, would show up in a general decrease in stocks or increase in order books, which would provide the information on the basis of which the national or regional planning commission would initiate the process of negotiating an adjustment. Production units and regional and local government would have contingency reserves and access to credit. Thus, macroeconomic balance, that is, a redefined concept of full employment and an absence of inflation, while not automatically guaranteed, should be achievable through continuous social action. Macroeconomic balance is considered further in chapter 10.

A central principle of the model is openness of information. Since production units would not be autarchic, atomistic competitors, although they would compete, the suffocating influence of commercial secrecy would be absent. All the information relating to the activities of production units would be publicly available – to their negotiated coordination body, to other production units, to government and social bodies, to anyone who was interested. Given the generalized possession of expertise, the availability of alternative opinions from experts in specific areas, the rotation of functional tasks, the cross-cutting representation of affected interests on the governing bodies of production units and on negotiated coordination bodies, information bias would be minimized.

Thus, regular audits would provide information on the use being made of society's productive resources by each production unit. This information would be used by negotiated coordination bodies, along with other relevant information, when making their decisions about investment and disinvestment. Information about the activities of negotiated coordination bodies would similarly be available when it came to decisions about sectoral coordination and major investment. In so far as society had developed to the stage of self-determination and self-government, this openness of information would be the basis for the administration of things. To the extent to which this had not yet been achieved, the information would enable people to be held accountable for their actions and, if necessary, would be the basis on which sanctions would be applied.

Sanctions in relation to production units that were judged to be performing unsatisfactorily would take the form of not agreeing to new investment and of withholding credit or subsidies for current production. Such decisions would be taken by the relevant negotiated coordination body or the banking system in discussion with it. The production units affected would be involved in the process leading up to the decision and would have had the opportunity to take corrective action before any sanctions were applied. The operation of sanctions at the level of the production unit as a whole is discussed further in chapter 10. Sanctions within the production unit are discussed in the next chapter. However, while it is important to establish that sanctions are possible within the model, and would in fact be extremely effective because they would be informed by detailed local knowledge, they are not an integral part of the model. The problem for a self-governing society is not to assume that people need to be coerced and to devise means of coercing them, but to ensure that self-activating people have the information on the basis of which to decide how their actions best contribute to the overall social interest as defined by them.

8.5   The Conscious Allocation of Resources

This chapter has been concerned primarily with planning at the level of society as a whole, with the collective social determination of the framework within which decentralized decision-making takes place. Consciously determined broad social priorities, disaggregated and made specific by the groups and individuals who are the ultimate users of the resources involved, result in a pattern of demand. These broad priorities also determine the primary input prices used by production units in setting their prices. Thus, production units are aware of what it is socially useful for them to produce and of the social cost of the resources they need to produce it. They can then combine this knowledge, reflecting overall social priorities, with their local knowledge of the detailed circumstances of their workplaces and communities to decide how they can best use their productive capacity in the social interest.

Major investment decisions are taken centrally and coordinated *ex ante* by the centre. Minor investment decisions are taken by negotiated coordination bodies and coordinated *ex ante* by them. It has been suggested that, since investment goods are produced with existing capacity, it is contradictory for investment to be the responsibility of the centre, or by extension of negotiated coordination bodies, while at the same time the use of existing capacity is the responsibility of production units (Salter 1983). However, the implementation of investment decisions is achieved by making purchasing power available to the relevant negotiated coordination body, and eventually production unit, which then uses it to buy the investment goods required. Thus, investment decisions taken at levels above the production unit become effective in the form of demand for the current output of the production units which have the capacity to produce investment goods. In this way the apparent paradox is removed.

Democratic planning involves the conscious determination of social priorities, at all levels, through a political process. Politics, participatory politics involving equal people, is central to it. In this fundamental respect it is the diametric opposite of the new right and market socialist objective of depoliticizing economic life. It also differs fundamentally from the classical Marxist view that with the abolition of exploitation and oppression, when all that remains is the administration of things, politics comes to an end. The social interest is seldom transparently evident. Self-activating equal subjects need to engage together continuously at each level of decision-making in order to decide themselves what in detail constitutes the social interest in any situation.

The closer we get to a self-governing society, the less of a problem motivation and incentives become. At issue is not whether material or moral incentives are preferable, but rather the difference between a situation in which external incentives, of whatever sort, are needed and a situation of autonomous self-activation (Elliott 1976, p. 151). As Horvat puts it, the aim is to replace 'incentives by self-determination, competition by cooperation, exchange by solidarity, accumulation of things by personal development, having by being' (Horvat 1982, p. 503).

In a society based on the model of negotiated coordination between equals and openness of information the activities of production units would be subject to public scrutiny – from their negotiated coordination body, other production units, customers, government bodies and any other interested groups. The same principle of open accountability would apply to all economic, social and government bodies. Since decision-making would involve all the different interests affected by the decision, sectional interests would be under pressure to modify their behaviour. There is, of course, always the possibility that the result would be stagnation rather than transformation, if the ethos of consensus enabled affected interests to veto change (Olson 1982). However, sanctions would be available if necessary and sooner or later experience of stagnation and social crisis would create the conditions for change.

The crucial motivational element in the model is its transformatory dynamic – the personalization of interdependence. Negotiated coordination requires personal interaction with others. It is a learning process in the course of which people have the opportunity to become aware of and concerned about the aspirations and potentialities of others, rather than being confirmed in a concern only for their own. It enables the use of society's resources to be consciously planned, at all levels, and thus enables people to decide, collectively and individually, what they need for their self-development, their self-transformation. Democratic planning through negotiated coordination is a necessary part of a fully democratic self-governing society.

9

Communities and Production Units

9.1 Local and Regional Planning

This chapter is concerned with the institutions through which a self-governing society would determine the social interest at levels below that of the society as a whole, that is, with the detailed social construction of the social interest within the broad framework determined at the national (or international) level. The discussion of democracy in chapter 6 identified two guiding principles: first, that decisions and their implementation should be the responsibility of those affected by them; and second, that, while the concept of self-government is relevant for civil society, the appropriate concept for the administrative structures of the state and for economic units is self-management.

Ultimate political power in a democracy must rest with the representative assembly at the level at which the decision is taken: local, regional or national. Decisions would be taken at the local level unless there were good reasons for them to be taken at a more general level. Such good reasons have in common the fact that the decisions in question affect a wider group of people than those at a particular local level. First, there are strategic decisions affecting the direction of development of a region or society as a whole. Second, there are decisions concerning redistribution between localities or regions. Third, there are decisions about activities that have effects external to the locality or region within which they take place. However, given the importance attached to pluralism and direct participation, there would be a strong presumption in favour of decentralization.

The principle of the maximum decentralization consistent with non-exclusion of affected groups would apply not only to the political power of representative assemblies but also to responsibility for functional activities. Collective responsibility for functional activities would probably include: infrastructural services like housing, water, communications, public health and the environment; education, training and recreation; science and the arts; and health and welfare. Such responsibilities would be devolved to social bodies that would themselves be decentralized in accordance with the principle of non-exclusion. The result of this functional and vertical balance between centralization and decentralization would be an interdependent matrix of representative and functional social bodies, each with clearly defined responsibilities, powers and resources. The organization of these activities involves significant interdependence which would be accommodated in the first instance by negotiated coordination between the relevant functional bodies, with ultimate responsibility in the event of failure to agree resting with the appropriate representative body. The result would be a pattern of demand for the output of production units reflecting social priorities in relation to collective activities.

In addition to their residual responsibilities for functional services if functional bodies failed to agree, local and regional representative assemblies would have an overall responsibility for economic activity in their area of jurisdiction. They would establish planning commissions with the task of giving effect to the social priorities determined through the local and regional democratic political process, within the overall national framework. These planning commissions would consist of representatives of the local or regional government, of the regional or national government, of the production units located in their area of jurisdiction, of the negotiated coordination bodies of those production units, and of relevant interest and cause groups. They would in turn be represented on the regional or national planning commissions, on the governing bodies of production units within their area of jurisdiction and on the negotiated coordination bodies of those units.

The local and regional planning commissions would have the function of ensuring that the quantity and quality of economic activity in their areas was such as to provide everyone with the opportunity to undertake their fair share of the different categories of social activity identified in chapter 7. This can be thought of as ensuring both full employment and an economic structure in which the distribution of the different categories of social activity – unskilled and repetitive, skilled, nurturing, creative, planning and running – was not too different from the national average. To achieve this would involve negotiating at the regional or national level over the location of major new investment and the *ex ante* coordination of such investment in their locality or region. It would also require resources at the disposal of the local or regional representative assemblies.

Responsibility for the final determination of local or regional priorities would rest with the representative assembly which, as at the national level, would have before it the report of the local or regional chamber of interests. These chambers would bring together all the interest and cause groups that wished to be represented in order to negotiate as far as possible an agreed approach. Areas of both agreement and dis-agreement would be forwarded to the representative assembly to inform its decision-making. Once again, the process of negotiated coordination involved, while recognizing the existence of differences of interest and perception, would incorporate a transformatory dynamic. In this way, the social construction of the social interest, begun at the national level, would be continued through the regional and local political process.

As in the economy as a whole, the level and pattern of demand originating within a locality or a region would be made up of: social consumption and investment, as disaggregated through negotiation between the different levels of representative assembly and functional bodies; centrally determined major investment that it had been decided to locate in the area; minor investment by production units in the area, as authorized by the relevant negotiated coordination bodies; personal consumption; and derived demand. Since localities and regions, as of course the country as a whole, would not be self-sufficient, not all the demand originating in an area would be spent on goods and services produced there, while some local production would be sold outside the area. However, the location of economic activity would not be determined by market forces but by the national and regional planning commissions and negotiated coordination bodies in the light of socially determined priorities with respect to regional development and redistri-bution.

At this stage in the discussion it is necessary to consider the local and regional levels separately. The process of negotiated coordination at the regional level would follow closely that at the national level. A possible framework is set out in figure 9.1, which should be considered together with figure 8.1 in the previous chapter. The regional planning commiss-ion would be guided by society's overall priorities as determined at the national level, the decisions of the national planning commission in implementing those priorities, and the regional priorities determined by the regional representative assembly in the light of the views of the regional chamber of interest. It would be represented in the section of the national planning commission dealing with regional distribution and on the negotiated coordination bodies of branches of production organized on an integrated national basis. It would also be represented on regional negotiated coordination bodies which would cover both nationally organized production units located in the region and regionally organized production units.

The regional planning commission would be responsible for sectoral coordination within the region, major investment in the region, and local

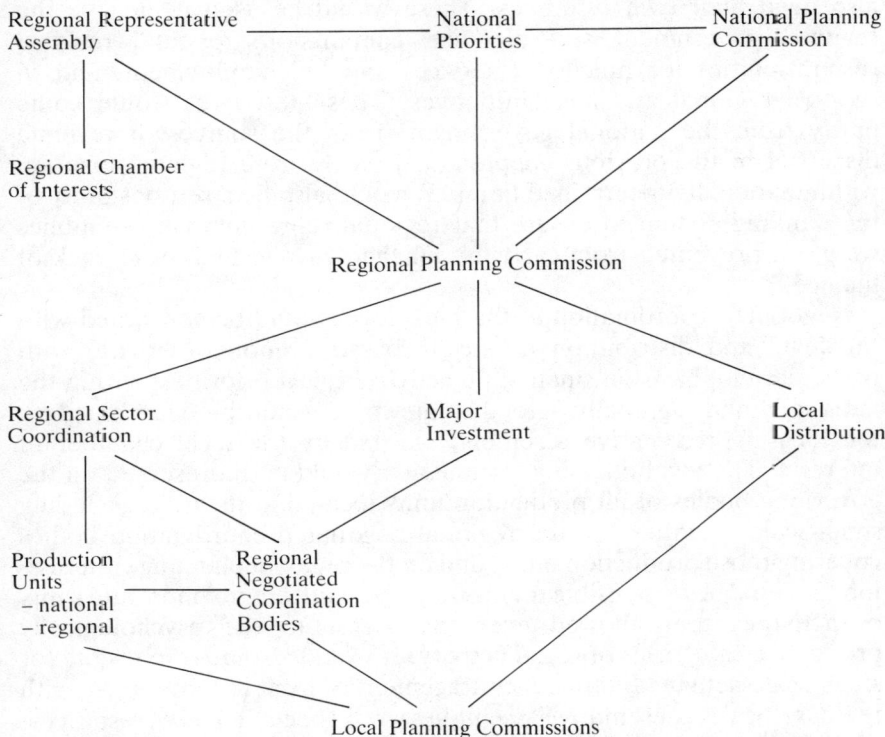

Regional Representative _____ National _____ National Planning
Assembly   Priorities   Commission

Regional Chamber
of Interests

Regional Planning Commission

Regional Sector   Major   Local
Coordination   Investment   Distribution

Production   Regional
Units   Negotiated
– national _____   Coordination
– regional   Bodies

Local Planning Commissions

Figure 9.1 Framework for regional negotiated coordination

distribution. It would have an overall view of the existing state and
expected future development of the region's economy. If national or
regional negotiated coordination bodies were contemplating the
creation or expansion, closure or contraction, of production units in the
region the regional planning commission would be able to assess how
the proposed changes meshed with one another and how the level and
character of economic activity in the region would be affected. It would
then make sure that this information was taken into account by the
negotiated coordination bodies when they were making their decisions.
Thus, decisions about changes in the allocation of resources would be
based on more complete information about the social interest than
would be provided solely by cost and profitability calculations based on
nationally determined primary input prices, the productivity of
production units and demand.

   In addition to negotiating with the national planning commission and
negotiated coordination bodies over the location of major investment
and changes in the capacity of existing production units, regions would

also need their own resources. These would be used to finance the regional government and planning commission, to fulfil residual responsibilities for functional services and full employment, and to support regional and local initiatives. These resources would come partly from the national government, from the sources of revenue discussed in the previous chapter, and partly from regional taxation within nationally determined limits. It would also be a responsibility of the banking system to ensure that regional representative assemblies were not prevented from carrying out their responsibilities by lack of finance.

Negotiated coordination at the local level would be concerned with the level and distribution of locally based economic activity, with particular emphasis on small-scale activity. Local priorities, within the nationally and regionally agreed framework, would be determined by the local representative assembly, assisted by the local chamber of interests. The local planning commission would be represented on the governing bodies of all production units located in its area, excluding small-scale activities, on the regional negotiated coordination bodies covering those production units, and on the regional planning commission. It would be responsible for ensuring local full employment and a mix of activities that allowed everyone access to the psychologically productive categories of social activity. It would also be responsible for small-scale activity and the encouragement of local initiatives. As with regions, local representative assemblies would need their own resources, derived from the region and from local taxation, and also access to the banking system. A possible framework for local negotiated coordination is set out in figure 9.2.

The framework for regional and local planning sketched in this section is designed to complement the framework for the determination and implementation of national priorities set out in the previous chapter. There, the way in which the broad distribution of resources and primary input prices would be arrived at on the basis of national priorities was discussed. Here, the way in which that broad distribution would be disaggregated and community interests would be incorporated has been elaborated. Although the role of the regional and local chambers of interests has been referred to it has not yet been considered in detail. However, it would be of central importance. References to the chambers of interests stand for the input of the self-governing bodies of civil society, discussed in chapter 6, into the process of constructing in detail the social interest. These self-governing bodies would embrace both interest groups and cause groups. Together with representative assemblies and functional bodies they would constitute the institutions through which a self-governing society would run itself. Their role is discussed further in the next section.

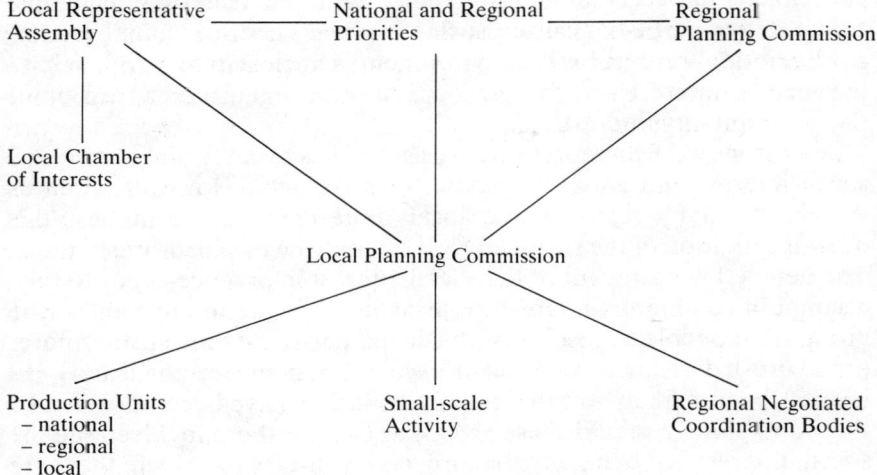

Figure 9.2   Framework for local negotiated coordination

Claims on resources in the form of purchasing power and prices that reflect costs of production are indispensable quantitative indicators of what constitutes socially useful production. However, qualitative considerations are equally indispensable. The interaction of representative institutions, community interests and consumer/user interests would generate the qualitative knowledge that has to be taken into account by production units and negotiated coordination bodies when deciding on what constitutes the social interest in any situation. The way in which community and consumer/user interests would be articulated is discussed in the next two sections, setting the scene for a detailed consideration of production units and negotiated coordination bodies in the final two sections of this chapter.

9.2   Community Interests

We belong to a society as a whole at the level of the nation state and to the international community as citizens of the world. We also belong to smaller communities consisting of people affected by or interested in similar things. These communities are not only geographically based, like the area or region in which we live, but involve us in all aspects of our lives: as members of different genders or ethnic groups; as tenants or owner occupiers; as people responsible for the care and nurturing of others; as practitioners of particular skills or professions; as workers; as users of collectively organized services; as individual consumers; as participants in particular cultural and recreational activities; as people committed to particular causes, such as women's liberation, anti-racism, gay liberation, respect for the environment, a nuclear-free world. What I have called interest and cause groups are the organized expression of these community interests.

As citizens we elect representative assemblies to determine the overall social interest and allocate resources accordingly. However, even as disaggregated by regional and local representative assemblies, this overall definition of the social interest can only be in broad-brush terms. The detailed working out of the social interest in practice needs to take account of community interests as articulated by the interest and cause groups that people choose to establish and participate in. Furthermore, broad brush decisions on overall priorities at national, regional and local levels are more likely to carry conviction if they have been informed by the views of interest and cause groups as to what those involved see the social interest as being in the aspects of life with which they are concerned. The relationship between political parties offering alternative articulations of community interests and the interest and cause groups expressing those interests has been discussed in chapters 6 and 8.

Autonomous, self-governing interest and cause groups would participate in the construction of the social interest both through their input into the process of determining the overall allocation of resources and through involvement in the detailed implementation of that allocation. First, groups would seek to stimulate public discussion of the interests with which they were concerned with the aim of influencing the general climate of opinion in society. They would also be able to engage in whatever forms of campaigning and struggle were legally recognized, and no doubt if they felt strongly enough they would also take action outside the law, in order to bring pressure to bear on the decision-making bodies. Disagreement, conflict and struggle cannot be assumed away and the scope for dissent and action to back it up is a basic democratic right.

Second, groups would be able to participate in taking the decisions on overall resource allocation through the national, regional and local chambers of interests. To the extent that the representatives of the different groups in these chambers reached broad agreement about priorities for the period under consideration, and the allocation of resources implied by them, the representative assembly would be unlikely to disagree. However, if widespread agreement could not be reached in the chamber of interests the representative assembly would have to decide itself. Even so, it would probably first refer the matter back to the chamber since without the agreement of the major interests involved any allocation of resources decided on would be in danger of proving unworkable, particularly in a society of self-governing equals.

Third, when it came to implementation interest and cause groups would participate in deciding on the detailed use of resources, either in partnership with the various functional social bodies or through the use themselves of collectively provided resources made available on an enabling basis. Thus, community interests would be involved in various ways in the process of determining in detail what was to count as the social interest. One expression of this process would be the pattern of demand that emerged. This, together with primary input prices, would provide the general information needed by production units in order to decide how best to use their existing capacity in the social interest.

However, community interest in production units would not be confined to influencing the pattern of demand. Interest and cause groups would also seek to influence directly the activities of production units that affected the issues with which they were concerned. For instance, equal opportunity groups would be interested in training and employment policy, environmental groups in methods of production and waste disposal, residents' groups in levels of pollution and local traffic. For such interests to receive serious attention the groups involved would need the right to be represented on the governing bodies of production units and on their negotiated coordination bodies. The basis of representation would differ according to whether the production units concerned were organized nationally, regionally or locally. Groups that felt there were no current or likely future issues requiring attention in their areas of concern might, of course, choose not to exercise their right of representation.

Although in the course of their lives people would typically undertake their fair share of society's necessary planning and running functions they would also undertake activities at less general levels in the functional hierarchy. While the objective is that the performance of functionally dependent tasks should not be associated with personal dependence, this will be achieved only gradually. Trade unions are likely to be necessary for the foreseeable future, both to insist on this principle within production units and, to the extent that the principle has not been achieved, to safeguard the interests of those still subject to personal dependence arising from their performance of functionally dependent tasks. Trade unions would also be interested in the implementation within production units of any incomes policy that they had been involved in negotiating at the national level. Thus, trade unions would always have the right to be represented on the governing bodies of production units and on negotiated coordination bodies and would almost certainly always wish to exercise that right. Again, the basis of representation would depend on the sort of production unit and negotiated coordination body involved.

9.3   Consumer and User Interests

Whatever else has to be taken into account by production units and
negotiated coordination bodies, as they seek to define how they can
best contribute to the social interest, satisfying consumers and users
must be central. There is no point in producing what people or other
production units do not want to use. Although the doctrine of
consumer sovereignty is usually discussed in a way that ignores the
interests of people as members of communities and as producers,
sectional trade unionism that sees production only in terms of jobs and
conditions of work, without reference to what is produced, is equally
unacceptable. How, then, are the interests of consumers and other
users to be represented in the process of determining socially useful
production? There are two ways: first, the deployment of purchasing
power by government and functional social bodies, individuals and
production units; second, the representation of consumers and other
users on the governing bodies of production units and on negotiated
coordination bodies.

For the use of purchasing power to be effective in representing
consumer and user interests there should ideally be alternative sources
of supply, so that customer choice provides behavioural information on
the extent to which different production units are producing what is
wanted. This may not always be possible, as when the characteristics of
the production process are such that all the output demanded can be
produced most efficiently by a single unit, or in the case of natural
monopolies such as telecommunications, railways, electricity, gas and
water, when it would be wasteful to duplicate channels of distribution.
Nevertheless, there should be a strong presumption in favour of
alternative sources of supply, a presumption supported also by the
general preference in a participatory society for activities on the
smallest scale that is sensible. This is one of the considerations that
would be taken into account in decisions on the sort of technology
society wished to develop.

Although the primary way in which consumer and user interests
would make themselves felt would be through effective demand,
representation of organized consumer and user groups on the governing bodies of production units and on negotiated coordination
bodies would also be necessary. The collective experience and views of
customers is likely to provide valuable information about how suppliers
could improve their performance in producing socially useful output.
Given an absence of commercial secrecy and a complete openness of
information, less successful production units would be able to discover
not only the fact that they were providing a less satisfactory service but

also the reasons why customers preferred the output of more successful production units. Qualitative information would supplement the quantitative information available from effective demand.

Representation of organized consumer and user groups on the governing bodies of production units would ensure that any tendency for them to use their local knowledge in their own sectional interests would be difficult to sustain. It would also be a safeguard against the tendency that people have to perceive things primarily from their own standpoint, even when they are genuinely committed to doing what is best for the overall interest. Decisions on how production units should use their existing capacity would be made by representatives of the consumers/users and the producers, along with the representatives of other interested groups. Thus, potential conflicts of interest and different perceptions of reality would become explicit and would have to be taken into account when arriving at decisions. The process would have a transformatory dynamic.

Consumer and user representation on the governing bodies of production units and on negotiated coordination bodies would also provide information about the ways in which customers' requirements were likely to change and about the new products and services that they would like to see developed. It would therefore be an important input into the process of anticipating change through the *ex ante* coordination of investment decisions to meet expected future demand. Furthermore, it would provide an impetus to innovation, not for its own sake, but in a considered way, planned to meet changes in the evolving definition of social need. This qualitative information cannot be provided by the quantitative impact of effective demand but requires direct representation.

Consumer interests would be articulated by consumer consultative committees for specific services, general consumers' associations and activist groups. In addition to assessing effectiveness, conducting surveys of reliability, testing products for safety, and recommending best buys, these organizations and groups would be represented on the governing bodies of production units and on negotiated coordination bodies. They would have the information and expertise to evaluate the estimates that these bodies would themselves presumably be making of their performance, helped by an across-the-board knowledge of consumers' experiences of comparable production units. They would also be in tune with changing preferences and so could contribute to decisions about innovation. Thus, the information available for decision-making would be far richer than that provided by the raw quantitative data about changes in sales, inventories and orders on their own.

Government and functional bodies would also be represented on the governing bodies of production units and on their negotiated coordination bodies, if they were major customers. Similarly, production units that were major users of the output of other production units would be represented on the governing bodies of those units. Finally, negotiated coordination bodies responsible for branches of production that were major users of the output of other branches would be represented on the negotiated coordination bodies for those branches. This network of representation would provide information, similar to that supplied by consumers' organizations, about the extent to which production units were meeting the requirements of collective consumption and of other production units and about where improvement or change was needed.

The interests of consumers and users, as of producers and communities, would also be the general responsibility of the national, regional and local planning commissions. They would monitor changes in technology and preferences and, through their representation on the governing bodies of production units and on negotiated coordination bodies, check that desirable changes were being undertaken and new developments were being taken up. Thus, attention to the interests of consumers and users would be achieved through a combination of the quantitative impact of demand on the financial performance of production units and the qualitative influence of consumer/user and planning commission representation on their decision-making bodies.

9.4   Production Units: Forms and Structure

Organizations undertaking economic activity are usually referred to as firms or enterprises. I have used the clumsier term production unit in order to avoid any suggestion of atomized decision-making, coordinated *ex post* by market forces, and to emphasize the socialized character of production in a self-governing society. However, nothing turns on the terminology and my production units can be thought of as the more familiar firms or enterprises, operating, however, in a clearly defined branch of production, or industry. Two principles apply to the organization of production units in the model of negotiated coordination: first, the social character of the productive resources incorporated in them, with the corollary that the use of those resources should be determined socially; and, second, the desirability of economic pluralism and a presumption in favour of small scale.

The first principle underlies the distinction I draw between the composition of the governing body of a production unit, which should be representative of all those affected by its activities, and its internal

COMMUNITIES AND PRODUCTION UNITS223

operation, which should be organized on the basis of self-management. This arrangement is quite different from that of the Yugoslav worker or labour self-managed enterprise, and from similar arrangements that populate market socialist models, in which the workers alone elect the governing body of their enterprise. However, even Horvat, the doyen of Yugoslav political economists, recognizes the force of the argument that complete autonomy for production units is incompatible with their social character, although he does not follow through the implications of that recognition (Horvat 1964, p. 119; 1982, p. 248).

Apart from very small-scale local activity, all economic activity would be undertaken by socially owned and controlled production units. There would be no private ownership or control of production units, with private here being used in the sense discussed in chapter 5 to include both capitalist and sectional worker ownership. As part of society's productive potential, production units should be socially owned. Here the distinction between state, or public, and social ownership is of great importance. As argued in chapter 5, socialization of the means of production requires democratic social control of both the overall disposition of resources and their detailed use. What it means for a production unit to be socially owned and controlled will therefore depend on how it fits into the overall picture and will differ according to the character of the economic activity involved.

Production units would be organized on a national, regional or local basis. Nationally organized economic activities would be of two sorts: those that needed to be nationally integrated, involving interdependent networks, particularly communications and some forms of energy; and those whose efficient scale of operation was too large for them to be sensibly undertaken separately in each region. Of course, in both cases production units would be actually located in one or more region and locality, but their operation would be organized on a national basis. The same principle would be used to decide which activities needed to be organized regionally rather than locally.

Thus, the principle of maximum decentralization subject to the non-exclusion of affected groups would determine the level at which production units were organized. If integrated activities were fragmented or production occurred on too small a scale productive resources would be wasted and everyone would be adversely affected. However, given the desirability of decentralization and economic pluralism, the maximum number of production units consistent with achieving a sensible scale of output would be established at each level. For instance, while the minimum sensible scale for a particular productive activity might be too large for there to be a production unit in each region, it might be small enough for there to be more than one production unit in the country as a whole, and similarly at the local/regional levels. I have used the term minimum sensible scale rather than minimum efficient scale since there would need to be socially agreed guidelines as to what loss of narrow economic efficiency was acceptable in order to achieve greater decentralization and economic pluralism.

The application of these principles would produce an array of production units, each with a differently composed governing body. The differences would reflect the factors determining the form of consumer/user and interest/cause representation, namely, the level at which the unit was organized, the region and locality in which it was located, and what it was producing. Individual choices by people as workers and consumers, and choices by collective users and other production units, would provide quantitative indicators of how the working conditions and output of a production unit were viewed. The response to this information and plans for longer term change would be decided in the first instance by the governing body of the production unit in the light of the available qualitative information. Each production unit would belong to a negotiated coordination body in which plans for changes in capacity, whether initiated by the production unit itself or elsewhere, would be negotiated and eventually decided. Negotiated coordination bodies are discussed in detail in the next section and the next chapter.

So far, the principle that the governing body of a production unit should be representative of those affected by its activities has been asserted and the potential constituencies have been identified in general terms. What can be said about the detailed composition of governing bodies? The Bullock Report on Industrial Democracy in the UK (Department of Trade 1977) provided for equal representation of shareholders and workers, plus a co-opted group forming less than one third of the total – the $2x + y$ formula. The co-opted group had the dual function of mediating between the representatives of capital and labour and bringing wider experience and considerations to bear. It was to be made up of senior personnel from other companies, people with special expertise, like solicitors and accountants, and trade unionists who were not employees of the company.

Specific representation of consumers was rejected, on the grounds that their interests were different in kind from those of shareholders and workers, best safeguarded by legislation and competition, and that in any case there would be problems in defining a consumer constituency. Worker representation was to be controlled by the trade unions, based on the existing structure of union and shop steward organization. It was argued that collective bargaining and worker representation in management were complementary and the suggestion that worker representatives should relinquish trade union positions was rejected. Despite the corporatist character of the Bullock proposals, they were opposed by most employers, effectively rejected by most unions, and came to nothing.

The Communist Party's evidence to the Bullock Commission (Ramelson 1975) insisted on public ownership and rejected syndicalism. It argued that four interests should be represented: the workers in the enterprise concerned; the Trades Union Congress, representing the working class as a whole; the government; and other bodies with a legitimate interest, such as local authorities. Representatives of workers in the enterprise were to be in a minority themselves, to avoid syndicalism, but together with TUC representatives would constitute a majority, thus ensuring control by the working class as a whole. This is a more acceptable position than that of the Bullock Report itself, in that it dispenses with private capital, but it is one-dimensionally workerist, privileging the role of people as producers over all other aspects of their lives.

It is not obvious what principle should guide the proportions in which different interests should be represented on the governing bodies of production units. It could be argued that all that matters is that each affected interest should be represented, since the emphasis is on negotiation and reaching agreement. However, decision-making based on unanimity is probably too restrictive and would increase the possibility of veto by sectional interests. At the other extreme, by analogy with the relationship between representative assembly and chamber of interests, it could be argued that ultimate control should rest with the representative of the relevant level planning commission on behalf of the community as a whole, in the form of a sort of golden share. However, this would run the danger of turning the process of negotiation into a mere formality.

In the end, the matter would be decided on the basis of experience through the democratic political process. As a starting point, my inclination is to go for equal representation of four categories of interest: planning commissions and the negotiated coordination body for the relevant branch of production, on behalf of the general interest; consumers' associations, government and functional bodies, other production units and other negotiated coordination bodies, representing consumers, users and suppliers; interest and cause groups, representing community interests as defined in section 9.2; and those working in the production unit, and their trade unions, representing themselves. Since no one interest would dominate, a premium would be placed on reaching agreement with other interests. There might be a danger that external interests would squeeze the interests of those working in the production unit. However, issues of disagreement would become public knowledge and the reasons for them would be subject to

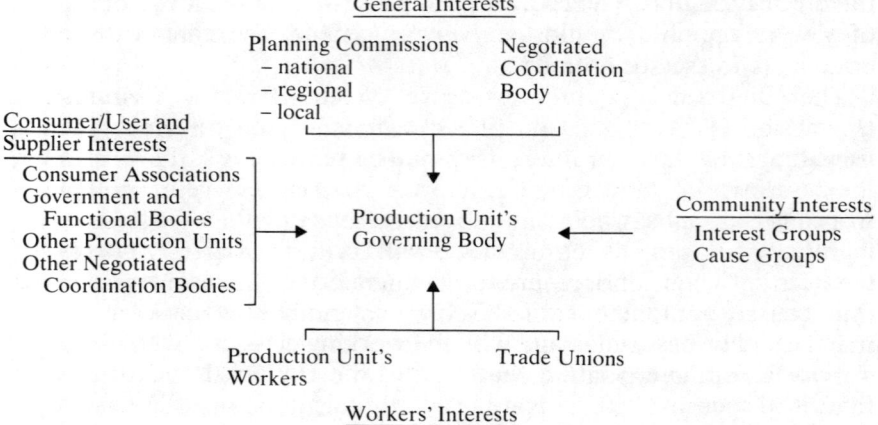

Figure 9.3   Possible composition of a production unit's governing body

public scrutiny and debate. Furthermore, included among the groups represented would be the trade unions to which the production unit's workers belonged. As a last resort, workers would always be able to take industrial action if they felt sufficiently aggrieved. Figure 9.3 illustrates this possible composition of a production unit's governing body.

A powerful influence making for agreement in the governing body would be the role of the negotiated coordination body to which the production unit belonged. The production unit would be completely autonomous with respect to its day-to-day operation and the use it made of its existing productive capacity, subject only to regular audit. However, if it were unable to meet the socially determined rate of return on assets employed, it would require subsidization from its negotiated coordination body if it were not to go out of business. Furthermore, investment would have to be agreed with its negotiated coordination body. It seems likely that negotiated coordination bodies, when making decisions about subsidies and investment, would take into account the extent to which the governing bodies of production units were in agreement and the nature of any disagreement. Hence, there would be a premium on reaching agreement.

While the governing bodies of production units would be representative of those affected by their activities, including their workers, internal organization would be on the basis of self-management. This would further decentralize decision-making to those affected. Once its governing body had defined the social interest in relation to a production unit's activities, decisions on how best to use the unit's resources to further that interest would be made by those working in the production unit. They would be in possession of the most local level of knowledge and would be best placed to use that knowledge effectively in the social interest.

There has been very little discussion of the internal organization of production units in a self-governing society. In an earlier paper, I argued that at levels below the governing body the organization of work should be the responsibility of committees on which representatives of those whose work was being organized were in a majority, with minority management representation and a right of appeal upward in the event of major disagreement (Devine 1981, p. 121). The reason for this was to combine detailed self-management by workers of the specific work they undertake with overall coordination of the internal operations of the production unit as a whole. Although this still seems to me the right objective, I now think it could best be achieved on a somewhat different basis, with self-managing work groups operating within a framework of targets and guidelines, agreed with the governing body through its executive committee, and coordinating their activities by negotiation.

The governing body, on which those working in the production unit were represented, would appoint an overall executive committee responsible for planning and running the production unit as a whole in accordance with the governing body's definition of the social interest. Each section within the production unit would elect a sectional executive committee responsible for organizing the section's work. These sectional executive committees would be accountable to the overall executive committee for ensuring that the section operated in accordance with the targets and guidelines agreed between them. They would also be accountable to their section for the targets and guidelines they agreed to and for their practice in organizing the section's work in accordance with them. Detailed coordination between the activities of sections would be achieved by negotiation, with provision for adjudication in the event of failure to agree.

People working in a production unit at functional levels less general than that of its overall planning and running would typically not spend their whole lives undertaking functionally subordinate activities. In so far as the social division of labour had been overcome, they would themselves have been involved, at other times or in other aspects of their lives, in overall planning and running activities. They would, therefore, be likely to have developed an overall consciousness and so be able to participate in the work of the production unit, and interact with those currently having overall functional responsibility for it, on a basis of equality. The fact that membership of both the overall and sectional executive committees and of any intermediate structures would normally rotate would also make for equal social relationships.

In a similar way, to the extent that everyone was an expert in something in some aspect of their lives, people would be able to recognize and respect specific expertise without being mesmerized or oppressed by it.

Internal self-management would also be the best basis for implementing any nationally agreed pattern of wage differentials in the light of local circumstances. Wages would be determined by internal negotiation within the framework of a nationally agreed incomes policy and would enter directly into cost determined prices. If a production unit was unable to meet its target rate of return because its prices were too high in relation to those of other production units in the same branch of production, the reasons for this would be examined by its governing body and then by its negotiated coordination body. If it were found that the relatively high prices were due to unduly high wages, or unduly low productivity, the production unit would be allowed time to put things right, during which it would be subsidized, but at the end of the agreed period the subsidy would cease. If, however, the reasons for the failure to meet the target rate of return were judged to be socially acceptable, the size and duration of any necessary subsidy would be decided in the light of the overall situation, as discussed in the next chapter. Thus, the process of internal negotiation would be able to take into account a wider set of considerations than relative profitability, although the outcome would have to be externally justifiable.

The local knowledge available to self-managing sections would provide the basis for the workers involved to decide on how best to further the social interest as defined by the agreed targets and guidelines for their section. To the extent that those involved were not yet fully self-activating, it would also provide the basis for any incentives and sanctions thought necessary. Decisions about individual wage differentials, promotion and discipline are most efficiently and equitably taken by the peer group. People working together are in the best position to know about one another's relative performance and also have an interest in fairness. The general principle of openness of information, with each section's record open to scrutiny by any other, would provide a safeguard against the exploitation of one section by another.

Finally, there is the question of diversity and flexibility. I think it likely that a self-governing society would place less emphasis than existing societies on economic growth, change for its own sake, and the proliferation of new products, and more emphasis on conservation and quality. However, the diversity of human interests and the importance of flexibility would surely be greater. Human creativity and personal self-development require a society in which there is scope for the widest pluralism of initiative. In the sphere of economic activity this has implications for the way in which new production units are established and for how small-scale activity is organized.

Responsibility for establishing new production units would be widely spread. Except in the case of small-scale local activity, where different arrangements would apply, decisions about new production units within existing branches of production would be the responsibility of the relevant negotiated coordination body. They would be made on the basis of the quantitative and qualitative information available about both the need to expand capacity and the wider community interests that were relevant to the determination of the social interest in each particular case. Thus, responsibility would be spread between all the regional and national negotiated coordination bodies and the interests represented on them.

With respect to new branches of production, funds would come from national, regional or local government, channelled through newly established national or regional coordination bodies or, in the case of local activities, directly. Recommendations that funds should be made available would come from the relevant planning commission. However, the initiative in making the case for new branches of production could come from anywhere. Since new branches of production tend to grow out of existing ones, important sources of initiative would probably include the planning commissions themselves, research institutes, existing negotiated coordination bodies, existing production units, and consumer and user organizations. However, any individual or group could come up with a proposal. Proposals could be made to all planning commissions at all levels and there would therefore be a multiplicity of independent centres at local and regional level making decisions about new initiatives.

Small-scale activity is a vital source of flexibility, creativity and diversity. It currently spans maintenance and repair services, professional services, cafés and restaurants, arts and crafts, music and recreation, alternative medicine and personal growth. It is currently organized on the basis of small capitalist firms, partnerships, cooperatives, charities and self-employment. The scale and character of the activities involved are such that the system of negotiated coordination bodies for existing branches of production and planning commission decisions about the establishment of new branches would probably be too cumbersome. However, atomistic competition in these activities, coordinated *ex post* by market forces, leads to self-exploitation and sharp practice. Some arrangement is needed that promotes creativity and diversity within a framework of participatory democratic social control.

One possibility is an extension of the principle of partnership between local government and the local community. Local authorities could establish centres, with facilities and resources, where people wishing to engage in the sort of activities under discussion could base themselves. The number of centres would depend on the local demand for the services being provided. The centres would be self-managed, within guidelines drawn up by the local planning commission in consultation with the local chamber of interests and adopted by the local representative assembly. If the number of people wishing to practise from these centres exceeded their capacity, a system of selection and possibly rotation would have to be evolved.

However, people would also be able to practise outside the centres, perhaps living partially on their basic income if such a system were in operation. This would provide a check on whether the centres were meeting social need. Success in attracting customers or clients outside the centres would be one consideration taken into account when allocating places in them. For activities needing to be widely available on the ground – like pubs, cafés, local shops – there would also have to be a system of licensing, operated by a section of the local planning commission, again in consultation with the local chamber of interests, to ensure the necessary coordination and cooperation. It is also likely that people engaged in the same line of activity in a locality would form organizations to exchange information and represent their interests.

If individual or small-scale cooperative activities spread beyond their initial locality they would probably have reached a scale at which they would need to be constituted as local production units. This would mean that they would have a governing body and would participate in the regional negotiated coordination body for their activity. More generally, regional and national negotiated coordination bodies would assume responsibility for coordinating the activities of any local or regional production units whose scale of operation became such as to start affecting other localities or regions. The relevant principle, once again, is that of maximum decentralization subject to the non-exclusion of affected groups.

Thus, in summary, there would be production units organized at the national, regional and local levels, according to the character of the activity involved, plus a variety of small-scale local activities undertaken by cooperative groups or individuals, for the most part in some form of partnership with the local representative assembly and planning commission. Responsibility for establishing new production units would be widely diffused and new small-scale activities could be started relatively easily. Activities that were successful at their existing level and wished to expand could do so by reorganizing as production units of the relevant level and participating in the corresponding negotiated coordination body. Flexibility, creativity and diversity would be combined with democratic social control at the different levels at which productive activity is undertaken.

9.5   Negotiated Coordination Bodies

Negotiated coordination bodies would be responsible for clearly defined branches of production and in general production units would operate in only one branch of production. All nationally organized production units in a given branch of production would belong to the national negotiated coordination body for that branch and similarly at the regional level. In some circumstances nationally organized units might also belong to regional negotiated coordination bodies, as when two or more nationally organized units in the same branch of production were located in the same region, or when a nationally organized unit was located in a region which had regionally organized units operating in the same branch of production.

Nationally and regionally organized production units would have direct relations with the local planning commissions in the areas where they were located, as would locally organized production units. Since it is unlikely that more than one production unit in any particular branch of production would be located in the same local area, there would, in general, be no need for local negotiated coordination bodies. Of course, small-scale local activities, undertaken by individuals or cooperatives, would typically be duplicated and would operate under a different set of arrangements, discussed at the end of the previous section.

There would also be branches of production with only one production unit, in the country as a whole or in a particular region. Although the issue of *ex ante* coordination at the national or regional level would not arise within these branches, it would nevertheless be desirable for there to be some external body to interact with such single production units. One possibility would be for them to have a direct relationship with the national or regional planning commission. However, it would probably be better for there to be quasi-negotiated coordination bodies, representing essentially the same interests as those on the governing bodies of the production units, but with different personnel, in order to provide a second judgement when it came to investment decisions. They would then also be poised to become full negotiated coordination bodies if circumstances changed to make it possible to have more than one production unit in the branch of production they covered.

The model of *ex ante* negotiated coordination is focused on the process of resource reallocation between different branches of production and between production units within the same branch of production. The assumption that individual production units would operate within a single branch of production raises two issues. First, how would a branch of production be defined? Second, might there not be production units that operated in more than one branch of production? The issues are related since the broader the definition of each branch of production the fewer separate branches there would be and the less likely it would be that the activities of a production unit would be classified as falling within more than one branch.

A branch of production would cover existing productive capacity and expertise that was sufficiently similar to be more or less interchangeable. It would be defined on the basis of similarity of production process, although structural linkages would also be relevant. Thus, the degree of interdependence between production units within the same branch of production would be noticeably greater than that between production units in different branches of production. In general, given the presumption in favour of decentralization, productive capacity belonging to different branches of production would be organized in different production units. However, if there were good reasons for exceptions to this norm, production units operating in more than one branch of production would belong to more than one negotiated coordination body.

The composition of negotiated coordination bodies would be determined by applying the basic principle of self-government, representation of all affected interests, and would therefore vary according to the characteristics of the activity involved. Thus, negotiated coordination bodies for nationally organized activities would be made up of representatives of the following: all the production units in the branch of production; the national negotiated coordination bodies for major supplying and major user branches; government and functional user bodies and national consumers' organizations; the sections of the national planning commission concerned with sector coordination, major new investment and regional distribution; the relevant regional planning commissions; and the relevant national level interest and cause groups, including of course the trade unions. Similar principles would apply at the regional level. The linkages involved were partially illustrated in figure 8.1 for the national level and figure 9.1 for the regional level.

Negotiated coordination bodies would be responsible for deciding how changes in the capacity of their branch of production should be achieved and how differential performance between production units within the branch should be dealt with. Production units would decide themselves on the use of existing capacity but investment would have to be agreed with the negotiated coordination body. As discussed in chapter 8, production units would be expected to obtain the socially determined rate of return on the assets they employed. Part of this would be taxed away to finance social expenditure and major investment. What remained would be at the disposal of the negotiated coordination body to finance minor investment in its branch of production. Production units that did not obtain the expected rate of return would require a subsidy in order to continue operating and this would have to be agreed with the negotiated coordination body.

Thus, the negotiated coordination body is where the *ex ante* coordination of investment decisions within a branch of production would take place and where more general social control over the use of society's productive potential than is possible at the level of the individual production unit would be exercised. It would have before it the quantitative information on each production unit generated by the interaction of demand, reflecting consumer/user choice in the use of socially determined purchasing power, and cost of production, reflecting productivity and socially determined primary input prices. It would also have available to it three sorts of qualitative information: first, information about planned major investment, new technological developments, and expected changes in demand; second, information about the reasons for any differential performance by production units, including consumer/user opinion; and, third, information about the gamut of community interests discussed in section 9.2.

This quantitative and qualitative information would be the basis on which those affected, the interests represented on the negotiated coordination body, would between them construct their own definition of what constituted the social interest in relation to the decisions facing them. It would be an exercise in self-government that did not invoke a spuriously self-evident and unproblematic concept of the social interest. It would take place within a framework determined at a more general level and would in turn help to shape the framework within which self-government at a less general level took place. The process of negotiation involved would recognize differences of interest and perception and would present the representatives taking part, and eventually the groups they represented, with the challenge of arriving at an agreed, equitable outcome. It would therefore both recognize present reality and have a transformatory dynamic.

What would happen if those involved in the negotiation failed to reach agreement? In the end, decisions would have to be taken by majority vote. This raises the question of the proportions in which interests should be represented on negotiated coordination bodies. As with the governing bodies of production units, there is no obvious principle and considerations similar to those discussed in the previous section would apply. Perhaps as a starting point, to be modified by experience, there could be three categories with equal representation: first, the production units directly involved; second, users, in the form of related negotiated coordination bodies, government/functional bodies, and consumers' organizations; and, third, community interests, in the form of planning commissions and interest/cause groups. The actual proportions themselves and the detailed basis of representation within each category would have to be agreed by those involved, probably in accordance with national guidelines and with provision for arbitration in cases of disagreement.

Given the need for a balance between the interests of those identifiably affected by the activities of a branch of production and the general need of society for flexibility in the use of its productive capacity, there would probably need to be some provision for appeal and review. Representatives on a negotiated coordination body who felt that the interests of their constituencies had been unreasonably disregarded might have a right of appeal to the relevant level planning commission. Similarly, if the representatives of the planning commission felt that insufficient attention had been paid to more general interests they should probably be able to institute a review by the planning commission. The responsibility of planning commissions for making recommendations to representative assemblies about the financing of major investment, the establishment of new negotiated coordination bodies, and, as a last resort, the reconstitution of existing negotiated coordination bodies, would give their views great weight.

Thus, the system of democratic planning and decision-making through negotiated coordination would enable a self-governing society to run the economy on the basis of agreed, socially constructed definitions of the social interest. It is also consistent with the reality of a society in the process of becoming self-governing but not yet fully there. It incorporates both a transformatory dynamic and a system of checks and balances, with sanctions available if necessary. The process of negotiated coordination, in particular the work of the negotiated coordination bodies as an alternative to coordination by market forces or hierarchical command, is considered in more detail in the next chapter.

10

Negotiated Coordination

10.1   Models of Coordination

'There are horizontal links (market), there are vertical links (hierarchy). What other dimension is there?' (Nove 1983, p. 226). I ended Part II by asserting that, although there is no other dimension, vertical links do not have to be authoritarian and horizontal links do not have to be market-based. Instead, both can be based on negotiated coordination. Chapters 8 and 9 were concerned with the process through which a democratic, self-governing society could arrive at, first, a detailed pattern of demand and a structure of primary input prices that reflect its collectively and individually determined priorities and, second, an articulation of community, consumer/user and producer interests that are represented in the decision-making processes of production units. Thus, the basis has been laid for discussion of the way in which this quantitative and qualitative information can be brought together to determine the allocation and reallocation of society's productive resources without the vertical coercion of authoritarian imposition or the horizontal coercion of market forces.

The quantitative and qualitative information both result from a conscious process of negotiation between those affected, during which differences of interest and perception are recognized and an agreed coordinated outcome is sought. However, the sense in which economists use the term coordination is more specific. It refers to the fact that in non-subsistence economies the many discrete acts of production that take place need to be coordinated so that they add up to an aggregate output corresponding to what society collectively and individually wants. The two standard models of how this coordination of production can be achieved are the model of administrative command planning and the model of the invisible hand or market forces.[1]

In command planning, the centre in principle works everything out in advance and issues instructions to each enterprise such that between them they produce the aggregate output required. Coordination takes place *ex ante*. In a market economy, each enterprise decides separately to produce what it expects to be able to sell at a profit. Relatively profitable industries attract enterprises until the additional supply causes profitability to fall; relatively unprofitable industries lose enterprises until the reduced supply causes profitability to rise. Coordination takes place *ex post*. Parts I and II discussed the case for planned *ex ante* coordination and the problems that arise both with centralized command planning and with attempts to use market forces as an instrument of planning. This chapter develops an alternative model for coordinating decisions about production and investment, using neither administrative commands nor market forces but through negotiation.

It is important to recall the distinction between market exchange and market forces. Market exchange, the sale and purchase of commodities, does not imply the operation of market forces, in which production and investment decisions are made atomistically and coordinated *ex post*. The use customers make of their purchasing power in choosing between the output of different production units generates information that is relevant to investment decisions. The way in which that information is used, however, will depend on the economic system. It may be used by each individual enterprise separately to decide to reduce or expand its own production, in ignorance of what other enterprises are doing. It may, in theory, be used by a command planner to change the instructions issued to the enterprises involved. It may, alternatively, be part of the information available to production units and their negotiated coordination bodies when making decisions about production and investment.

Thus, the argument that only market forces can generate information about consumer or user preferences is based on a confusion of market forces with market exchange. It is similarly true that market research into consumer or user needs is not the prerogative of any one system. However, there are respects in which the three models of coordination do differ in their ability to respond to customer demand. Although information on consumer and user needs may in theory be available, centralized command planning necessarily suffers from information overload and is therefore unlikely to be able to make effective use of it. Although atomized decision-makers have information about the current demand for their own output, supplemented possibly by market research into future trends, they are necessarily unaware of what their rivals are intending to do and therefore the aggregate outcome of their separate decisions will only correspond to what is needed by chance.

Negotiated coordination, by contrast, allows decentralized decision-making that is able to take account of all the information available and arrive at a coordinated aggregate response that reflects the interests of all those affected.

In the model of negotiated coordination, production units are responsible for their day-to-day activities, for the use they make of their existing capacity. They set prices equal to long-run costs, calculated on the basis of socially determined primary input prices and their prevailing level of productivity, as discussed in the next section. The principal responsibility of production units is to use their existing capacity to meet customer demand. Since the pattern of consumer and user demand is the quantitative reflection of collectively and individually determined priorities, meeting it represents a first approximation to the way in which existing capacity can best be used in the social interest. The second approximation is arrived at by combining this quantitative information with the qualitative information contributed by the interests represented on the governing bodies of production units. Thus, the key issue for production units is to use their capacity to further the social interest as they see it, within the framework of the laws, regulations and guidelines arrived at through the self-governing political process.

While decisions about the use of existing capacity are made by production units, decisions about changes in capacity are made by negotiated coordination bodies. This enables investment decisions to be coordinated *ex ante* in the light of all the relevant information. When it comes to changes in capacity, quantitative information about current demand for the output of production units at existing cost-based prices remains important, of course, but the relative importance of qualitative information about community and producer interests and expected long-run change is enhanced. Investment and expansion, or lack of investment and contraction, affect regions and localities, interests and causes, workers in different production units, in ways that are qualitatively different from the effects of changes in the use made of existing capacity. At the same time, new trends in demand and foreseen changes in technology have to be taken into account, as have expected changes in relative scarcities and prices due to planned major investment elsewhere in the economy.

Thus, the model of negotiated coordination differs from coordination by centralized command in that decisions about investment within a branch of production are decentralized to the negotiated coordination body for that branch, which involves all production units in the branch and is able to make full use of all available information. It differs from coordination by market forces in that investment decisions within a branch of production are coordinated *ex ante*, on the basis of all the available information, not *ex post*, through attempts to correct wrong decisions that were made on the basis of only part of the available information. It differs from both the other models in that the people affected by investment decisions are the people who make the decisions, consciously, in the light of an awareness of their mutual interdependence. Unlike the other models, which appeal to people's narrow self-interest, negotiated coordination encourages people to transcend their narrow self-interest and has a transformatory dynamic. Thus, it provides better information than the other models and moves beyond coercion towards the self-development of self-activating subjects.

10.2   Price Formation: Costs and Demand

If arrived at as outlined in chapters 8 and 9, the structure of demand facing production units would reflect society's collectively and individually determined priorities. Purchasing power would be distributed between personal consumption, collective consumption and investment, and economic investment, and then disaggregated, according to those priorities. The output that people collectively and individually wished to buy with their purchasing power would be an indication of its social value. However, the pattern of demand depends not only on the distribution of purchasing power but also on the pattern of relative prices. For society to make best use of its productive capacity to meet social need, relative prices should correspond to relative costs of production. Decisions on the use of existing capacity should be made on the basis of existing relative costs; decisions about new capacity should be made on the basis of the relative costs, and therefore prices, expected to prevail during the life of the investment when it comes to fruition.

Production units would set prices equal to long-run cost of production. This is made up of the cost of intermediate inputs bought from other production units and the cost of primary inputs. Intermediate inputs are materials, energy and services, used up in a single period of production, and buildings, equipment and other fixed assets, whose use is spread over several periods of production. In order to calculate the notional cost of the fixed assets used up in a single production period a principle of depreciation would be needed. Primary inputs are labour, natural resources and, leaving aside the conceptual problems involved, use of part of society's stock of fixed assets. The determination of primary input prices in accordance with social priorities was discussed in chapter 8. Wage rates, the rentals on natural resource use, and the rate of return on assets employed (capital charge), would between them reflect the desired share of personal consumption in output, the importance attached to economizing in the use of different natural resources, and any desired change in the balance of labour-intensive and fixed asset-intensive methods of production.

Costs of production calculated in this way would represent real social cost. Prices equal to them would serve as an information base to guide decision-making. They would have an accounting function, enabling production units and functional social bodies to record contributions made to and use made of the social product. They would enable production units to know how much of a product was demanded at the price it cost to produce it and therefore whether the resources required could be better used producing something else. They would have a rationing function, since when collective bodies and individuals had used all their purchasing power they would have exhausted their share of the social product. They would, finally, serve as a guide to the choice of the most economic method of production when undertaking investment. However, prices equal to costs of production based on existing capacity, on the use of existing fixed assets, would be at best only rough guides to longer-run decisions. When the period under consideration is long enough for investment in new fixed assets to take effect various interdependencies have to be taken into account.

First, there is the question of the scale of production. If there are constant returns to scale, then cost per unit of output is unaffected by the quantity produced. If, however, there are decreasing or increasing returns to scale, then unit cost depends on the volume of output. Hence, investment decisions intended to decrease or increase capacity would have to take account of estimates of the way in which the change in scale would affect unit cost, price and therefore, depending on elasticity, demand. Second, there are the interdependencies that arise from the relationship between the rate of return on assets employed and labour costs. As already noted in chapter 8, this ratio will influence the choice of technique, or method of production, where alternatives differ in their degree of labour and fixed asset intensity. The rate of return also affects the valuation, and therefore the appropriate depreciation rate, of existing fixed assets. Hence, if social priorities and therefore the ratio between rate of return and labour costs have changed since existing capacity was installed, or are expected to change, prices equal to existing cost will only be a starting point for decisions about investment.[2]

Labour costs depend on the level of wages and labour productivity. Wages would be influenced by the socially determined wage rates set out in the nationally agreed incomes policy but would be finally decided through the process of internal negotiation discussed in chapter 9.

Labour productivity is determined by the technological characteristics of the method of production embodied in the fixed assets and the efficiency and work intensity with which it is operated. Thus, labour costs, while largely determined by factors outside a production unit's control, would nevertheless be influenced by the decisions of its governing body and the way in which they were implemented by its self-managing workers. Wages paid and conditions of work would feed through into costs and prices. They would, therefore, be unlikely to diverge too far from prevailing social norms, since prices would affect demand, the degree of capacity utilization, and hence the extent to which the socially determined rate of return was achieved. Differential rates of return between production units would be the starting point for discussions in the negotiated coordination body about the distribution of investment and the payment of subsidies.

There is a clear theoretical difference between variable and fixed inputs into the production process. Variable inputs, such as materials and energy, are bought on a continuous basis and hence the quantity bought can be varied as the level of output varies. Fixed inputs, most obviously fixed assets, are acquired discontinuously, at discrete intervals. Once acquired, their use is spread over more than one production period and the quantity cannot easily be changed in the short run to take account of changes in the level of output. The distinction is, of course, to some extent arbitrary. Materials and energy may be bought on the basis of long-term contracts that cannot easily be altered in the short run. Labour is usually considered to be a variable input but the extent to which this is in fact the case depends on the social relationships prevailing in the society. Even in capitalist economies the wages of some key workers are considered by their employers to be part of fixed costs, while in statist economies until recently it was virtually impossible for enterprises to reduce their labour force in the short run and to a large extent this remains the case.

Costs per unit of output, and therefore price, would be made up of these two components: first, the cost of the variable inputs, since they can be directly related to the unit of output; second, a mark-up on these variable costs to cover fixed costs, including any fixed rentals on natural resource use, and the capital charge. The size of the mark-up will depend on the the quantity of output, that is the number of units, over which the fixed costs and the surplus to cover the capital charge are to be spread. Hence, unit cost, and therefore price, must be calculated on the basis of an assumption about the quantity of output corresponding to full-capacity working. Given the fixed costs, the desired rate of return on the fixed assets employed by the production unit, and the value of those assets, the required excess of revenue over total variable costs is determined. The required addition to variable cost per unit of output is then arrived at by dividing this required surplus by the number of units that would be produced at the assumed full-capacity level of output.

Production units would offer their output for sale at cost-based prices calculated as outlined. It is therefore possible, indeed likely, that the prices of the output produced by production units in the same branch of production would differ. This might be because the characteristics of the products of different production units and the costs of producing them differed or it might be because the cost of producing essentially the same product differed between production units. Customers would choose between the alternative product characteristic/price combinations offered by production units. Production units, depending on the demand for their products, would find themselves operating at or below full capacity, or, since the full-capacity level of output assumed for the purpose of calculating the mark-up on direct cost is necessarily notional, conceivably above it. They would therefore find that the rate of return they actually obtained equalled, fell short of, or exceeded, the desired rate of return that had been incorporated in their prices.

The way in which realized rates of return, obtained on the basis of the use of existing capacity, would be taken into account by negotiated coordination bodies when making longer-term decisions affecting production units is discussed in the next section. First, however, it is necessary to consider whether demand, as well as cost, should influence price. To make the best use of society's available productive resources it is desirable that the pattern of relative prices, which guides decision-makers in their use of the socially determined distribution of purchasing power, should correspond to the pattern of relative costs. If this is not the case, then society's productive potential is not being used to best effect in satisfying society's needs. In the long run, therefore, the supply and demand for each product should correspond at prices equal to the socially defined minimum cost of production.[3] Demand will have an indirect influence on long-run cost of production when there are decreasing or increasing returns to scale since cost per unit of output will then vary with the quantity produced. In the case of constant returns to scale, however, costs alone would determine price and demand would determine the quantity produced at that price.

The argument that demand should influence price directly applies, if at all, to the short run, to situations in which, during the period it takes to adjust capacity, demand at a price equal to long-run cost would exceed or fall short of existing capacity. First, there is the argument that changes in price due to changes in demand, with supply or capacity remaining fixed, provide signals and, in the case of market economies, incentives for changes in capacity. If demand increases and supply does not price rises and, since costs have not changed, profits also rise, with the consequence that new resources are attracted into the industry. Similarly, if demand falls in relation to capacity prices and profits fall and resources leave the industry.

In the model of negotiated coordination, it is assumed that negotiated coordination bodies will wish to adjust capacity if they are aware of the need to do so. Hence, price changes in response to changes in demand would not be necessary in order to affect profits and thereby create an incentive for capacity changes. Nor are price changes necessary to provide the information that changes in capacity are needed. A change in demand first becomes apparent as a change in the quantity being sold at the existing price and is therefore reflected in changes in stocks or orders. Such changes are perfectly good indicators or signals that an imbalance between demand and current output has developed. If a change in demand for its products proved to be permanent, a production unit would find its stocks being run down and its order book lengthening, or its stocks increasing and orders falling. This information, together with any change in the production unit's realized rate of return due to any change in the degree of capacity utilization, would be available to the negotiated coordination body when making long-run decisions affecting the production unit. Price changes in response to changes in demand are therefore not necessary for the purpose of providing information about the need to adjust capacity.

The second argument in favour of allowing price to change in response to a change in demand is that to do so allows existing capacity to be used to best social effect during the period it takes for capacity adjustment to be carried through. If demand at the existing cost-determined price becomes greater than can be supplied with existing capacity, some form of rationing will be inevitable. The best form, the argument runs, is rationing by price, since this means that available output goes to those who are prepared to pay most for it and who presumably, therefore, value it most. Similarly, it is argued, if more can be produced with existing capacity than is demanded at the existing full-cost price, a lower price, provided it covers variable cost, would enable existing capacity to make some contribution to social need until it was scrapped.

Although there might be situations in which this second argument makes sense, it seems unlikely that it would have general validity. The cost of holding stocks adequate to accommodate most changes in demand until capacity adjustment was possible would probably be accepted as socially desirable in order to enable the planned allocation of resources to be achieved on the basis of long-term costs. Furthermore, while a distribution of purchasing power according to socially determined priorities as collectively and individually disaggregated would in general be a good first approximation to what constitutes socially useful production, price in excess of cost of production is in many cases unlikely to be acceptable as a rationing device in situations of temporary shortage. Rather than rationing by price, qualitative judgement, on the basis of guidelines agreed by representatives of those affected and detailed qualitative knowledge is often likely to prove the preferred method.

Dobb argues that quantity rather than price adjustment would be the normal method of adjustment to situations of disequilibrium between demand and current supply. However, he identifies two exceptions where price might sensibly be allowed to diverge from costs: first, so-called deficit goods, whose supply cannot be adjusted sufficiently within the planning period; and, second, close substitutes produced in different branches of production with different costs when, again, it is either not possible or not socially desirable for capacity adjustment to be undertaken within the planning period (Dobb 1967, pp. 201–2). A further exception arises in relation to perishable produce, at least in the case of a glut when the maintenance of price equal to planned cost would result in waste. In general, however, demand would influence price only indirectly, when returns to scale are variable rather than constant.

10.3   The Process of Negotiated Coordination

In the model of negotiated coordination, long-run responsibility for each branch of production rests with its negotiated coordination body. Production units are responsible for deciding on the use of their existing capacity but changes in capacity are the responsibility of the negotiated coordination body. Changes in the capacity of production units in a particular branch of production may be needed for two reasons: first, because of changes in the demand for the output of the branch of production as a whole; second, because differences in performance between production units make it socially desirable to increase the capacity of some units and reduce that of others.

Major increases in the capacity of a branch of production, requiring major investment, would be decided by the national planning commission, on the basis of changes in overall social priorities or strategic direction, and finance would be made available to the negotiated coordination body by the national representative assembly. The commission would also initiate major reductions in capacity on the same basis. Other increases or decreases in a branch of production's capacity would be decided by the negotiated coordination body itself, in response to expected changes in demand not originating from major national decisions. Production units would have to agree minor investment with the negotiated coordination body, although delegated responsibility would be possible. Minor investment would be financed using the post-tax surplus of the production units in the branch of production in question, or credit from the banking system, as discussed in the next section.

How would negotiated coordination bodies know when minor changes in capacity in order to meet incremental changes in demand were needed? First, they would have information about changes in the stocks and order books of the production units they covered. Although the experience of any one production unit might be due to circumstances specific to it, the average trend would represent the experience of the branch of production as a whole. The same would be true of realized rates of return in relation to the socially determined target rate incorporated in the cost-based prices. If realized rates of return on average fell short of the target rate, that would indicate that on average the branch of production was working at below the assumed full-capacity level. It might also be the case that realized rates exceeded the target rate, indicating that notional full-capacity levels were being exceeded. Second, negotiated coordination bodies would have available the results of market research and estimates from major users of how they saw their demand changing. The continuous interchange of information through the cross-cutting network of representation involved in the process of negotiated coordination, unimpeded by the requirements of commercial secrecy, is a major advantage of the model.

Thus, negotiated coordination bodies would know what changes in the capacity of the branches of production for which they were responsible were necessary, either to accommodate centrally-taken decisions or in response to their own estimates of expected incremental changes in demand. However, the fact that a change in branch capacity is socially necessary, in order to respond to actual or expected changes in demand, is not in itself enough to define what is in the social interest when thinking about the individual production units making up the branch. In addition to the quantitative indicator represented by the pattern of demand, qualitative considerations have also to be taken into account, as articulated by the interests represented on the negotiated coordination body.

This is likely to be especially important when the change involves reductions in capacity. Branches of production may be associated with valued ways of life. They may be central activities in certain localities. They may provide favourable opportunities for particular psychologically productive activities, less available in other branches of production. However, established ways of life may also be disrupted by the expansion of capacity. Either way, therefore, change in capacity needs to be planned and coordinated with other changes taking place in the economy, and in society more generally, so that the costs of change do not fall disproportionately on those most directly affected. It seems likely that the closer we get to a self-governing society the more the pace of change will be determined by the need to ensure that it is not destructive of the human spirit but occurs in a psychologically enhancing way.

The interests represented on a negotiated coordination body would between them decide on the pace of change they thought desirable. They would include the planning commission and other bodies representing a more general interest, as well as the production units and communities directly involved. Together, therefore, they would embrace the inevitable tension between the specific and the general interest, which would be explicitly recognized in the process of seeking a negotiated definition of the social interest in each particular case. In the event of unresolved disagreement there would be a right of appeal to the planning commission for a decision on behalf of the representative assembly. If the decision, however reached, meant that the socially determined target rate of return could not be realized in the branch of production as a whole, the negotiated coordination body would seek to negotiate an agreed shortfall or excess with the planning commission.

Once a negotiated coordination body had decided what change was needed in the overall capacity of the branch of production for which it was responsible, it would have to decide how the change should be distributed between the different production units. One of the principal considerations it would take into account would be the relative performance of the different units. Furthermore, even if no change was planned for the branch of production as a whole, differences in relative performance might be grounds for socially desirable changes in the relative size of production units. Thus, the negotiated coordination body would have to evaluate the performance of the production units in its branch of production, with the production units themselves, of course, taking part in the evaluation process.

The negotiated coordination body would have access to all the records and accounts of the production units. In the first instance, it would consider the realized rate of return of each production unit in relation to the socially determined target rate, that is, the rate of return incorporated in its cost calculations. The realized rate might differ from the target rate for three categories of reason, each with potentially different implications. First, there are reasons within the control of the production unit. Thus, decisions about wage levels and conditions of work that differed from the social norm might have resulted in a product characteristic/price combination that was less, or more, attractive to customers than those of other production units in the same branch of production. As a consequence the production unit would be operating below, or above, its assumed full-capacity level and its realized rate of return would therefore fall short of, or exceed, the target rate.

Second, a production unit's product characteristic/price combination might be relatively unattractive, or attractive, to customers for reasons beyond its control. In particular, it might be in an objectively less, or more, favourable location than other production units in the same branch of production. Again, the consequence would be a realized rate of return lower, or higher, than the target rate. Third, the level of demand for the output of the branch of production as a whole might have fallen, or increased, so that, assuming their product characteristic/price combinations were equally attractive, all production units would have realized rates of return lower, or higher, than the target rate.

The problem for the negotiated coordination body would be to identify which one, or more, of these three situations was responsible for any divergence between the realized and target rates of return and then decide how to respond. In none of the three situations is the socially desirable response obvious without detailed local information.

In the first situation, a production unit might be a pioneer, experimenting with new forms of work organization to enrich the social relationships and psychological rewards of the people working in it. Its interpretation of national guidelines calling for the relative importance of such considerations to be enhanced might be in advance of that of other production units. On reflection, the representatives of other production units, and of wider interests, might agree with the pioneering interpretation. If so, the outcome of the discussion in the negotiated coordination body might be agreement on the general adoption of the new methods throughout the branch of production, with a recommendation to the planning commission that they should be more widely disseminated.

Thus, although the pioneering production unit's realized rate of return would have been below the realized rates of return of the other production units because its costs were higher, the conclusion would be not that its costs were too high but that their costs were too low. This would imply a revision of previously agreed social priorities since the higher prices would reduce the real value of purchasing power. Alternatively, of course, the negotiated coordination body might decide that the production unit in question had gone beyond what was socially desirable and agree a time limit for it to move back to the prevailing social norm. While adjustment was taking place production units with realized rates of return below the target rate would be subsidized. By the end of the adjustment period they would be expected to be realizing the target rate and the subsidy would end.

More generally, if production units, as a result of their own decisions, were turning in differential performances that the negotiated coordination body did not consider to be socially justified, they would be allowed time for adjustment during which those with higher rates of return would subsidize those with lower rates. Since the reasons for the differential performance would have been clarified, as a basis for forming a view about whether or not it could be justified, production units would have the benefit of one another's experience and socially agreed best practice would be effectively disseminated. In this way, sectionally influenced perceptions resulting in socially unacceptable levels of narrow economic efficiency would be challenged, while socially desirable innovation would be encouraged and diffused.

In the case of differential realized rates of return due to factors specific to production units, but this time beyond their control, the socially desirable response is again not obvious without detailed local knowledge. An objectively unfavourable location, in terms of narrow economic efficiency, might be a good reason for a production unit to close, if there were other branches of production that needed to expand for which the location was more favourable. However, if the location was generally unfavourable for all branches of production, or the branches of production for which it was favourable did not need to expand or provided less psychologically productive employment, then it might be socially desirable for a production unit to continue in that location even though it realized less than the target rate of return. The social interest in such cases needs to take account both of the detailed local situation, known only by those most closely involved, and of more general considerations. Once again, it would be decided in the negotiated coordination body by the representatives of all the interests affected, specific and general.

Finally, realized rates of return might diverge from the target rate because of a change in demand for the output of a branch of production as a whole. The pace at which adjustment would occur in such cases would be determined by the need to ensure that the costs of change were not borne disproportionately by those most directly affected. This is in fact the situation discussed earlier in this section when considering changes in the size of a branch of production as a whole.

Thus, when realized rates of return differ from the target rate, for whatever reason, a judgement has to be made about what constitutes the social interest in each case. In some cases, the reason for the difference might be considered socially desirable and long-run subsidies would be agreed. In other cases, the reason for differential performance would not be considered socially acceptable and a limited subsidy only would be agreed, to allow for a period of adjustment. The first approximation to the social interest, the interaction of socially determined demand and cost-based prices, represents a quantification of the general social interest. This initial quantitative indication is then refined in the negotiated coordination bodies in the light of the qualitative considerations brought to bear by the representatives of the particular interests affected. The outcome is a second approximation, a modification of the initial quantitative representation of the social interest. It is given effect through a pattern of consciously decided and agreed subsidies. The process is one of the social construction of the social interest at ever more specific levels.

Individually, negotiated coordination bodies would coordinate investment, or disinvestment, to bring about any necessary change in capacity in the particular branch of production for which they were responsible. They would do so *ex ante*, in advance of the commitment of resources, in the light of the fullest possible local knowledge of the circumstances of each production unit and of the communities and interests affected by them. Collectively, interacting with the national and regional planning commissions, negotiated coordination bodies would coordinate the implementation of major investment decisions within the economy as a whole. Negotiated coordination bodies would enable economic decisions to be coordinated consciously, yet without central administrative command, in the light of the overall situation, yet on a sufficiently decentralized basis to make effective use of local knowledge. They are the central institution of the model of negotiated coordination and are what essentially distinguishes it from the administrative command and market forces models.

Having established that negotiated coordination bodies would have the information they would need to define the social interest, and to coordinate investment decisions in accordance with it, there remains the question of motivation. In the longer term, the closer we get to a self-governing society of autonomous, self-activating subjects the more the availability of the relevant information would in itself be sufficient, since people would increasingly wish to act on the basis of their perceptions of the social interest. Even then, however, people would initially be likely to evaluate the same information differently, since their perceptions would differ according to their different experiences. In the shorter term, the weight of continuing narrow sectional and self-interest has also to be taken into account.

The pattern of cross-cutting representation that lies at the heart of the system of negotiated coordination is the principal means for containing the anti-social impact of narrow self-interest and promoting its transformation. It is also the means by which people's initial perceptions would be modified in the light of those of others. First, it provides a safeguard against information bias. The records and accounts of all economic organizations – the self-managing sections of production units, production units as a whole, negotiated coordination bodies, planning commissions – would be open, subject to regular audit and available for public scrutiny by any organization, group or individual. It is unlikely that distorted information would long survive in such an environment, particularly if it was being used to justify exceptional treatment. Since the governing bodies of production units and the negotiated coordination bodies would contain representatives of other production units and negotiated coordination bodies, as well as of customers, interest and cause groups, and planning commissions, the possibilities for systematic distortion of information would be remote.

Second, openness of information would provide the basis for any incentives and sanctions that might be considered necessary. Within the self-managing sections of production units, decisions about individual incentives and discipline would be taken by the peer group, subject to the right of trade union representation, as outlined in chapter 9. Production units themselves would have governing bodies representative of all affected groups and so no one group could insist on its sectional interest predominating. Of course, the possibility of a sectional corporate consciousness developing in a governing body, embracing the representatives of all the affected interests, cannot be ruled out. However, the representatives would themselves be accountable to those they were representing. Furthermore, in the long run the production unit would need the agreement of its negotiated coordination body for any subsidy and for investment. Corporate consciousness could only be sustained in the long run if it resulted in externally justifiable decisions accepted by the negotiated coordination body as being in the social interest. In a similar way, negotiated coordination bodies would have to be able to justify their decisions to other negotiated coordination bodies and to the planning commissions.

Thus, within a system of negotiated coordination, the anti-social impact of narrowly sectional or self-interested motivation could be contained. However, containing narrow self-interest is not the same thing as seeking to harness it and set it to work by designing an incentive system that rewards and therefore reinforces it. The model of negotiated coordination is prefigurative, in that it anticipates a society in which people wish in principle to act in the social interest and the problem is for them to decide together what that means in practice. At the same time, the model is able to accommodate situations in which this principle is not fully operative. However, its dynamic is transformatory. It cannot legislate narrow self-interest away, but neither does it reward it. Instead, it institutionalizes the requirement that specific interests are made explicit, brought up against one another, confronted with representatives of more general interests and encouraged to arrive at an integrated view through negotiation. Negotiated coordination is a process in the course of which learning occurs, perceptions change and consciousness may be transformed.

As the process of self-transformation takes place, the extent to which people are the objects of decisions taken by others diminishes and people increasingly become self-activating subjects who themselves take the decisions that affect them. As argued in chapter 7, this transformation from subaltern to hegemonic consciousness is likely to be accompanied by a change from compensatory to emancipatory activity. The more the psychological need for compensatory consumption gives way to a need for psychologically productive activities, the greater the weight likely to be given to qualitative considerations in the process of defining the social interest. Thus, negotiated coordination may be expected to become less concerned with planning the production of things and increasingly the means through which people plan their time budgets and the creation of the psychologically productive activities contributing to their further self-development.

10.4 Macroeconomic Balance

As discussed in chapter 8, the allocation of claims on society's productive potential in accordance with social priorities would result in an aggregate level of demand, a value of total expenditure, equal to the value of the full employment level of output at the cost determined prices. The required rate of return on assets employed and the rentals on natural resource use would be set at levels that between them would produce a surplus equal to the planned value of social expenditure and economic investment. The surplus would be taxed at a rate that yielded a revenue equal to the planned value of social expenditure and major investment. The post-tax surplus would then equal the planned value of minor investment. This basic framework might be modified by the use of other taxes, in particular a turnover tax and a tax on wages. The question of macroeconomic balance arises because, although planned expenditure would equal the value of the full employment level of output, actual expenditure might not always equal planned expenditure.

Government and functional social bodies might spend less, or more, than planned in a given period, adding to, or running down, their contingency reserves. Negotiated coordination bodies might not be able to ensure that all the funds made available for major investment were spent within the planning period. The actual personal saving rate might differ from the one that had been assumed for planning purposes. Thus, the planned pattern of expenditure would be modified by unanticipated saving and dissaving, involuntary on the part of collective bodies, voluntary on the part of individuals. However, in the absence of the systemic cyclical reasons for deliberately postponing or advancing planned expenditure that exist in capitalist and statist societies, unanticipated saving and dissaving would tend to offset one another. Although the planning commission would have to monitor the situation carefully, actual and planned aggregate expenditure would for the most part broadly coincide.

A further complication arises from the fact that the post-tax surplus, intended to finance minor investment, would not necessarily be distributed between branches of production and production units in accordance with the socially desirable distribution of minor investment that emerged from the decisions of the negotiated coordination bodies. Branches of production that were expanding might need to make use of some of the post-tax surplus of branches that were contracting. Production units it had been decided should expand might need to use some of the post-tax surplus of units it had been decided should contract. This redistribution of purchasing power in accordance with what was required by the socially constructed definitions of the social interest would be undertaken by the planning commissions, the negotiated coordination bodies and the banking system.

The national, regional and local planning commissions, and the corresponding representative assemblies, would be responsible for ensuring full employment in their areas of jurisdiction. If it appeared that effective demand in the country as a whole, or in a region or locality, was falling short of the level required for full employment, the relevant planning commission would recommend that contingency reserves or credit should be used to increase aggregate expenditure, distributed in accordance with current priorities. Regional and local planning commissions would also be ultimately responsible for dealing with the consequences of reductions in capacity and employment by production units in their areas and also of any disciplinary action resulting in loss of employment.

Although negotiated coordination bodies could not themselves directly run down or close production units, their decisions on subsidies and investment could indirectly have the same effect in the longer term. Regional and local planning commissions would be represented on all negotiated coordination bodies covering production units in their areas. They would be aware of all the changes potentially affecting their regions and localities that were under consideration in the different negotiated coordination bodies. Thus, they would have a crucial role to play in ensuring that decisions about the contraction and expansion of production units in their areas were coordinated. In the last resort, however, the residual task of ensuring that work was available for all those seeking it would fall to the local planning commissions and representative assemblies. They would use their contingency reserves and access to credit from the banking system to finance any necessary provision. There would be no reason in the model for real resources to be unemployed because of lack of finance.

Since prices would be cost-determined, macroeconomic imbalance in the form of actual effective demand in excess of the planned level of expenditure would not result in inflation. Excess demand would become apparent in the form of falling stocks and lengthening order books. In relation to any one branch of production this might be due to a change in the pattern of expenditure, in which case it would be accompanied by falling demand, rising stocks and idle capacity in other branches. The necessary reallocation of resources would then take place through the negotiated coordination bodies and the planning commissions, as already outlined. In the event of generalized excess demand, however, the national planning commission would recommend a reduction in planned aggregate expenditure, distributed according to prevailing social priorities.

Price increases could only occur in response to cost increases, which could only be due to increases in primary input prices or reductions in productivity. Since the relationship between the rate of return and rentals on natural resource use, on the one hand, and wages, on the other, would be determined by decisions about the desired overall allocation of resources at the national level, the only internal source of inflation, apart from falling productivity, would be money wage increases. If these exceeded on average the non-inflationary increase agreed in the nationally negotiated incomes policy, derived from the agreed share of personal consumption in total output, then prices would be higher than those assumed in planning the allocation of purchasing power. The result would be that agreed social priorities would not be achieved. The same would be true if productivity levels fell below those assumed when calculating total available national output. Inflation, as always in modern society, would be the result of conflict arising from a failure to agree over the distribution of time, effort or output.

The one additional factor that could cause inflation is the influence of higher import prices, affecting both imported consumer goods and domestic output produced with imported inputs. A deterioration in the terms of trade represents a reduction in the total output available for domestic use. The distribution of that reduction would in principle be determined through the political and planning process, in accordance with prevailing social priorities. If the agreed reduction in claims on real output was not accepted by some groups and they decided to increase their money wages to compensate for the increased price level, then costs would increase further and the result would be the start of an inflationary spiral.

This last consideration has introduced for the first time the international dimension. Although macroeconomic balance is usually interpreted to include balance of payments equilibrium, the international dimension is not discussed in this book. Nevertheless. I believe the principles underlying the model of negotiated coordination could be applied to international economic transactions. In particular, the need to combine the quantitative indicators generated by exchange at cost-based prices with the qualitative considerations articulated by community interests is as valid at the international as at the national level, although the form in which it would be institutionalized and operated would inevitably differ.

10.5 An Assessment

The model of democratic planning through negotiated coordination outlined in the last three chapters has been designed with two purposes in mind: first, as the economic aspect of a self-governing society, a third way different from both capitalism and statism; and, second, as a guide to transformatory practice in the process of consciously working for change in both existing systems. It is intended as an alternative to market socialism as the way forward, an alternative premised on the possibility of moving towards a fully democratic, self-governing society made up of autonomous, self-activating subjects. In my view, it is the prevailing mood of profound pessimism about this possibility that underlies the current vogue for market socialism.

Kornai has recently distinguished between the naive reformers, who pioneered the idea of regulated market socialism in Eastern Europe, and the radical reformers, who emerged as a trend among Hungarian economists in the late 1970s in response to their experience of the New Economic Mechanism. He considers himself to have started as naive and to have become radical. He argues that the view that 'the market is an "instrument" in the hands of the central policy maker. . . . The faith placed in the harmonious, mutually correcting duality of "plan" and "market" . . . is the centerpiece of the pioneers' naïveté' (Kornai 1986b, p. 1729). He now advocates 'market-clearing prices . . . firms should be stimulated to increase their net worth as their primary goal . . . the hardening of the budget constraint . . . a flexible capital market. The possibility of bankruptcy must be an ultimate threat . . . prosperous firms must have the opportunity to expand quickly by self-financing, by loans or by raising capital on the capital market' (Kornai 1986b, p. 1733). The role of the state is confined to macroeconomic management, monopoly regulation, infrastructure, dealing with harmful externalities and income redistribution.

Kornai's pioneers were not real market socialists. They advocated decentralized profit-maximizing decisions motivated by narrow self-interest in relation to current production, within a regulated environment, but investment was to be decided centrally. Thus, although there was to be market exchange, resources would not be reallocated by market forces. The radicals certainly are marketeers, in that investment in their models would be determined by market forces, but it is less clear in what sense they are socialist. In particular, planning seems to have disappeared, even as a desirable objective. What is so significant, I think, about the developments reported by Kornai is that they represent the full logic of attempts to harness narrow self-interest through profit related incentives and market forces. Most market socialists continue to believe that it is possible to combine planning with the use of market forces. However, both the logic of the way in which market forces operate and the Hungarian experience suggest that this belief is naive.

The model of negotiated coordination is an attempt to demonstrate that it is possible to achieve the necessary balance between centralized and decentralized decision-making without recourse to either hierarchic command or market forces. I have tried to show that planning and the effective use of local knowledge are complementary not incompatible, that investment can be coordinated *ex ante* and secondary uncertainty minimized without administrative command planning, and that horizontal transactions can be mediated by market exchange without that involving market forces. I have also attempted to establish that negotiated coordination has a transformatory dynamic and to place it in the context of a self-governing society.

For negotiated coordination to be accepted as a serious alternative model of coordination, it must be found convincing in relation to the central requirements of information and motivation. In relation to the first requirement, the model's combination of quantitative and qualitative information is, I think, convincing. It allows general and specific, overall and local, information to be integrated by representatives of those affected in the social construction of an ever more disaggregated definition of the social interest. The national representative assembly, advised by the chamber of interests, after public discussion, informed by the input of the national planning commission, decides on overall priorities. These are incorporated in a broad allocation of resources and a set of primary input prices. Decisions about the disaggregated use of those resources are decentralized horizontally to functional social bodies and vertically to the regional and local levels. The governing bodies of production units and negotiated coordination bodies, consisting of representatives of all affected groups, integrate the quantitative and qualitative information to arrive through negotiation at a definition of the social interest in relation to current production and the type and distribution of investment.

The two other models of planning, administrative command and regulated market, are both unable to make effective use of local knowledge. In neither case does the centre have the local knowledge necessary to specify adequately the constraints, whether administrative instructions or regulated determinants of post-tax profitability, that determine what people as producers do. The result is plan bargaining or the regulator game. In the model of negotiated coordination, people decide themselves what to do, along with others affected by the decision, in the light of their knowledge of general considerations and their own local knowledge.

It is important to establish that the model of negotiated coordination meets the information requirement, in order to counter the argument that the only alternative to vertical hierarchy is horizontal market and that, even if people wished to act in the social interest, they could only know what this involved on the basis of information generated by market forces. In the model of negotiated coordination, information generated by market exchange is one input into the decision-making process, but the operation of market forces, in the sense of atomistic responses to profit opportunities, is not what determines investment and leads to the reallocation of resources. However, the most powerful argument for market forces, in my view, is not that only they can generate adequate information but rather that they are incentive compatible, that is, they reward effective response to the information they generate, where reward is in terms of narrow self-interest. The enduring appeal of market forces to realists, or cynics, is the argument that the invisible hand harnesses private vice to public good.

In the end, the issues of information and motivation are inseparable. Market forces cannot generate all the information needed for decision-making in the social interest. The orthodox theoretical recognition of this is the concept of market failure. It leads to a concern with attempts to modify the framework of constraints within which narrow self-interest is pursued, through fiscal and monetary policy, on the one hand, and the respecification of property rights, on the other. However, attempts to harness narrow self-interest inevitably result in the use of local knowledge to get round regulation, rather than in it being made available by those who possess it for use in the social interest. The consequence is an unending regulator game that is not really a game at all since it is wasteful of human creativity and morally corrosive.

More generally, the concerns that I have referred to as the qualitative interests that have to be taken into account when defining the social interest already make themselves felt in both statist and capitalist economies, but in perverse forms – through direct action, pressure groups, lobbying, personal influence and corruption. Since they are motivated by defensive sectional or narrow self-interest, such attempts to modify the outcome of market forces or manipulate the administrative structure are necessarily subaltern or self-seeking, without regard for the specific interests of others or for more general interests. They eventually produce a reaction against the politicization of economic decision-making and a demand either for parametric regulation or for no regulation at all. Ironically, the attempt to supersede or control market forces through collective action and the bureaucratic intervention of the state has resulted in a reassertion of market ideology that is in danger of becoming hegemonic.

If the model of negotiated coordination meets the information requirement, as I believe it does, is it also convincing in relation to motivation, or is it hopelessly utopian? Again, I think the requirement it incorporates for affected interests to negotiate an agreed course of action, with cross-cutting representation on decision-making bodies, provision for majority decision-making, openness of information, rights of appeal, and residual sanctions in the form of collective decisions about subsidies and the distribution of investment, is convincing. Of course, the model is also utopian, but not hopelessly so. It looks forward to a self-activating, self-governing society but it incorporates a transformatory dynamic. In the end, judgement about the motivational content of the model will probably depend on the view taken of what people are capable of becomimg and hence of whether or not a self-governing society is possible.

Would an economy based on negotiated coordination be efficient? It would certainly not be Pareto-optimal within the static neo-classical welfare economic framework. Stock levels adequate to allow time for adjustment through negotiated coordination, without disruptive bottlenecks or inconvenient shortages, would tie up productive resources. Where agreement could not be reached, it would take time for sanctions coupled with further discussion to result in adjustment. Resources, by comparison with the static welfare economic general equilibrium ideal, would be wasted. However, Pareto optimality is neither possible nor necessarily desirable. When compared with actual existing systems and market socialist models, I see no *a priori* reason why the model of negotiated coordination should be less efficient. Indeed, the advantages of the model in relation to information and motivation suggest just the opposite.

Perhaps more to the point is the question of innovation. Would negotiated coordination be so cumbersome, would the weight attached to reaching agreement be such, that innovation was inhibited? This is a complex issue. The sources of ideas and prototypes for innovation would be widely dispersed, ranging from small-scale activities, through research institutions, to existing production units and negotiated coordination bodies. Decision-making on proposals for innovation would also be widely dispersed, with the planning commissions at all levels having resources available to finance innovation requiring major investment and negotiated coordination bodies similarly able to adopt and finance innovations involving minor investment. At the next stage, cross-cutting representation on decision-making bodies would ensure the rapid diffusion of successful innovations. On the other hand, the need to obtain agreement might limit the scope for the single-minded obsessional pursuit of an idea against all odds. However, the extent to which institutional agreement is already needed for innovation in capitalist and statist economies should not be forgotten and speculative innovative work could be encouraged by earmarking some resources specifically for that purpose.

It is likely that both the rate and character of innovation would be influenced by being determined through negotiated coordination. Representatives of workers, consumers and users, of conservation and environmental groups, of other interested groups, would all be involved in the decision-making process. They would have a direct say in the sort of innovation that was supported and adopted. Thus, by contrast with the sluggish innovative performance of the statist countries and the out of social control combination of socially harmful, wastefully trivial and socially useful innovation in capitalist economies, innovation in a society based on negotiated coordination would be subject to conscious social choice.

One consequence of this, in the context of a movement from subaltern to hegemonic consciousness, from compensatory to emancipatory activity, would probably be a greater harmony between the economy and the environment, with the rate of growth of material production increasingly tending towards zero. Although far in the future, this raises the possibility that the balance between centralization and decentralization in society would shift further towards the latter. To the extent that production becomes routine, involving established patterns of exchange, the need for continuous coordination of change diminishes. Active planning and coordination are most necessary in conditions of rapid change. This would mean that decision-making by production units would become relatively more important and by negotiated coordination bodies relatively less important.

Finally, there is the question of whether the process of negotiated coordination would not be too complicated, too time-consuming. Perhaps people have better things to do with their lives than spend them in meetings and negotiations to organize production, not to mention similar involvement in relation to their self-governing activities in civil society. I think that this is an important consideration making for opposition to the trend towards the politicization of economic life, but that it is misconceived. It ignores the long-term historical trend towards the commitment of an increasing proportion of time and other resources to the conscious negotiation of social interaction. The reasons for this trend are the increasing socialization of production, the growing interdependence of social life in general, and the trend towards greater equality, although this latter still has a long way to go. People are less and less prepared to allow things to be done, or just to happen, to them and are more and more potentially able to assert active, conscious control over their lives. This is discussed further in the next chapter.

I believe that the way forward is not to depersonalize interdependence by elevating the role of impersonal market forces but to personalize it through negotiated coordination and the democratization of politics. Interdependence can be based either on inequality, the universal situation to date historically, or on equality, the dream of visionaries through the ages. If it is based on inequality it can only be sustained by coercion, whether in the form of one of the infinite varieties of personal dependence or of dependence on the outcome of impersonal market forces. The loss of nerve over the possibility, perhaps even the desirability, of achieving equality is what underlies today's love affair with the market. Faced with a choice between direct personal dependence and the apparent personal autonomy of an actor in a formally equal competition, even though mediated by market forces and therefore in practice inevitably unequal, most people would probably choose the latter. However, that is not the real choice.

On the one hand, the conflicts engendered by inequality are unlikely to be more than temporarily suppressed by the depersonalized coercion of market forces. Sooner or later the long arm of history makes itself felt through uncontrolled and uncontrollable behaviour, whether in the form of vested interests that paralyse or destabilize a society, civil unrest, coups, corruption that morally corrodes a society, irrationalism, fundamentalism or illiberalism. On the other hand, there is an alternative. The model of democratic planning through negotiated coordination is offered as a vision of a society and an economic system committed to equality; equality of access to material resources but above all equality of access to psychologically productive activity. The final chapter of this book considers trends within the advanced capitalist and statist societies, as the twentieth century approaches its end, that might be developed and transformed as part of a process of transition towards such a fully democratic, self-governing society.

PART V

Conclusion

11

Conclusion

11.1 Introduction

Part III set out the objectives of democratic planning, as I see them: bringing the production process under social control, so that productive resources are used to meet social need; participatory democracy, so that people define social need for themselves; and the abolition of the social division of labour, so that everyone has equal access to psychologically productive activity. The overall objective was summarized as self-determination by self-activating subjects in a self-governing society. Part IV then outlined a model of democratic planning that would further these objectives. In it the coordination of economic decisions is achieved through negotiation between those who are affected by them, rather than through the coercion of the state or of impersonal market forces.

In this concluding chapter I speculate on the prospects for transition to a self-governing society based on negotiated coordination. In my view what is involved, in both East and West, is the continuation of a long-run historical trend towards political and economic democracy. The developments in the Soviet Union under Gorbachev give hope that sooner or later pressures for democratization make themselves felt. Perestroika at its most radical is seen as a revolutionary democratic reconstruction of Soviet society. It can be interpreted as an application of Brus's argument, set out in chapter 3, that in modern societies democracy is one of the principal forces of production. At the same time, the emergence of the new right in the West is a salutary reminder that there is nothing inevitable about the continuation of the democratic trend. What happens depends on what people do, on social and political action.

During the past decade, in both East and West, people have reacted against state control. In the context of a vision of movement towards a self-governing society, this is to be welcomed. However, it is important to remember that the growth of state control in modern times has been to a large extent a response to the inadequacies and excesses of market forces. In the Soviet Union, state control made possible a planned economy and the use of productive resources to further the national objective of economic development, in a way that would not have been possible by relying on market forces. In the West, the role of the state in the economy has also been to supersede or regulate private ownership and market forces. In both, the growth in the role of the state has been a historically progressive development, part of the process of achieving social control over production.

Reaction against the state has occurred because people have experienced state action as oppressive, arbitrary and inefficient. In the statist countries the experience has been of a monolithic political system, chronic shortage and a lack of dynamism, which have given rise to alienation, apathy and conformism. In the capitalist countries it has taken the form of welfare paternalism, state sector insensitivity to consumers and users, corporatism and inefficiency due to the partial suspension of the restructuring function of capitalist economic crises. The result in both systems has been a rediscovery or re-evaluation of the supposed virtues of the market mechanism.

State control consists of bureaucratic action. It is experienced as alien because it smothers people's impulses towards self-help and their desire for self-determination. It is not socially controlled collective action that is personally enabling. Nevertheless, as argued in chapter 5, it is crucial not to lose sight of the public or common aspect of the state. The way forward is not to resurrect private enterprise, whether capitalist or sectional, but to complement the public aspect of state ownership and activity with increasing social control over the state and new forms of social ownership and control. Economic pluralism should not be equated with a mixed economy in which public and private ownership coexist. Social control requires political and economic democracy and is therefore incompatible with both statism and private ownership.

In the West, the new right has hegemonized the reaction against state control. It has successfully argued the case for market forces as the only way to allow scope for personal initiative and harness it to the general good. It has led, interpreted, shaped and integrated all impulses for self-help and self-determination in the direction of individualism and private enterprise. Although this is essentially a reactionary devel-opment, it has gained its strength by addressing real issues that the traditional left has decried or ignored. The dominant response of non-dogmatic socialists in the West, disoriented by the success of the new right and lacking any credible alternative, has been to argue for market socialism as the way forward. It is claimed that this avoids the dangers of statism and enables the advantages of planning to be combined with decentralization in a form of regulated market mechanism.

This claim was examined in chapter 4 and found wanting. Theoretical analysis and historical experience both lead to the conclusion that planning and the operation of market forces are incompatible. The growth of organized groups pursuing their sectional interests is one of the best documented characteristics of developed societies. In a market-based economy these groups seek to frustrate the working of market forces when it affects them adversely. Pressure develops for state action to offset the instability and inequality inherent in a market economy. However, the narrow self-interest that provides the motivation of a market economy carries over into the political sphere in the form of special pleading, lobbying, corruption, direct action, and any other action available to influence state decisions. The result, as already noted, is that state control is experienced as oppressive, with people's creativity being used to get round it rather than to further democratically agreed collective action. Thus, the political conditions for deregulation and rolling back the state are created.

While the reaction against state control in the West has been hegemonized in a reactionary direction, developments in the Soviet Union have a quite different feel to them. Glasnost and perestroika are advocated as revolutionary policies intended to bring about qualitative, systemic changes in Soviet society. Since the objective of a self-governing society has democracy at its heart, these developments have to be judged primarily in terms of their democratic impetus. At the moment they represent an attempt at revolution from above. The legacy of statism in the Soviet Union is an alienated, passive, conformist, subaltern consciousness on the part of most people outside the ruling group, and many inside it. The development of autonomous organized groups has been inhibited by the monolithic political system and the suffocating dominance of the party/state. Autonomy and self-activation, necessary preconditions for self-government, have to be learned through generations of struggle and participation by people in defining and demanding what they perceive as being in their interests. The absence of such experience is presumably what Gorbachev means when he refers to the lack of a democratic tradition in the Soviet Union.

Whatever contributes to the development of such a tradition clearly represents progress in the Soviet context. Glasnost and perestroika appear to be releasing a wave of creativity and popular energy. The beginnings of open democratic discussion and action within the party and the intelligentsia are apparent. Some independent groups and associations have emerged and may be allowed to contest elections. In the economic sphere the emphasis is on more autonomy for enterprises, with wages related to efficiency and output quality. There is also talk of introducing a central role for market forces in the longer term, although what is intended here remains vague and the crucial question of how planning and market forces might be combined remains unaddressed. All these changes are seen as part of a general move to break the bureaucratic power of the state and to promote an ethos of personal responsibility.

One way of interpreting perestroika is as an attempt to replace an incompetent and venal bureaucracy by a more competent meritocracy, invoking the assistance of the masses to do so. There is a sense in which the drive for modernization, efficiency, higher output, better quality, and incentives related to ability, skill and effort, parallel the attempted Czech reform of 1968, characterized by Bahro as the glorious revolution of the intelligentsia (Bahro 1978, p. 189). At the same time, however, the changes are being undertaken in the name of democracy. It seems possible that they may interact with the power of the democratic ideal and the evident tensions and conflicts of interest in Soviet society to produce an era of social conflict and struggle that cannot be orchestrated and ultimately controlled from above.

There are certainly many issues around which struggle is likely to develop. The changes seem to be creating expectations and releasing aspirations for a better life and, perhaps, for more popular control of the everyday conditions of that life. However, the process of removing subsidies and moving towards a cost-based price structure, together with the upheaval in income differentials as relatively low-paid professional workers gain at the expense of relatively high-paid skilled or semi-skilled workers, will result in a major redistribution of real income. Furthermore, although so far the maintenance of full employment has been guaranteed, the threat of closure in the event of persistent unprofitability is bound to be perceived as a threat to job security. Finally, any move towards the geographical decentralization of political power will come up against pressures of national separatism akin to those that have been so destabilizing in Yugoslavia.

Thus, the process of transition from the monolithic statist system towards a self-governing society is bound to be traumatic and it is hard to see how prolonged social upheaval and conflict can be avoided. It is impossible for a non-specialist in Soviet affairs to speculate on which institutions in Soviet society are likely to be transformed as the process gets underway, what new institutions are likely to be created, how genuine pluralism in civil society and at the interface with the state is likely to develop. It is equally impossible to be sure that the process of democratization and modernization will not be cut short as the inevitable tensions and conflicts make themselves felt. However, sooner or later Soviet society will have to democratize if it is not to continue to stagnate. As it does, there will be a generalization to the society as a whole of the process of negotiation and mutual accommodation that already takes place within the ruling group. As this generalization occurs the interests involved in the negotiation will become more explicit and those affected will increasingly articulate what their interests are themselves.

While the Gorbachev era promises to be exciting, signs of progress in the West are harder to come by. From the standpoint of democratic advance and transition towards a self-governing society the situation in the capitalist countries is contradictory. The role of the state in economic and social life has been partially redefined and reshaped. Popular aspirations for autonomy and self-determination have been hegemonized by the new right. The regulated market economy shows no sign of being able to produce an economic and social performance that meets people's longer term aspirations. New social movements have developed, along with a growing crisis of traditional politics, particularly on the left. What is needed is a political movement and practice that breaks the impasse by making democracy and self-government the organizing principles of social action.

11.2   Negotiation: Retrospect and Prospect

A major objection to the model of negotiated coordination outlined in Part IV is likely to be the demands it would make on time, the proliferation of meetings it is assumed would be involved. However, I think this objection is misconceived. In modern societies a large and possibly increasing proportion of overall social time is already spent on administration, on negotiation, on organizing and running systems and people. This is partly due to the growing complexity of economic and social life and the tendency for people to seek more conscious control over their lives as material, educational and cultural standards rise. However, in existing societies much of this activity is also concerned with commercial rivalry and the management of the social conflict and consequences of alienation that stem from exploitation, oppression, inequality and subalternity. One recent estimate has suggested that as much as half the GNP of advanced western countries may now be accounted for by transaction costs arising from increasing division of labour and the growth of alienation associated with it (North 1984).

Thus, there is no *a priori* reason to suppose that the aggregate time devoted to running a self-governing society based on negotiated coordination would be greater than the time devoted to the administration of people and things in existing societies. However, aggregate time would be differently composed, differently focused and, of course, differently distributed among people. If administration is conceptualized as production, then negotiated coordination can be thought of as a revolution in both the process of production and in its output, without necessarily requiring any significant increase in the aggregate input of time.[1] Furthermore, as argued in chapter 7, it is a mistake to regard time spent running things as inherently unproductive psychologically. Of course, if it did turn out that people began to feel too much time was being spent on administration, then that would become an issue for public discussion and reform.

In existing capitalist societies, negotiation takes place within and between economic enterprises and state bodies, within and between self-governing organizations, and between the former and the latter. The process of transition towards a self-governing society consists of widening the scope of this negotiation, extending it to new areas, working for the inclusion of all affected groups, and creating the conditions in which the negotiation is increasingly between equals. Since the Second World War there have been three main areas within the economic sphere in which experience relevant to this process has been gained: the trend to neo-corporatism, with the evolution of procedures for reaching a broad consensus on priorities among the principal interests in the economy; arrangements for coordinating the activities of enterprises in individual industries or sectors; and moves towards industrial democracy. The first two were discussed in chapter 2 and the third in chapters 6 and 9.

These developments opened up the possibility of subordinate classes and groups having a direct influence on the decisions that affect them. The state and its agencies became terrains of struggle, with the conflicting interests seeking to negotiate an agreed course of action. Moves towards industrial democracy raised the possibility of a similar development in the boards of enterprises. As in all negotiations, the outcome depended on the relative strengths of the interests involved, on the prevailing balance of power. Given the privileged position of business in capitalist society, of course, there was always the danger that subordinate interests would achieve only token representation, or would become incorporated, and in general this is what happened. Trade union influence has been limited to certain corporate gains and at times the exercise of a veto.

Even so, when state intervention and worker involvement break the spell of inevitability cast by market forces, a potential threat to the established order arises. By the mid-1970s the inflationary consequences of full employment and the popular discontent created by state paternalism had undermined the post-war consensus and created the conditions for the emergence of the new right. In the UK, this occurred in a context of post-imperial decline and the paralysis induced by the defensive strength of the trade unions and the result was Thatcherism. Thatcherism has broken with neo-corporatism, rejecting tripartite negotiation with the unions and management, has adopted an arm's length relationship with a private sector greatly enlarged by privatization, and has weakened the power of the unions through unemployment, legislation and the ideology of self-determination through individual rather than collective action.

The response of the left and some trade unions to the approaching end of consensus was the alternative economic strategy. However, in the key areas of economic planning and popular participation it remained underdeveloped. The principal concept to emerge was that of the planning agreement, a tripartite agreement to be negotiated between the government, on the one hand, and the management and unions of each major public and private enterprise, on the other. The planning agreement system was intended to ensure that the strategic decisions of each enterprise were in conformity with overall national economic priorities and at the same time in the interests of the enterprise's workers. Incentives were envisaged in the form of financial assistance linked to the objectives set out in the planning agreement. Thus, the system presupposed the existence of a democratically determined set of national priorities, worker involvement in strategic decision-making within the enterprise, and a way of fusing national priorities and worker interests into operational guidelines and indicators for performance assessment at the level of the enterprise.[2]

During the 1980s the alternative economic strategy began to attract criticism from some of its originators and earlier supporters on four grounds: that it was statist in conception, a programme primarily for government action, with scant attention to popular involvement; it was parochial rather than internationalist in orientation; it ignored environmental constraints; and it was focused on white male sectional priorities, ignored the feminist demands articulated during the 1970s and was devoid of any vision of a society based on new human and social relationships, on new moral values (Aaronovitch 1986). This criticism was part of the reaction against state control and paternalism that had already been successfully hegemonized by the new right.

The alternative economic strategy was the nearest the left has come in the post-war period to developing a hegemonic strategy. However, it suffered from the left's general political weakness and was effectively abandoned as the left became marginalized by the advance of Thatcherism. At the same time, the success of the new right in national politics gave added impetus to a gathering trend on the left towards an emphasis on decentralization and local initiatives, with particular interest in the possibilities of municipal socialism. The work of the Greater London Council (GLC) between 1981 and its abolition in 1986 was the most striking example of this and provides a rich body of experience to draw on.

The GLC sought to create a partnership between the local state and popular involvement in the struggle for jobs, socially useful production and social control. It rejected the concept of planning as a blueprint imposed from above, advocating instead a process of popular planning in which power is shared between workers, users and communities, all involved from the beginning in drawing up strategic plans for their particular workplaces, industry sectors and localities. This insistence on the politics of production, on planning as a conscious political process, as opposed to seeing production as a purely technical matter of either implementing a blueprint drawn up by others or responding to market forces, was a major advance. It held out the possibility of reuniting the ideals of democracy and planning and went alongside a more general orientation towards creating a democratic partnership between the state and civil society (Campbell and Jacques 1986).

However, the prospect of popular democratic planning remained for the most part a vision rather than becoming a reality. The two fundamental reasons for this were the pressure of market forces and the level of development of the human resources involved. Attempts to work against the logic of market forces were hindered by private ownership, the GLC's limited powers and the hostile central government. They also suffered from a lack of clarity about how to mesh the immediate interests of the workers and communities directly affected with more general interests. The problems in relation to human resources had two aspects to them, both of far-reaching significance for the development of a self-governing society. There was a shortage of skilled personnel committed to the objectives of the GLC's strategy, which turned out to be more serious than any shortage of finance. Equally inhibiting, however, was the absence of flourishing autonomous groups in civil society, of a network of self-governing groups representing the self-organization of the people of London.[3]

This was part of a more general, political, problem. The GLC was committed to the public sector and the voluntary sector, to the state and to civil society. Yet civil society, and particularly the trade unions, proved unable to rise to the challenge of the partnership that was offered. As Campbell and Jacques argue,

> The GLC defined, sensitised, inspired new constituencies of support – ethnic groups, women, gays and lesbians, arts groups, transport users. It fashioned a new progressive coalition. But two things remained problematic in this enterprise and were never resolved, the Labour Party

and the trade unions. The Labour Party remained essentially external to these developments, it did not feature as an active agent in the process we have been describing and was never transformed by them. Likewise, the trade unions outside County Hall never found a new place, a new role for themselves. The politicians learnt from *Red Bologna*, but the trade unions didn't. In short, the GLC, an administration, was transformed, the labour movement was not. (Campbell and Jacques 1986, p. 10)[4]

Negotiation today is primarily between those who possess power as part of the group that runs society. In capitalist societies in the economic sphere it complements and modifies the influence of market forces, which remain dominant. Subordinate groups have forced their way into the negotiation as they have become more powerful as a result of their self-organization and action, helped by the moral force of the democratic ideal. However, their lack of economic power and their subaltern consciousness means that they remain subordinate, oscillating between incorporation and oppositionism. In a way, negotiated coordination, embryonic and underdeveloped, already exists. The task is to transform and extend it so that its potential dynamic for movement towards a self-governing society is increasingly realized.

Institutional developments in three key areas are currently required for the assertion of greater social control over production through conscious negotiated coordination. These are, first, forms of worker involvement in strategic decision-making in the enterprise, followed by consumer and community group involvement; second, moves towards industry or sector working groups, comprising representatives of the major enterprises, trade unions and other interests, to discuss sectoral strategies and exchange information on investment; and, third, a revival of the National Economic Development Council, or a comparable body, to discuss overall priorities, including macroeconomic policies and a voluntary incomes policy informed by the need to avoid inflation in the context of movement towards a redefined full employment and greater equality. All three developments are possible within the medium term, make no assumptions about concurrent changes in legal ownership, and have the force of the argument for economic democracy behind them.

However, the crucial requirement for democratic advance is a quantitative and qualitative strengthening and transformation of the autonomous self-governing organizations of civil society – trade unions, consumer/user groups, other interest and cause groups. This necessarily involves the transition from subaltern to hegemonic consciousness and hence the role of political parties. This process is considered in the next section.

11.3   Struggle, Participation and Transformation

Although the argument for it is compelling, democracy is achieved only as a result of struggle, primarily by those who are currently excluded from participation in the decisions that affect them. The first stage in collective action is struggle around specific demands: for higher wages, shorter waiting-lists, a pedestrian crossing, a new arts' centre; against a dangerous production process, an unfair dismissal, a proposal for nuclear dumping. These struggles may have great importance in strengthening collective organization, yet in themselves they do not lead beyond the specific issue. The need is to transform them into the democratic demand for participation in the decision-making process, with eventual recognition that decisions on these issues are interdependent and need to be taken in the light of one another.

As long as subordinate groups pursue their separate interests and demands independently of one another they cannot effectively challenge the position of the dominant group in society. As argued in chapter 7, within the functional division of labour there is a category of planning and running activities, activities concerned with the system as a whole. In a society in which the social division of labour has not been abolished, the people who perform these activities constitute the dominant group and enjoy privileged access to the society's material and psychologically productive resources. The group's actions have a twofold character: they fulfil necessary overall social functions and they maintain the dominant position of the group. However, they appear primarily in their first role, as necessary actions in the general good, with the consequence that their effect in reproducing inequality and privilege is obscured. In this way, the hegemonic position of the ruling group is maintained.

For subordinate groups to make the transition from subaltern to hegemonic consciousness requires a combination of action outside and participation inside the decision-making bodies of society. Each group needs to organize itself and formulate its own interests as it currently perceives them and then confront those interests with the interests of other groups as formulated by them. This is necessary in order for groups to develop an awareness of how their particular interests and decisions relate to one another and need to be modified so that they can be integrated into a definition of the overall or general interest that provides a coherent alternative to the definition offered by the ruling group.

The process of transition is bound to be immensely difficult since what is involved is a redistribution of power. The reason why subordinate groups have a subaltern consciousness is that they are subordinate. They are relatively powerless to influence the decisions that affect them and spend most of their time in psychologically unproductive and compensatory activities. Collective behaviour that is defensive and sectional, individual behaviour that is narrowly self-seeking, appear to be the only forms of action open to people. Yet, as long as subordinate groups retain a subaltern consciousness they will remain subordinate. One manifestation of this problem has been the inability of the trade union movement to develop a strategy for economic democracy at the level of the enterprise (Lane 1987). Another has been the tendency for left councils to make authoritarian use of the local state, in pursuit of apparently progressive policies, as a substitute for the involvement of civil society on the basis of a transformed consciousness. This authoritarianism inevitably feeds new right ideology and thus creates the conditions for the eventual isolation of the councils (Campbell 1987).

In the absence of hegemonic consciousness and developed procedures for negotiated coordination, decentralization of decision-making to the groups most immediately involved is likely to have contradictory effects. Control by residents' associations of estates, or by parents' associations of schools, may result in racist or social class-based discrimination. Worker-controlled enterprises may pursue sectional interests or engage in self-exploitation. More generally, the growth of decentralized centres of power, in the absence of unifying institutions and values, is more likely to lead to sectional conflict, institutional sclerosis and social stalemate than to result in harmonious cooperation. If it does, there is likely to be a reaction against the conflict and inefficiency involved, with the dominant group in society leading a turn to state authoritarianism, or to impersonal market forces, or a combination of the two, and thus reasserting its hegemonic position.

The alternative is for sectional interests to become transformed so that they work together on the basis of an agreed definition of an overall social interest different from that offered by the dominant group. This would enable a challenge to to be made to the dominant group's hegemonic position. The question is how this can be achieved. The general answer, I think, is to be found in a democratic political practice, combining respect for the autonomy of different social movements and self-governing organizations with a commitment to equality. Such a political practice cannot, therefore, be based on simply adding up the demands of different groups of people, or of the same people in different aspects of their lives. As they now are, groups have differential access to resources and different partial consciousnesses. There is no reason to suppose that their different demands will be consistent with one another and every reason to suppose that they will conflict. What is required is transformatory experience involving social interaction in a context of argument about what would promote equality in each concrete situation.

Part of that experience will be living through the social crises that result from failure to reach agreement over the distribution of resources and failure to respect the rights of others. The consequences of accelerating inflation due to a struggle between temporarily equally powerful social groups over real income, or of racial conflict due to prejudice and inequality, can be severe. Social crises can be thought of as learning situations, providing opportunities for reappraisal and motivating change. Of course, the direction of change is not predetermined. Crisis normally produces reaction. Progressive advance requires a political and moral climate informed by the values of democracy and equality, and the existence of credible and realizable measures that will further those values in the specific situation.

Laclau and Mouffe have argued that the logic of democracy 'is only a logic of the elimination of relations of subordination and of inequalities' and that it needs to be combined with 'a set of proposals for the positive organization of the social' if it is to be part of a hegemonic project (Laclau and Mouffe 1985, pp. 188, 189). It is not within the scope of their book to make suggestions as to what such proposals might be, nor do they discuss the agency that might articulate a hegemonic project around such proposals. I believe that at the institutional level the model of negotiated coordination provides such a set of proposals, a vision of what the social organization of a radical democracy might look like. It can be seen as a development from existing institutions and practices already present in the state and in economic enterprises. It also points to ways in which existing institutions of civil society might be developed, for example, trades councils or associations of voluntary groups.

The agency for articulating a hegemonic challenge, or competing challenges, to the hegemony of the existing dominant group can only, in my view, be the transformed political party. At the level of society as a whole, the process of simultaneous articulation and transformation involves an interaction between political parties and philosophies and the various interest groups. Different political parties pursue different hegemonic strategies, based on different values and visions, seeking to transform and articulate the different group interests in different ways, each claiming to represent the overall interest. In unequal societies, parties based on the values and interests of the dominant groups have a privileged position in the political process of deciding between these alternatives.

The challenge facing the parties that seek to articulate the interests of subordinate groups on the basis of emancipatory values and equality is to contribute to a simultaneous transformation of consciousness and change in the balance of forces in society. This requires that the parties are themselves transformed by learning to respect the different interests represented within them while at the same time articulating those interests on the basis of shared values and a common strategic outlook. Of course, articulation in this sense does not mean the current practice of pretending to a spurious unity that obscures real differences and fractures at the first sign of strain. It means arriving, through negotiation in the course of which initial positions are modified, at a coherent set of policies that recognizes both real differences and common values.

As power is redistributed and greater equality is achieved, the process of struggle and transition towards a self-governing society moves on to the next stage. This process of struggle, participation and transformation provides the only ultimately convincing answer to the question of motivation in the model of negotiated coordination. Pateman expresses the issue exactly: 'The problem is that any form of radical social and political change seems to presuppose that Rousseau's second great transformation of human nature has already taken place; the form of consciousness needed for, and that will be further developed within, the new social order must, it seems, already be in existence or change will not be possible.' She also suggests the answer: 'It is during their social life together that individuals learn how to cooperate and . . . develop the capacities necessary for the creation and maintenance of a voluntarist social order. Hopes for the future depend upon the potentiality for social and political education, and upon social and political action and organization' (Pateman 1979, pp. 176, 177).

11.4 A Self-activating, Self-governing Society

Although democratic planning through negotiated coordination is a model of economic organization for a self-governing society of self-activating subjects, it seems likely that in a self-governing society negotiated coordination would be the appropriate organizing principle for all aspects of social life. Unless the social interest is assumed, wrongly, to be self-evident and unproblematic, it can only be socially constructed by the people whose interest it is.

Decisions as a result of conscious social interaction, through negotiation, are already the norm in modern societies, with the major exception of those economic decisions coordinated by market forces. Even in relation to economic activity, the long-term trend in both capitalist and statist countries has been for the impersonal outcome of the operation of market forces to be modified or replaced by the administrative actions of the state, involving negotiation. However, at the moment the negotiation is typically not between equals, with the result that the outcome is still largely determined by the distribution of power. The less equally is power distributed, the more the outcome is dictated by the powerful; the more equal people are, the greater the extent to which the outcome is determined by conscious decisions arrived at through negotiation informed by the agreed values of the society.

The absence of adequate social control over the state has produced a reaction against the historical trend towards the modification and eventual supersession of market forces. There is a danger that a countertrend may be becoming established. Instead of major economic decisions being brought increasingly under conscious social control, a trend is emerging for them to be returned to the domain of impersonal market forces, with outcomes that no one willed but which reproduce inequality and benefit the powerful. In both capitalist and statist countries the option of moving towards greater social control over the economy has for the time being lost ground, with the market option gaining support. Given the existing distributions of power in the two systems this is perhaps not surprising. Ruling groups do not voluntarily give up their dominant position.

There are, thus, two interconnected aspects to the process of moving towards a self-governing society: first, the achievement of equality, so that negotiation is between equals; and, second, the replacement of impersonal market forces by conscious control over planned economic activity. The two aspects are interconnected because neither is possible without the other. Equality is impossible without replacing market forces as the coordinating mechanism for economic decisions, because market forces operate through and reproduce inequality. The replacement of coordination through market forces by negotiated coordination is impossible without equality, since faced with a choice between unequal relationships of personal dependence and relationships based on formal equality, with actual inequality mediated by the coercion of market forces, people eventually settle for the latter.

The historical trend towards equality still has a long way to go and may even have been temporarily reversed. Once formal political equality as citizens has been won, the next objective is to win economic equality, which is in any case necessary for full political equality. Unearned income deriving from the unequal ownership of property is incompatible with economic equality and in modern society this is the moral part of the case for the common, social ownership of the means of production. While there may be a case, during the process of transition to a self-governing society, for earned income inequalities, on incentive grounds or to influence job choice between different

industries and localities, differentials need to be publicly and continuously justified in the light of a presumption in favour of equality.
Equality of access to the output of society's productive resources is an
essential part of economic and political equality.

However, if a self-governing society of self-activating subjects is to
be achieved, the crucial inequality that has to be overcome is inequality
of access to society's psychologically productive activities. It is just
about theoretically possible to conceive of a society in which people
enjoy formal political equality and equal income, yet are divided into
doers and the done to, organizers and the organized, planners and the
planned, runners and the run. However, such a society would not be
self-governing, people would not be self-activating, and they would not
be equal. Economic activity does not just produce output in the form of
goods and services to be consumed. Political activity does not just
create a well- or ill-governed social order. The characteristics of the
activities, of the relationships, that people are involved in determine
their possibilities for self-development. These activities and relationships are the way in which people produce, people create,
themselves.

Thus, the central requirement for advance to a self-governing society
of equal subjects is movement towards more equal access to the
material and psychological resources necessary for self-development.
Abolition of the social division of labour is the precondition for ending
the oldest forms of oppression and inequality, between men and
women and between mental and manual labour. It is also a precondition for achieving global ecological balance, since the end of
subalternity and alienation will enable people to transform their
unconscious need for compensatory consumption into a conscious need
for emancipatory activity. If capitalism and statism have today in their
different ways created the objective and subjective possibilities for
advance to socialism, communism and self-government, it is up to us to
decide whether to act on those possibilities, whether to draw on the
internal and external resources available to us to transform both our
circumstances and ourselves.

If we decide to do so, we have to find ways of going beyond reliance
on the operation of impersonal market forces for the coordination of
our economic activity. The model of democratic planning through
negotiated coordination outlined in Part IV is an attempt to show that
this is possible without recourse to administrative command planning.
It is an attempt to demonstrate that there is a third way that is both
realistic and yet has a transformatory dynamic. The only other third
way that has been proposed, regulated market socialism, is neither
realistic nor transformatory. It is based on an internally inconsistent
political economy in which people undertake economic activity on the

basis of narrow self-interest yet regulate themselves by non-narrowly self-interested political action in the social interest. Democratic planning through negotiated coordination, by contrast, is a model that offers us the possibility of taking responsibility for our lives and in so doing transforming ourselves.

Movement towards democratic planning and a self-governing society requires political action informed by a hegemonic political strategy. Without the development of autonomous, self-governing groups in civil society, struggling to assert their interests in relation to the state and the economy, there can be no progress. Without such groups finding the way to transform their existing subaltern, sectional, consciousness into hegemonic, overall, consciousness, there can be no challenge to the dominant position of the ruling hegemonic group. Transformatory political action has to be informed by a credible vision of a better society. One of the factors inhibiting such action has been the crisis of the traditional socialist vision, not least the loss of confidence in the possibility of combining freedom and democracy with planning. I hope that the model of democratic planning through negotiated coordination will contribute to thinking about how, particularly in relation to the economy, optimism about the possibility of a better society can be combined with realism about how people are and what we can become, what together we can make of ourselves.

Notes

Chapter 1   Introduction

1 It is difficult to decide what term to use for the Soviet Union and the countries of Eastern Europe, not to mention China and Cuba. In this book, for reasons discussed in chapter 5, I use the term *statist* when referring to the overall character of these societies, and *centrally planned* or *command* when referring specifically to their economic systems.

2 In a fundamental sense exploitation occurs through the domination of capitalists or their agents over workers in the labour process, see Rowthorn (1980, ch. 1). For a classic text on Marxist political economy, see Sweezy (1962). For a discussion of recent theoretical work, see Roemer (1986).

3 Of course, such attempts have invariably been part of a political upheaval. However, official proposals for economic reform have typically not included workers' councils or other elements of industrial democracy based on genuinely autonomous worker involvement, although this may be changing with Gorbachev.

4 For a technical treatment of competitive general equilibrium, see Arrow and Hahn (1971); for a defence of its use, see Hahn (1973); and for a non-technical summary, see Hahn (1982). On methodological individualism, see Levine, Sober and Wright (1987); Lukes (1973, ch. 17). Western theoretical literature on economic planning has been dominated by the construction of models of decentralized planning designed to achieve outcomes comparable to that of competitive general equilibrium analysis, one reason why it has been so largely beside the point; for a survey, see Cave and Hare (1981, ch. 6).

5 This is referred to in the literature as the trade off between (Pareto) efficiency and equality; see Meade (1964). For a discussion of the same issue in the context of the experience of the market-oriented reform in Hungary, see Kornai (1980a).

6 This is not to deny that some planning occurs in capitalist economies; see chapter 2. Nor would I suggest that the potential advantages of planning

are fully realized in the statist countries; see chapter 3. I am discussing here a democratic socialist economy, yet to be achieved.

7 The same argument applies to the choice of which method of production should be used when more than one is available. Decisions are made on the basis of estimates of the pattern of relative costs and prices that will prevail during the life of the capacity to be installed. However, in the absence of planning these estimates are affected by secondary as well as primary uncertainty. Two further considerations should also be noted. First, in general relative prices cannot be determined until either the real wage or the rate of profits is known; see Sraffa (1960). Second, the above discussion in terms of rational decision-making is concerned with narrowly economic questions of resource use. Broader social questions are also relevant to decisions about investment and choice of technique and are discussed below.

8 For three differing analyses of the waste arising from oligopolistic rivalry, see Aaronovitch and Sawyer (1975), Baran and Sweezy (1968) and Cowling and Mueller (1978).

9 Although Dobb has been interpreted as espousing market socialism in one of his last works (Dobb 1974), he clearly rejects market forces in the sense outlined here. Any ambiguity arises from a usage that does not distinguish precisely enough between market exchange and market forces.

10 The established pattern is related to Kornai's concept of vegetative, or autonomous, control; see Kornai (1980b, p. 148). There are also similarities with the behavioural theory; see Cyert and March (1963).

11 The same point in a political context has been made by Beetham (1983), who argues that the nation state as a decision-making unit is too large for some decisions and too small for others.

Chapter 2   Capitalist Planning

1 The last three paragraphs are based on Hancock and Gowing (1949, chs XI and XV); and Robinson (1951, pp. 43–54).

2 For an account of how the foundations of the welfare state were laid by work undertaken within the machinery of government of the British wartime coalition, see Addison (1975).

3 For a more detailed account of the budgeting process, see Mitchell (1966, pp. 56–60).

4 Whether the unprecedented period of prolonged full employment between 1945 and the late 1960s was due to demand management or to other factors has been a subject of controversy; see Bleaney (1985, ch. 4). Britain's experience differs from that of other countries in the timing of both the commitment to and the achievement of full employment. It also differs in the forms of intervention adopted. However, at the most general level a common pattern is evident. For an authoritative, if optimistic, survey, see Shonfield (1965); see also Tobin (1980, pp. 46–8).

5 For a discussion along these lines applying a logic of collective action based on game theoretic coalitions to historical situations, see Olson (1982).

6   Adaptive expectations – people form their expectations on the basis of lagged adaptation to past experience; rational expectations – people understand how the economy works, are immediately aware of the ultimate effect of any change and immediately alter their behaviour accordingly. By contrast, Keynes believed expectations were character-ized by animal spirits, with businessmen exhibiting a herd instinct and careering about wildly together.

7   Cf. 'Monetarism is the incomes policy of Karl Marx. By deliberately setting out to base the viability of the capitalist system on the maintenance of a large "industrial reserve army", monetarists validate Marx's analysis' (Balogh 1982, pp. 177–8).

8   The split between macro and micro policies has been noticeably sharp in Britain. At one level of explanation this is because of the *laissez-faire* arm's length tradition (Shonfield 1965, ch. VI); at another it is because of the finely balanced relationship between the classes, which made micro-intervention potentially more subversive of capitalism in Britain than elsewhere (Smith 1981, p. 82).

9   Richardson has argued convincingly that the logic of the standard model of perfect competition, based on perfect knowledge and atomized decision-making, is paralysis, since an opportunity for all is an opportunity for none (Richardson 1960, p. 57). In practice firms can only act if there are imperfections which to some extent insulate them from instantaneous competition. If imperfections do not exist then firms seek to create them (Richardson 1965; 1967). It follows that pure indicative planning, by perfecting the information available to firms, may have the opposite effect to that intended (Richardson 1971). This underlines the fact that the problem with atomized decision making is not primarily inadequate information on the part of decision makers but rather the absence of consciously coordinated decision-making.

10 For assessments of the National Plan, see Brittan (1969, ch. 10); Budd (1978, ch. 6); Meadows (1978); Shanks (1977, chs 1–2); Surrey (1972).

11 See also McArthur and Scott (1969, p. 26). For assessments of French planning, see Cave and Hare (1981, ch. 4); Cohen (1977); Estrin and Holmes (1983); Shonfield (1965, chs V, VII, VIII).

12 This analysis of Japan's industrial policy is based on Boltho (1985) and Brown (1980). Boltho's discussion is an examination of recent work suggesting that the importance of Japan's industrial policy has been generally overstated, a suggestion Boltho rejects.

Chapter 3   *Central Planning*

1   For overviews of the Soviet-type system of central planning, see Cave and Hare (1981, ch. 2); Dobb (1966, chs 14, 15); Ellman (1979); Gregory and Stuart (1986); Nove (1977); Zimbalist and Sherman (1984, chs 7–9).

2   For a bitter indictment of the system and its problems by previously sympathetic critics from the Budapest school, see Feher, Heller and Markus (1983).

3   The system of material balances is primarily concerned with consistency and starts from the existing structure of the economy and pattern of inter-enterprise transfers. While it may approximate to a consistent plan, it is in no sense able even to approximate to an analytically optimal plan, that is, one that would maximize the achievement of the planners' objective function, if of any degree of complexity. However, such optimal planning cannot sensibly be taken as an ideal for purposes of comparison or evaluation since it is entirely technical, not socially based, and implies the existence of perfect knowledge. Nevertheless, the need to use resources efficiently, to take account of differences in the real costs of production involved in achieving given objectives in different ways, is central to the technical content of planning. The structure of relative prices, however determined, and the criteria for investment decisions are crucial here. Similarly, although input–output analysis takes account of the secondary effects that arise from the material balance system's revision of output targets and input requirements in the attempt to achieve consistency, it is based on known, fixed technical coefficients and is therefore not a substitute for that system. Nevertheless, much can be learned from its use as a supplementary technique. For discussion of these issues, see Augustinovics (1975); Cave and Hare (1981, ch. 10); Dobb (1955, ch. III; 1960; 1967, Part 5; 1970b, Part II); Gregory and Stuart (1986, pp. 171–7, 193–202, 245–53); Nove (1983, pp. 90–106); Zimbalist and Sherman (1984, pp. 240–6, ch. 9).

4   For an early but authoritative discussion of overcentralization, see Kornai (1959).

5   See Portes (1979, p. 124); Radner (1975, p. 112); Rosenberg and Birdzell (1986, p. 30).

6   The Czech experiment was cut off by the Warsaw Pact invasion in 1968. For its design, see Holesovsky (1973).

7   On the reform in the GDR, see Gregory and Stuart (1980, ch. 8); Karen (1973); Selucky (1972, ch. 3). On economic reform in the Soviet Union and Eastern Europe generally, see Bornstein (1979); Brus (1975, pp. 148–71); Cave and Hare (1981, chs 3, 9); Ellman (1968); Gregory and Stuart (1986, ch. 13); Holesovsky (1977, pp. 216–222); Nove (1980); Nove and Nuti (1972, Part Four); Portes (1972); Selucky (1972); Zimbalist and Sherman (1984, ch. 11).

8   See Gomulka (1986, ch. 1). Gomulka's position on this is more or less identical to that of Bahro (1978, Part One); see chapter 5.

9   This summary is based on Hanson (1986; 1987).

Chapter 4   Market Socialism

1   Lange's model is sometimes included in this family, but such an interpretation is probably unfair. It fails to take account of Lange's principal concern: 'The real issue is *whether the further maintenance of the capitalist system is compatible with economic progress*' (Lange 1938,

p. 110); and also of his judgement that '*the real danger of socialism is that of a bureaucratization of economic life*' (Lange 1938, p. 109).

2   In the UK the long process of coming to terms with reality and creating the conditions for a democratic socialist renewal is best documented in the pages of *Marxism Today*; see Hall and Jacques (1983); Jacques and Mulhern (1981).

3   On the structure and early experience of the NEM, see Balassa (1973); Morva (1975); Portes (1972); Selucky (1972, ch. 6).

4   A hard budget constraint, of course, is what is assumed to confront the price-taking firm in a perfectly or imperfectly competitive market. Competition policy in capitalist economies is an attempt in the context of oligopolistic or monopolized markets to safeguard or substitute for competition as a control mechanism. See Devine et al. (1985, ch. 9).

5   On the experience of the NEM up to the end of the 1970s, see Cave and Hare (1981, ch. 3); Galasi and Sziraczki (1985); Gregory and Stuart (1980, ch. 8); Hare (1977); Hare et al. (1981); Kornai (1980a); Zimbalist and Sherman (1984, ch. 15)

6   Commenting on the NEM in its introductory period Portes argued that the fundamental unresolved problem in systems of state ownership was the absence of a dynamic capital market: 'The structural transformation of the economy cannot proceed very far without diversification, mergers and liquidations in response to profit opportunities, or their absence' (Portes 1972, pp. 656–7). Thornton made essentially the same point from a different angle: 'The Hungarian case shows, however, that simply establishing market incentives does not necessarily result in efficient performance in economic units unless property rights in the firm's assets are fully exercised. The present socialist ownership arrangements are likely to provide for short-run and monopoly behaviour and to generate income differentials that may reflect differential access to economic rents in the system' (Thornton 1975, p. 322). Kornai, arguing that even after 1979 the budget constraint remained soft, writes: 'Enduring losses do not lead to "death", to the liquidation of the enterprise; and conversely "death", the liquidation of the enterprise and its absorption into other units, may occur by administrative decision, independently of considerations of profitability. It is not the market that performs natural selection, it is the government office that orders decimation' (Kornai 1986a, p. 92).

7   The terminology used reflects the Yugoslav ideology of self-government, in which society not the state owns the means of production. Given the absence of political democracy and the presence of continued social stratification, this is at best self-government of the political and economic bureaucracy. The conditions necessary for genuine socialization of the means of production are discussed in chapter 5.

8   Zimbalist and Sherman cite in particular three studies: Adizes (1971); Comisso (1979); Hunnius (1972). They note a diversity of results from regions differing in level of development and ethnic make-up.

9   On the evolution and experience of the Yugoslav system, see Flaherty (1982); Gregory and Stuart (1980, ch. 8); Neuberger and James (1973);

Pejovich (1973); Sacks (1984; 1985); Schrenk and Ardalen (1979); World
Bank (1979); Zimbalist and Sherman (1984, ch. 16).

10 For example, see Horvat (1982); Selucky (1979); Sik (1976).

11 It could be argued that market forces do not have to rely on narrow
self-interest for their operation. Those responsible for running enterprises
might follow rules laid down by the centre because they thought that was
the right thing to do, even if their own narrow self-interest were
unaffected by the outcome of their decisions. Lange's model, in which
managers follow certain non-profit-maximizing rules on the basis of prices
set by the centre and adjusted by it through trial and error to clear
markets, appears to be such a case (Lange 1938, sections III, IV).
However, the assumption that the problem of motivation has been
overcome goes against the grain of current advocacy of market socialism.
Furthermore, market exchange as a means of generating information is
not the same thing as the operation of market forces. In Lange's model the
former exists but the latter does not.

12 Detailed references are not given except for quotations. For Brus, see his
(1972, ch. 5; 1973, ch. 1); for Nove, see his (1983, Part 5).

13 For a fundamentalist response, see Mandel (1986).

14 Kornai has moved in the opposite direction and now regards his own and
Brus's early work as naive in believing in the possibility of a planned
regulated market: 'The faith placed in the harmonious, mutually
correcting duality of "plan" and "market" . . . is the centerpiece of the
pioneers' naïveté' (Kornai 1986b, p. 1729). He now appears to believe in
fully-fledged market socialism, with little, if any, pretence at planning
(Kornai 1986b, section VII.D).

15 Even if people are in some sense involved in setting the parameters, or at
least agree with them in general, there will always be grounds for
exceptions in the light of local circumstances. Even if the legitimate
grounds for exception are specified and agreed in advance, there will
always be unforeseen cases and unforeseen outcomes, with those affected
sooner or later seeking special treatment.

Chapter 5   The Socialization of Production

1 With both, of course, having themselves been preceded by varieties of
primitive communal society; see Hobsbawm (1964); Leacock (1972).

2 For a defence of the traditional interpretation, see Cohen (1978). For a
recent survey, see McLennan (1983).

3 The sense, if any, in which pre-revolutionary Russia was stagnant is, of
course, a matter of controversy. Lenin, in his criticizm of the Narodniks,
argued that capitalism was in fact developing in Tsarist Russia (Lenin
1960).

4 Pre-revolutionary Russia, the actually existing socialist countries of the
Third World, and most of the East European countries, were all subject to
imperialist domination and were ripe for an industrializing and modernizing social formation when their current regimes were established. The

exceptions were Czechoslovakia and the GDR. However, they, like the other East European countries, had the statist social formation imposed on them by the then Stalinist Soviet Union.

5 The general impossibility of defining production relations without reference to the superstructure, in particular to law and ideology, has been increasingly asserted by modern Marxists. For a brief discussion, see (Hodgson 1984, Appendix A).

6 In the Soviet Union and the less developed statist countries the statist mode of production initially probably did accelerate economic development. However, the Soviet model was also imposed on countries with relatively developed economies and very different traditions, in particular Czechoslovakia and the GDR. In these countries the retarding and inhibiting effect was probably dominant from the beginning.

7 More accurately, there is political democracy in the developed capitalist countries. There are, of course, plenty of capitalist countries which do not have political democracy, probably most. On the other hand, no countries with command planning systems have political democracy. See (Lindblom 1977, ch. 12).

8 Although Brus's central reasons for rejecting this argument, discussed in the rest of this section, are compelling, he adduces one reason which, in my opinion, is wrong. Focusing on Djilas's 'new class' (Djilas 1958), he argues against the view that the bureaucracy constitutes an exploiting class and in doing so appears to reject the view that statism represents a new mode of production (Brus 1973, pp. 94–6). However, he does not consider the view, discussed in the first section of this chapter, that statism is a mode of production *sui generis*. Along with Bahro and Horvat, I agree with Brus that the concept of a new property-owning class is inappropriate but nevertheless also hold the view that statism is a new mode of production characterized by contradiction between the apparatus, or bureaucracy, and the masses, or the people.

9 Hirst, in the main theme article of a symposium on the future of socialism, starts by arguing against administrative command planning and for what he calls associationalist socialism, with which I am in broad sympathy. However, he ends up arguing against any form of planning. See Hirst (1987, pp. 9–10).

10 For an inspiring 'gay contribution to human survival' that poses the choice eloquently and starkly, see Fernbach (1981).

Chapter 6   Democracy

1 Primarily the theorists of participatory democracy, see Macpherson (1977); Pateman (1979); but, see also the neo-pluralists Dahl (1985); Lindblom (1977).

2 Significant possible exceptions are Bahro and Horvat, since they both reject political party pluralism. The same is true of Burnheim, who rejects democratic representation through election altogether in favour of demarchic selection by lot of decision makers who are statistically

     representative of those affected by the decision. See Bahro (1978, pp. 350–1); Burnheim (1985, pp. 101, 111); Horvat (1982, p. 321).

3   Throughout the chapter discussion of what a self-governing society might look like merges with consideration of possible ways of moving towards it. This reflects the fact that although end state and transition are conceptually distinct there is continuity in the processes involved.

4   Although there is no perfect method of election, some system of proportional representation is clearly desirable, the particular form depending on the relative importance attached to precise proportionality and minority representation.

5   The title of a book outlining the approach adopted by some feminists in the 1970s in struggles over welfare provision; see London to Edinburgh Weekend Return Group (1979). For an evaluation of that experience, see Rowbotham (1986, pp. 98–104).

6   Classical Marxism's emphasis on the primacy of production derives from its concern with what Marx called the pre-history of human society, the period during which the preconditions for socialism and communism were being created. However justified this emphasis may have been in classical Marxism, it cannot be carried over into the era of human autonomy and self-government.

7   Of course, not all political theorists take this view. Indeed, with Nozick and Hayek as exemplars of the new right's legal democracy, Held notes a new polarization of democratic ideals (Held 1987, ch. 9). Nevertheless, the tendency for the incompatibility thesis to gain ground has been a marked feature of the past decade.

8   Held places community services, 'childcare, health centres, education', within civil society (Held 1987, p. 290). This is in the context of his model of democratic autonomy in which, presumably, the coercive element present in these services as currently provided by the state has been overcome. At the moment, these services involve both coercive and voluntary relationships and so have a contradictory location.

9   This taxonomy is similar to Horvat's, except that he argues for the legal prohibition of political parties and their replacement by political societies, like the Fabians, on the grounds that political parties promote political passivity rather than political participation (Horvat 1982, pp. 320–2).

10   It may be that the interest group category is too broad and should be divided into economically-based interests, such as trade unions and professional bodies and, in capitalist societies, employers' groups, on the one hand, and the rest, on the other. This would make sense if, as seems likely, the characteristics of the groups and the nature of their interests differ significantly between these subcategories.

11   The contrast between East and West in terms of the degree of development of civil society was, of course, emphasized by Gramsci in relation to the situation existing before the 1917 Russian revolution (Gramsci 1971, p. 238).

12   On the power relationships underlying women's oppression, see Barrett (1980). For an influential general discussion of the dimensions of power, see Lukes (1974).

13   On the difficult experience of the West German Greens in seeking through direct democracy, mandation and rotation to combine partici-pation and the avoidance of oligarchy with leadership and expertise, see Ware (1986, pp. 122–5).

14   In fact, I think compulsion might be justified in terms of Held's principle of autonomy, although I certainly would not wish to do so. The principle is set out as follows: 'individuals should be free and equal in the determination of the conditions of their own lives; that is, they should enjoy equal rights (and, accordingly, equal obligations) in the specifi-cation of the framework which generates and limits the opportunities available to them, so long as they do not deploy this framework to negate the rights of others' (Held 1987, p. 271). Since public life has to be conducted, people who choose not to undertake their fair share of public responsibilities are negating the right of at least some others only to undertake their fair share of such responsibilities and hence their right to live a balanced life.

Chapter 7   Abolition of the Social Division of Labour

1   Rattansi argues that although Marx in his early writings conflated the functional and the social division of labour he did not do so in his mature work, where he accepted the necessity of a functional division of labour and concentrated on the abolition of the social (Rattansi calls it class) division of labour, especially that between mental and manual labour (Rattansi 1981).

2   Bahro's book appeared as *Die Alternative* (the alternative) in German but as *The Alternative in Eastern Europe* in the English translation. This is unfortunate, since although the analysis is primarily of Eastern Europe, the alternative offered is intended to replace capitalism as well as statism.

3   Since the interrelated themes of the social division of labour and the dimensions of social consciousness recur throughout Bahro's book, references are given only for quotations. On absorbed consciousness, see especially Bahro (1978, ch. 6); on surplus consciousness, see especially Bahro (1978, ch. 10).

4   This is, of course, a greatly simplified account. For a fuller discussion of the characteristics, dimensions and structure of work from the standpoint of this chapter, see Bahro (1978, ch. 6); Hegedus (1977, ch. 5).

5   For a related argument in the context of an explanation of inflation in terms of rising real income expectations eventually outstripping any achievable rate of increase in labour productivity, see Devine (1974, pp. 81–2).

6   Positional goods are either '(1) scarce in some absolute or socially imposed sense or (2) subject to congestion or crowding through more extensive use' (Hirsch 1977, p. 27). The positional character of culture in existing societies that is referred to here is social, i.e. the aspect of the satisfaction derived from culture that depends on the exclusion of others.

7   Hirsch argues for a reduction of income inequality on these grounds in his
    discussion of positional jobs – jobs towards the top of functional hierarchies
    which, without distinguishing between the functional and social division of
    labour, he asserts are necessarily limited in number; see Hirsch (1977, pp.
    41, 183–4).

Chapter 8   National Priorities and Planning

1   In an open economy, the cost of imports has to be taken into consideration
    at the level of the economy as a whole and the cost of imported intermediate
    inputs enters into the cost of production at the level of the production unit.
2   Sraffa uses the term rate of profits not rate of return.
3   In times of natural disaster or other crisis it is conceivable that a decrease in
    real and therefore money income would be necessary.
4   For further discussion of these issues concerning investment, choice of
    technique and prices, see (Dobb 1967, Part 5; Dobb 1970b, chs 8–9).

Chapter 10   Negotiated Coordination

1   Kornai (1986b, p. 1690) refers to these as bureaucratic and market
    coordination. He recognizes that other forms of coordination exist, without
    specifying them, but conducts his discussion of the Hungarian reform
    process entirely in terms of the changing balance between these two
    standard forms.
2   In fact, the situation is still more complicated. The degree of fixed asset
    intensity itself is not given independently of the rate of return. It can be
    thought of as depending on the interrelationship between the length of the
    production period of the fixed assets, the time profile of when within that
    period the resources required for their production are used, and the rate of
    return. This gives rise to the phenomenon of 'reswitching' or 'capital
    reversal'; for a survey, see Harcourt (1972). It also gives rise to the
    indeterminacy referred to in chapter 8, an interdependence between
    relative prices and technical coefficients, which is broken by the central
    determination at the macro level of the share of investment in total output.
3   Socially defined in the sense that both the wage level and the factors
    influencing productivity would have been determined through the social
    interaction constituting the interlocking processes of negotiated coordi-
    nation and would therefore have been publicly justified and accepted.

Chapter 11   Conclusion

1   I owe this point to David Purdy.
2   On the alternative economic strategy, see Conference of Socialist
    Economists (1980); Aaronovitch (1981); Cobham (1984). For a detailed

NOTES TO CHAPTER II

model of economic planning in Britain close to the 'gradualist' version of the alternative economic strategy, see Hare (1985, chs 5–8).
3   On the experience of the GLC, see Murray (1984); Greater London Council (1985); Palmer (1986); Rustin (1986); Mackintosh and Wainwright (1987).
4   The relationship between the communist administration in Bologna and the community has been widely considered to be a particularly successful and in many respects unique example of a partnership between the local state and local civil society; see Jaggi, Muller and Schmid (1977).

Bibliography

Aaronovitch, S. (1981): *The Road from Thatcherism* (London, Lawrence & Wishart).

Aaronovitch, S. (1986): 'The Alternative Economic Strategy: Goodbye to All That?', *Marxism Today* (February).

Aaronovitch, S. and Sawyer, M. (1975): *Big Business* (London, Macmillan).

Aaronovitch, S. et al. (1981): *The Political Economy of British Capitalism* (Maidenhead, McGraw-Hill).

Abramsky, C. (ed.) (1974): *Essays in Honour of E.H. Carr* (London, Macmillan).

Adam, J. (1980): 'The Present Soviet Incentive System', *Soviet Studies*.

Addison, P. (1975): *The Road to 1945* (London, Cape).

Adizes, I. (1971): *Industrial Democracy: Yugoslav Style* (New York, The Free Press).

Arrow, K. and Hahn, F. (1971): *General Competitive Analysis* (San Francisco, Holden-Day).

Augustinovics, M. (1975): 'Integration of Mathematical and Traditional Methods of Planning', in Bornstein, M. (ed.) (1975).

Bahro, R. (1977): 'The Alternative in Eastern Europe', *New Left Review*, 106.

Bahro, R. (1978): *The Alternative in Eastern Europe* (London, New Left Books).

Bakunin, M. (1977): *God and the State*, in Woodcock, G. (ed.) (1977).

Balassa, B. (1973): 'The Firm in the New Economic Mechanism in Hungary', in Bornstein, M. (ed.) (1973).

Balogh, T. (1982): *The Irrelevance of Conventional Economics* (London, Weidenfeld and Nicholson).

Baran, P. and Sweezy, P. (1968): *Monopoly Capital* (Harmondsworth, Penguin).

Barrett, M. (1980): *Women's Oppression Today* (London, Verso).

Beetham, D. (1981): 'Beyond Liberal Democracy', *The Socialist Register*.

Beetham, D. (1983): 'The End of the Nation State?', *University of Leeds Review*.

Bettelheim, C. (1976a): *Class Struggles in the USSR, First Period 1917–23* (Brighton, Harvester).

Bettelheim, C. (1976b): *Economic Calculation and Forms of Property* (London, Routledge & Kegan Paul).

Beveridge, W. (1944): *Full Employment in a Free Society* (London, Allen & Unwin).

Blackaby, F. (ed.) (1978): *British Economic Policy, 1960–74* (Cambridge, Cambridge University Press).

Bleaney, M. (1985): *The Rise and Fall of Keynesian Economics* (Basingstoke, Macmillan).

Bliss, C. (1972): 'Prices, Markets and Planning', *Economic Journal*.

Boltho, A. (1985): 'Was Japan's Industrial Policy Successful?', *Cambridge Journal of Economics*.

Bornstein, M. (1979): 'Economic Reform in Eastern Europe', in Bornstein, M. (ed.) (1979).

Bornstein, M. (ed.) (1973): *Plan and Market* (New Haven, Yale University Press).

Bornstein, M. (ed.) (1975): *Economic Planning, East and West* (Cambridge, Mass., Ballinger).

Bornstein, M. (ed.) (1979): *Comparative Economic Systems* (4th edn; Homewood, Ill., Irwin).

Bornstein, M. (ed.) (1985): *Comparative Economic Systems* (5th edn; Homewood, Ill., Irwin).

Brittan, S. (1969): *Steering the Economy* (London, Secker & Warburg).

Brown, C. (1980): 'Industrial Policy and Economic Planning in Japan and France', *National Institute Economic Review*.

Brus, W. (1972): *The Market in a Socialist Economy* (London, Routledge & Kegan Paul).

Brus, W. (1973): *The Economics and Politics of Socialism* (London, Routledge & Kegan Paul).

Brus, W. (1975): *Socialist Ownership and Political Systems* (London, Routledge & Kegan Paul).

Brus, W. (1980): 'Political System and Economic Efficiency: The East European Context', *Journal of Comparative Economics*; reprinted in Gomulka (1986).

Brus, W. (1985): 'Socialism – Feasible and Viable?', *New Left Review*, 153.

Budd, A. (1978): *The Politics of Economic Planning* (Manchester, Manchester University Press).

Burnheim, J. (1985): *Is Democracy Possible?* (Cambridge, Polity Press).

Cairncross, A. (1970): 'Introduction' to Devons. E. (1970).

Campbell, B. (1987): 'Labour's Left Councils: Charge of the Light Brigade', *Marxism Today* (February).

Campbell, B. and Jacques, M. (1986): 'Goodbye to the GLC', *Marxism Today* (April).

Cave, M. and Hare, P. (1981): *Alternative Approaches to Economic Planning* (London, Macmillan).

Chester, D. (1951): 'The Central Machinery for Economic Policy', in Chester, D. (ed.) (1951).

290 BIBLIOGRAPHY

Chester, D. (ed.) (1951): *Lessons of the British War Economy* (Cambridge, Cambridge University Press).

Cobham, D. (1984): 'Popular Political Strategies for the UK Economy', *Three Banks Review*.

Cohen, G. (1978): *Karl Marx's Theory of History: A Defence* (Oxford, Oxford University Press).

Cohen, S. (1977): *Modern Capitalist Planning: The French Model* (Berkeley, University of California Press).

Comisso, E. (1979): *Workers' Control Under Plan and Market* (New Haven, Yale University Press).

Conference of Socialist Economists, London Working Group (1980); *The Alternative Economic Strategy* (London, Conference of Socialist Economists).

Cowling, K. and Mueller, D. (1978): 'The Social Costs of Monopoly Power', *Economic Journal*.

Cox, A. (1986): 'State, Finance and Industry in Comparative Perspective', in Cox, A. (ed.) (1986).

Cox, A. (ed.) (1986): *The State, Finance and Industry* (Brighton, Wheatsheaf).

Cyert, R. and March, J. (1963): *A Behavioral Theory of the Firm* (Englewood Cliffs, Prentice-Hall).

Dahl, R. (1985): *A Preface to Economic Democracy* (Berkeley, University of California Press).

Department of Economic Affairs (1965): *The National Plan* (Cmnd 2764; London, HMSO).

Department of Trade (1977): *Report of the Committee of Inquiry on Industrial Democracy*, chaired by Lord Bullock, (Cmnd 6706; London, HMSO).

Deutscher, I. (1972): *Marxism in Our Time* (London, Cape).

Devine, P. (1974): 'Inflation and Marxist Theory', *Marxism Today* (March).

Devine, P. (1981): 'Principles of Democratic Planning', *Socialist Economic Review*.

Devine, P. et al. (1985): *An Introduction to Industrial Economics* (4th edn; London, Allen & Unwin).

Devons, E. (1951): 'The Problem of Coordination in Aircraft Production', in Chester, D. (ed.) (1951).

Devons, E. (1970): *Papers on Planning and Economic Management*, edited by Cairncross, A. (Manchester, Manchester University Press).

Djilas, M. (1958): *The New Class* (London, Thames & Hudson).

Dobb, M. (1946): *Studies in the Development of Capitalism* (London, Routledge).

Dobb, M. (1955): *On Economic Theory and Socialism* (London, Routledge & Kegan Paul).

Dobb, M. (1960): *An Essay on Economic Growth and Planning* (London, Routledge & Kegan Paul).

Dobb, M. (1966): *Soviet Economic Development since 1917* (6th edn; London, Routledge & Kegan Paul).

Dobb, M. (1967): *Papers on Capitalism, Development and Planning* (London, Routledge & Kegan Paul).

Dobb, M. (1970a): *Socialist Planning: Some Problems* (London, Lawrence and Wishart).

Dobb, M. (1970b): *Welfare Economics and the Economics of Socialism* (Cambridge, Cambridge University Press).

Dobb, M. (1974): 'Some Historical Reflections on Planning and the Market', in Abramsky, C. (ed.) (1974).

Dow, J. (1964): *The Management of the British Economy, 1945–60* (Cambridge, Cambridge University Press).

Dyson, K. (1986): 'The State, Banks and Industry: the West German Case', in Cox, A. (ed.) (1986).

Elliott, J. (1978): *Conflict or Cooperation? The Growth of Industrial Democracy* (London, Kogan Page).

Elliott, J. E. (1976): 'Marx and Contemporary Models of Socialist Economy', *History of Political Economy*.

Ellman, M. (1968): 'Lessons of the Soviet Economic Reform', *The Socialist Register*.

Ellman, M. (1979): *Socialist Planning* (Cambridge, Cambridge University Press).

Engels, F. (1972): *The Origin of the Family, Private Property and the State*, edited by Leacock, E. (London, Lawrence and Wishart).

Estrin, S. and Holmes, P. (1983): *French Planning in Theory and Practice* (London, Allen & Unwin).

Feher, F., Heller, A. and Markus, G. (1983): *Dictatorship Over Needs* (Oxford, Basil Blackwell).

Feinstein, C. (ed.) (1967): *Socialism, Capitalism and Economic Growth: Essays Presented to Maurice Dobb* (Cambridge, Cambridge University Press).

Fernbach, D. (1981): *The Spiral Path* (London, Gay Men's Press).

Flaherty, D. (1982): 'Economic Reform and Foreign Trade in Yugoslavia', *Cambridge Journal of Economics*.

Forbes, I. (ed.) (1986): *Market Socialism* (London, Fabian Society).

Galasi, P. and Sziraczki, G. (1985): 'State Regulation, Enterprise Behaviour and the Labour Market in Hungary', *Cambridge Journal of Economics*.

Gomulka, S. (1986): *Growth, Innovation and Reform in Eastern Europe* (Brighton, Wheatsheaf).

Gomulka, S. and Ostojic, S. (1986): 'Innovative Activity in the Yugoslav Economy', in Gomulka, S. (1986).

Gorbachev, M. (1987): Speech to the Central Committee of the Communist Party of the Soviet Union on January 27, 1987, *The Guardian* (February 2, 1987).

Gough, I. (1979): *The Political Economy of the Welfare State* (London, Macmillan).

Gramsci, A. (1971): *Selections from the Prison Notebooks*, edited by Hoare, Q. and Nowell Smith, G. (London, Lawrence and Wishart).

Greater London Council (1985): *The London Industrial Strategy* (London, Greater London Council).

Gregory, P. and Stuart, R. (1980): *Comparative Economic Systems* (Boston, Houghton Mifflin).

Gregory, P. and Stuart, R. (1986): *Soviet Economic Structure and Performance* (3rd edn; New York, Harper & Row).

292   BIBLIOGRAPHY

Griffiths, R. (ed.) (1977): *Government, Business and Labour in European Capitalism* (London, Europotentials Press).

Hahn, F. (1973): 'The Winter of Our Discontent', *Economica*.

Hahn, F. (1982): 'Reflections on the Invisible Hand', *Lloyds Bank Review*.

Hall, S. and Jacques, M. (eds) (1983): *The Politics of Thatcherism* (London, Lawrence and Wishart).

Hancock, W. and Gowing, M. (1949): *The British War Economy* (London, HMSO).

Hanson, P. (1986): 'The Shape of Gorbachev's Economic Reform', *Soviet Economy*.

Hanson, P. (1987): 'The Enterprise Law and the Reform Process', *Radio Liberty Research Bulletin* RL269/87 (July 14).

Harcourt, G. (1972): *Some Cambridge Controversies in the Theory of Capital* (Cambridge, Cambridge University Press).

Hare, P. (1977): 'Economic Reform in Hungary: Problems and Prospects', *Cambridge Journal of Economics*.

Hare, P. (1985): *Planning the British Economy* (Basingstoke, Macmillan).

Hare, P., Radice, H. and Swain, N. (eds) (1981): *Hungary: A Decade of Economic Reform* (London, Allen & Unwin).

Hayek, F. von (1945): 'The Use of Knowledge in Society', *American Economic Review*.

Hegedus, A. (1976): *Socialism and Bureaucracy* (London, Allison and Busby).

Hegedus, A. (1977): *The Structure of Socialist Society* (London, Constable).

Hegedus, A. et al. (1976): *The Humanisation of Socialism* (London, Allison and Busby).

Held, D. (1986): 'Introduction: New Forms of Democracy', in Held D. and Pollitt, C. (eds) (1986).

Held, D. (1987): *Models of Democracy* (Cambridge, Polity).

Held, D. and Pollitt, C. (eds) (1986): *New Forms of Democracy* (London, Sage).

Hilton, R. et al. (1976): *The Transformation from Feudalism to Capitalism* (London, New Left Books).

Hirsch, F. (1977): *Social Limits to Growth* (London, Routledge & Kegan Paul).

Hirst, P. (1987): 'Can Socialism Live?', in *The New Statesman* (1987).

Hobsbawm, E. (1964): 'Introduction' to Marx, K. (1964).

Hobsbawm, E. (1987): 'Offering a Good Society', in *The New Statesman* (1987).

Hodgson, G. (1984): *The Democratic Economy* (Harmondsworth, Penguin).

Holesovsky, V. (1973): 'Planning and Market in the Czechoslovak Reform', in Bornstein, M. (ed.) (1973).

Holesovsky, V. (1977): *Economic Systems: Analysis and Comparison* (New York, McGraw-Hill).

Horvat, B. (1964): *Towards a Theory of Planned Economy* (Belgrade, Yugoslav Institute of Economic Research).

Horvat, B. (1982): *The Political Economy of Socialism* (Oxford, Martin Robertson).

Hunnius, G. (1972): 'Workers' Self-Management in Yugoslavia', in Hunnius, G. et al. (eds) (1972).

Hunnius, G. et al. (eds) (1972): *Workers' Control* (New York, Vintage).

Jacques, M. and Mulhern, F. (eds) (1981): *The Forward March of Labour Halted?* (London, Verso in association with *Marxism Today*).

Jaggi, M., Muller, R. and Schmid, S. (1977): *Red Bologna* (London, Writers and Readers).

Karen, M. (1973): 'Concentration Amid Devolution in East Germany's Reforms', in Bornstein, M. (ed.) (1973).

Kellner, P. (1984): 'Are Markets Compatible with Socialism?', in Pimlott, B. (ed.) (1984).

Kiloh, M. (1986): 'Industrial Democracy', in Held, D. and Pollitt, C. (eds) (1986).

Kilpatrick, A. and Lawson, T. (1980): 'On the Nature of Industrial Decline in the United Kingdom', *Cambridge Journal of Economics*.

Koopmans, T. (1957): *Three Essays on the State of Economic Science* (New York, McGraw-Hill).

Kornai, J. (1959): *Overcentralisation in Economic Administration* (Oxford, Oxford University Press).

Kornai, J. (1980a): 'The Dilemmas of a Socialist Economy: The Hungarian Experience', *Cambridge Journal of Economics*.

Kornai, J. (1980b): *The Economics of Shortage* (Amsterdam, North-Holland).

Kornai, J. (1986a): *Contradictions and Dilemmas* (Cambridge, Mass., MIT Press).

Kornai, J. (1986b): 'The Hungarian Reform Process: Visions, Hopes, and Reality', *Journal of Economic Literature*.

Laclau, E. and Mouffe, C. (1985): *Hegemony and Socialist Strategy* (London, Verso).

Lane, T. (1987): 'Unions: Fit for Active Service?', *Marxism Today* (February).

Lange, O. (1938): 'On the Economic Theory of Socialism', in Lange, O. and Taylor, F. (1938).

Lange, O. and Taylor, F. (1938): *On The Economic Theory of Socialism* (Minneapolis, University of Minnesota Press).

Leacock, E. (1972): 'Introduction' to Engels, F. (1972).

Lenin, V. (1960): *The Development of Capitalism in Russia* (Moscow, Foreign Languages Publishing House).

Levine, A., Sober, E. and Wright, E. (1987): 'Marxism and Methodological Individualism', *New Left Review*, 162.

Lindblom, C. (1977): *Politics and Markets* (New York, Basic Books).

Lively, J. (1979): *Democracy* (Oxford, Basil Blackwell).

London to Edinburgh Weekend Return Group (1979): *In and Against the State* (London, Pluto).

Lukes, S. (1973): *Individualism* (Oxford, Basil Blackwell).

Lukes, S. (1974): *Power: a Radical View* (London, Macmillan).

Lukes, S. (1984): 'The Future of British Socialism?', in Pimlott, B. (ed.) (1984).

McArthur, J. and Scott, B. (1969): *Industrial Planning in France* (Cambridge Mass., Harvard University Press).

Mackintosh, M. and Wainwright, H. (eds) (1987): *A Taste of Power* (London, Verso).

McLellan, D. (1977): *Karl Marx: Selected Writings* (Oxford, Oxford University Press).

McLennan, G. (1983): 'Historical Materialism Today: Some Variations and Problems', in Matthews, B. (ed.) (1983).

Macpherson, C. (1977): *The Life and Times of Liberal Democracy* (Oxford, Oxford University Press).

Mandel, E. (1986): 'In Defence of Socialist Planning', *New Left Review*, 159.

Marer, P. (1985): 'Economic Reform in Hungary', in Bornstein, M. (ed.) (1985).

Markus, M. and Hegedus, A. (1976): 'Free Time and the Division of Labour', in Hegedus, A. et al. (1976).

Marx, K. (1909): *Capital*, Volume III (Chicago, Kerr).

Marx, K. (1964): *Pre-Capitalist Formations*, edited by Hobsbawm, E, (London, Lawrence and Wishart).

Marx, K. (1974): *Critique of the Gotha Programme,* in *The First International and After* (Harmondsworth, Penguin in association with *New Left Review*).

Marx, K. (1976): *Capital*, Volume I (Harmondsworth, Penguin in association with *New Left Review*).

Matthews, B. (ed.) (1983): *Marx: A Hundred Years On* (London, Lawrence and Wishart).

Meade, J. (1964): *Efficiency, Equality and the Ownership of Property* (London, Allen & Unwin).

Meade, J. (1970): *The Theory of Indicative Planning* (Manchester, Manchester University Press).

Meadows, P. (1978): 'Planning', in Blackaby, F. (ed.) (1978).

Middlemas, K. (1979): *Politics in Industrial Society* (London, André Deutsch).

Mitchell, J. (1966): *Groundwork to Economic Planning* (London, Secker and Warburg).

Morris, D. (ed.) (1985): *The Economic System in the UK* (3rd edn, Oxford, Oxford University Press).

Morris, D. and Stout, D. (1985): 'Industrial Policy', in Morris, D. (ed.) (1985).

Morva, T. (1975): 'Planning in Hungary', in Bornstein, M. (ed.) (1975).

Mottershead, P. (1978): 'Industrial Policy', in Blackaby, F. (ed.) (1978).

Murray, R. (1984): 'New Directions in Municipal Socialism', in Pimlott, B. (ed.) (1984).

Myant, M. (1984): 'Yugoslavia: An Experiment in Crisis', *Marxism Today* (February).

Neuberger, E. and James, E. (1973): 'The Yugoslav Self-managed Economy: a Systemic Approach', in Bornstein, M. (ed.) (1973).

Nolan, P. and Paine, S. (eds) (1986): *Rethinking Socialist Economics* (Cambridge, Polity).

North, D. (1984): 'Transaction Costs, Institutions and Economic History', *Zeitschrift für die gesamte Staatswissenschaft* (*Journal of Institutional and Theoretical Economics*).

Nove, A. (1977): *The Soviet Economic System* (London, Allen & Unwin).

Nove, A. (1980): 'The Soviet Economy: Problems and Prospects', *New Left Review*, 119.

Nove, A. (1983): *The Economics of Feasible Socialism* (London, Allen & Unwin).

Nove, A. (1986): *Marxism and 'Really Existing Socialism'* (London, Harwood).

Nove, A. and Nuti, M. (eds) (1972): *Socialist Economics* (Harmondsworth, Penguin).

Nuti, M. (1978): 'Investment, Interest and Degree of Centralisation in Maurice Dobb's Theory of the Socialist Economy', *Cambridge Journal of Economics*.

Nuti, M. (1979): 'The Contradictions of Socialist Economies: A Marxian Interpretation', *The Socialist Register*.

Olson, M. (1982): *The Decline and Fall of Nations* (New Haven, Yale University Press).

Palmer, J. (1986): 'Municipal Enterprise and Popular Planning', *New Left Review*, 159.

Pateman, C. (1979): *The Problem of Political Obligation* (Chichester, John Wiley).

Pejovich, S. (1973): 'The Banking System and the Investment Behaviour of the Yugoslav firm', in Bornstein, M. (ed.) (1973).

Pimlott, B. (ed.) (1984): *Fabian Essays in Socialist Thought* (London, Heinemann).

Portes, R. (1972): 'The Strategy and Tactics of Economic Decentralization: Concepts and Problems', *Soviet Studies*.

Portes, R. (1979): 'The Control of Inflation: Lessons from East European Experience', in Bornstein, M. (ed.) (1979).

Poulantzas, N. (1978): *State, Power, Socialism* (London, New Left Books).

Purdy, D. (forthcoming): *Social Power and the Labour Market* (Basingstoke, Macmillan).

Radford, R. (1945): 'The Economic Organisation of a P.o.W. Camp', *Economica*.

Radner, R. (1975): 'Economic Planning Under Uncertainty: Recent Theoretical Developments', in Bornstein, M. (ed.) (1975).

Ramelson, B. (1975): 'Public Ownership and Industrial Democracy', *Comment* (March 22).

Rattansi, R. (1982): *Marx and the Division of Labour* (London, Macmillan).

Richardson, G. (1960): *Information and Investment* (London, Oxford University Press).

Richardson, G. (1965): 'The Theory of Restrictive Trade Practices', *Oxford Economic Papers*.

Richardson, G. (1967): 'Price Notification Schemes', *Oxford Economic Papers*.

Richardson, G. (1971): 'Planning versus Competition', *Soviet Studies*.

Robinson, E. (1951): 'The Overall Allocation of Resources', in Chester, D. (ed.) (1951).

Roemer, J. (1986): *Value, Exploitation and Class* (London, Harwood).

Rosenberg, N. and Birdzell, L. (1986): *How the West Grew Rich* (London, Tauris).

Rowbotham, S. (1986): 'Feminism and Democracy', in Held, D. and Pollitt, C. (eds) (1986).

Rowthorn, R. (1980): *Capitalism, Conflict and Inflation* (London, Lawrence and Wishart).

Runciman, W. and Sen, A. (1965): 'Games, Justice and the General Will', *Mind*.

Rustin, M. (1986): 'Lessons of the London Industrial Strategy', *New Left Review*, 159.

Sacks, S. (1984): *Self-Management in Large Corporations: The Yugoslav Case* (London, Allen & Unwin).

Sacks, S. (1985): 'The Yugoslav Firm', in Bornstein, M. (ed.) (1985).

Salter, J. (1983): 'Review' of Nove, A. (1983), *Manchester School*.

Schrenk, M. and Ardalan, C. (1979): *Yugoslavia: Self-Management Socialism* (Oxford, Oxford University Press).

Selucky, R. (1972): *Economic Reforms in Eastern Europe* (New York, Praeger).

Selucky, R. (1979): *Marxism, Socialism, Freedom* (London, Macmillan).

Shanks, M. (1977): *Planning and Politics: The British Experience, 1960–76* (London, Allen & Unwin).

Shonfield, A. (1965): *Modern Capitalism* (London, Oxford University Press).

Sik, O. (1967): 'Socialist Market Relations', in Feinstein, C. (ed.) (1967).

Sik, O. (1976): *The Third Way* (London, Wildwood).

Simon, R. (1982): *Gramsci's Political Thought* (London, Lawrence and Wishart).

Singh, A. (1977): 'UK Industry and the World Economy: A Case of Deindustrialisation?', *Cambridge Journal of Economics*.

Smith, R. (1981): 'The Historical Decline of the UK', in Aaronovitch, S. et al. (1981).

Smith, T. (1979): *The Politics of the Corporate Economy* (Oxford, Martin Robertson).

Sraffa, P. (1960): *Production of Commodities by Means of Commodities* (Cambridge, Cambridge University Press).

Surrey, M. (1972): 'The National Plan in Retrospect', *Bulletin of the Oxford University Institute of Economics and Statistics*.

Sweezy, P. (1962): *The Theory of Capitalist Development* (London, Dobson).

The New Statesman (1987): Symposium on 'Does Socialism Have A Future?' (March 6).

Thornton, J. (1975): 'Comments on Porwit and Morva', in Bornstein, M. (ed.) (1975).

Tobin, J. (1980): *Asset Accumulation and Economic Activity* (Oxford, Basil Blackwell).

Walker, K. (1977): 'Workers' Participation in Management', *Bulletin of the International Institute for Labour Studies* (Geneva).

Ware, A. (1986): 'Political Parties', in Held, D. and Pollitt, C. (eds) (1986).

Watson, M. (1977): 'The Character and Contradictions of Western Style Planning', in Griffiths, R. (ed.) (1977).

Williams, R. (1980): 'Beyond Actually Existing Socialism', *New Left Review*, 120.

Woodcock, G. (ed.) (1977): *The Anarchist Reader* (Brighton, Harvester).

World Bank (1979): 'The Decentralized Self-Managed Economic System of Yugoslavia', in Bornstein, M. (ed.) (1979).

Young, S. with Lowe, A. (1974): *Intervention in the Mixed Economy* (London, Croom Helm).

Zimbalist, A. and Sherman, H. (1984): *Comparing Economic Systems* (London, Academic Press).

Zysman, J. (1983): *Governments, Markets and Growth: Financial Systems and the Politics of Industrial Change* (Oxford, Martin Robertson).

Index